SAPIENS RISING

The View from 2100

A Manifesto for the Children of the 21st Century

Neil Freer

THE BOOK TREE
San Diego, California

ISBN 978-1-58509-146-1

Cover image creation and design
© Ursula Freer, http://www.ursulafreer.com

Cover layout by
Mike Sparrow

Published by
The Book Tree
P O Box 16476
San Diego, CA 92176
www.thebooktree.com
We provide fascinating and educational products to help awaken the public
to new ideas and information that would not be available otherwise.
Call 1 (800) 700-8733 for our FREE BOOK TREE CATALOG.

Contents

PROLOGUE

*The present evolutionary crisis of humans on planet Earth
is that of a final examination for their continuance in
Universe. It is not an examination of political, economic,
or religious systems, but of the integrity of each and all-
individual humans' responsible thinking and unselfish
response to the acceleration in evolution's evermore-
unprecedented events.*

—Buckminster Fuller

Our planet, this agonizingly beautiful little planet, is on hold. Seeking relief and release, in a perverse ecology we recycle outmoded, primitive paradigms, shuffling our feathers-and-molasses confusion between hands. In a time when we are required to deal with the politics of non-overlapping alien realities, we are not able to resolve the separations caused by our overlapping intra-species realities. It has rendered us theologically inane, philosophically naive, scientifically cramped, socially isolated, ecologically damaged, politically challenged and intellectually bewildered.

This white paper brief is submitted as a metanormative scenario addressing the current planetary, species Sapiens situation. It is intended as a perspective from the leading edge of our species' development from which to view and understand ourselves now, socially, culturally, and evolutionarily, all these elements being brought to bear on the current socio-political arena. The primary focus is on how to overcome the obstacles and make the transition to the new human and new human society, how to bring about the transmutation of our species, how to step cleanly out of species adolescence and attain stellar citizenship.

I stand to speak for the planet, for all of us, the entire species Sapiens, because someone must, and soon. We are far into a time of profound, challenging novelty and stellar opportunity that we must recognize and understand for our and our children's sake. I ask for a crisis council of the entire world, not a trial, for we are also far into a time of planetary danger that no weapon can destroy, and there is no time for recriminations. We are already well into this century which we can recognize as the century of our transformation to the new human and a new human planetary and cosmic society or we can remain primitively and myopically terran centered and continue to slaughter each other and go down to self destruction. This is the time of individual declaration: each of us must decide and declare whether we are for our species' survival or not.

It is clearly evident, after thousands of years of trial and disastrous errors, that the relief and release from our racially adolescent immaturity we seek as individuals and as a planetary species will not come from yet another economic experiment, yet another U.N. negotiated conflict resolution, yet another religious ecumenical conference, new age vision, or yet another political format, much less some new twist on the MAD scenario, or some war to end all wars.

In the greatest overview, the current planetary state of the species manifests two main characteristics: we, the species Sapiens Sapiens, are being offered stellar citizenship by alien species who are, by now, quite obviously present around and on Earth. We have been given the rules: no weapons in space and we matriculate as a united, peaceful species or we do not get accepted. The major obstacle blocking us from peaceful species unity is a schizophrenic species identity crisis due most fundamentally to religio--cultural conflicts. Both of these major factors are being taken advantage of by human anti-species elements to manipulate world affairs for their own advantage. There is also a threat to the species, the severe to cataclysmic effects of the passing of the tenth planet of our system that is being suppressed that must be understood and dealt with because it can mean literal extinction.

The patterns of our brief history on this planet coupled with the evidence of our individual and collective behavior clearly indicate that we shall control and isolate the suppressive, predatory, anti-species element, attain a new human status, a profoundly new human planetary society and stellar citizenship. The perennial conflicts between religions as well as the religion vs. science, creationist vs. evolution conflicts can now be resolved due to our having recovered abundant information to restore and understand our history as a genetically engineered species by the Anunnaki/Nefilim, the alien species from the tenth planet in our solar system who colonized Earth and created us as a slave species to work their gold mines. Religion has been redefined as the continuation and sublimation of that ancient master-slave relationship. We can now attain a consensual, planetary understanding of ourselves as generic humans, beyond the "my god is better than your god" radically divisive conflicts, leading to planetary peace and unity.

A very fundamental, critical question, therefore: Is it even possible to arrive at an overarching new planetary paradigm so comprehensive and robust that it corrects, subsumes, completes and outmodes all previous partial paradigms, explains all our previous explanations, with the scope and power to unify and pacify the planet?

Unequivocally, yes. We are not incapable of getting off "maybe". We are blocked only by primitive, antique legacies and the way to expunge them from the fabric of our cultures is now available to us. I stand in planetary council to respectfully but urgently point out that there is, indeed, a new understanding of our beginnings and our history worthy of our collective wisdom which alone has the comprehensive power and truth to dispel our species bewilderment, restore our true history and dignity, and vaporize our divisions and conflicts by literally redefining us.

This world view only can activate all the elements required to achieve our transformation and will take us, in the light of a deepened knowledge of our species and ourselves, to a new level of species maturity and degree of freedom, unity, vision and peace beyond civilization and religion as we have known them. We must become an exosocial and exopolitical species. Some among us are already living even beyond that transformation as new humans. We will explore that now and future domain to sharpen our perspective and vision and get comfortable with our realevolutionary trajectory.

But how to transmute ourselves as a species to become the vision? What physical currency, what leverage, do we possess to enable us to transition through the radical social, political, economic, psychological changes and adjustments without major disruptions of the fabric of our every day existence? How convince the winners in this primitive phase of competition to move to planetary cooperation that will afford them even more than they possess and covet now --- as well as provide plenty equally for the former losers, the poor, indeed the entire planet?

We have the means, the methods. Developments in science, free --- "zeropoint"-energy and nanotechnology combined with artificial intelligence afford us the physical means of control, power, fabrication, distribution, response, remediation and education to provide for plenty for literally all on the planet. Economically, we have accumulated sufficient scientific and technical expertise in the sciences of nanotechnology and free energy to transition intelligently from the illusory primitive modality of competition for limited resources to a near leisure society with plenty for a 6 billion population or more without a great deal of transitional stress. A totally new economic of secure plenty for all removes the major obstacle of opposition by those who feel their accumulated wealth and control threatened. The educational system can be transformed by the implementation of advanced electronic communication devices and, eventually, by rapid direct information transfer to the brain. Immortality or, at least, highly extended lifespan will become a routine option and will radically alter the way human life is understood.

The engine driving the species to cosmic consciousness --- and, currently, crisis --- is the intrinsic collective consciousness expanding to understand, explore, encompass, master, experience and enjoy the universe as an integral part of it. The patterns of our brief history on this planet coupled with the evidence of our individual and collective behavior clearly indicate that we shall inevitably control and isolate the suppressive, predatory, anti-species element, attain a new human status, a profoundly new human planetary society and stellar citizenship.

To set this paper in historical perspective, in my natural view as a futant-futurist, we are still in the Dark Ages. Writing this paper has all the physical and psychological sensations of the twelfth century rather than the twenty-first. Our science and philosophy are only short stages ahead of the developments of the 17th century. Our planetary situation feels like a second rate medieval drama. The critical advantage and difference is that we have more than enough robust information and evidence to determine that this phase is really all over and some of us are not only ready to live but are living a whole other existence already.

Whether we chose to acknowledge it yet or not, we are already well into one of "...those Grand Moments when the whole scale of being is reevaluated" as friend, futurist John Petersen of the Arlington Institute has characterized it (http://www.arlingtoninstitute.org). To this point we have only cataloged the shadows and maladies in our collective psyche. While we have been focused on our problems in cramped terracentric myopia a set of profound factors has blossomed in our collective consciousness that contains the keys to unlocking the doors of our expanded perception and in which the resolution to the problems and obstacles deeply embedded in our species' and individual psyches' is to be found. These empowering factors range from the multidimensional to the econopolitical.

We are already into a profound transmutation of our species, which will characterize this 21st Century, and it is no longer feasible to think in partial terms of national, cultural, religious, or civilizational adjustments and solutions. The novel synthesis and world view advanced in this work subsumes partial glimpses of a new politic, humanistic new world order, enlightened eco-economics, a third culture, all knowledge united in a grand consilience, and cerebral turning points. We now have the keys to integrate our past with our present and future in the concept of generic humanity, the critical factor for achieving planetary peace, unity and matriculation into stellar society --- planetary, peaceful, cooperative unity being the only adequate benchmark in these times of profound transition to a new human society and cosmic citizenship. The political problems and conflicts of even recent history are cold ashes, symptoms of the perennial divisive Babel-factoring standstill we have been at that has allowed the ruthless and the predatory to learn to beat, then buy, the house, economically and financially, manipulate the masses and bring us to this obscene state of affairs.

The overview presented here is meant to be the broadest possible and, perforce, is partially exosociological as well as sociological although I bring it down to the immediate details of survival and socio-political adjustments. This briefing may present material that may not be otherwise in your purview but it is directly and critically related to the national and cultural and planetary interests and security both short and long term.

As a philosopher, futurist, futant and contactee and primarily as a generic human, I stand aside, but not separate, so that I may speak of everything, as far as possible beyond all totems and taboos. I speak here in the collective "we" and "us" to maintain the species' vision beyond our divisions as we take council together in the name of the children and their future. As each in our turn rises to say, "I think that we must…" let the cardinal rule of right conduct be that the intended "we" embraces the species and the planet, no less.

This the end time of our species' bewildered adolescence and our transformation into a mature stellar species has already begun. Let us reclaim our planetary identity, our own cosmic credentials and genetic wisdom, and prepare as a united planet, in the only adequate, truly planetary, new world order, to matriculate into the heavens, into space, into stellar society as, finally, Sapiens Sapiens, the truly doubly wise. I stand to speak for and to all of us, the species Sapiens, to urge us all to make it so for our children and ourselves. Welcome, the new human.

1

SAPIENS RISING:
THE ILLUSION OF STANDSTILL AT THE LEADING EDGE

Synopsis

We are a precocious species, puzzling even to ourselves because we are Babel-factored, divided and conflicted because of religious dogmas and cultural legacies, seemingly at standstill in our development into the future. Our children, us in the future, suffer because of this and we risk wiping ourselves out through wars, pollution, corruption, primitive competition. But we have recovered our true history, can arrive at planetary unity as generic humans and we have the memes and means now to achieve it.

Sapiens rising, staggering out of the mists of our puzzling past into the disconcerting present, facing a perplexing and awesome future. But rising, surely, inexorably, skirting the edges of various extinctions from our adolescent tinkering with nature and our nature itself, progressing in spite of mystifying retrogressive divisiveness and meanness, rising in greater and greater consciousness, evolving toward the stars in steady anticipation of contact with almost unimaginable, yet already familiar, alien rising Others.

Homo Erectus, by the paleontological records, took a million slow years to progress from rough flaked stone tools to smooth flaked stone tools. We, Sapiens Sapiens, have come from square one in east central Africa only 200,000 years ago, through a sudden blooming of civilization in Mesopotamia some 6000 years ago to hitting a golf ball around on the Moon a few years ago, considering an exploratory trip to Mars in the near future, and already having dispatched a probe beyond our solar system with a message of greeting.

Technologically, a measure preferred by some, we have come from living by our muscle, gambling on our skills to kill game, gathering the fruits of field and forest, transporting our possessions, protecting and defending ourselves, through the tool using stage, the machine age, are well into the electronic age and beginning to master molecule, microtubule and nanotechnology. To serve our needs we have progressed from the waterhole to Perrier, from taming fire to flirting with free energy --- in 200,000 years, less than a quarter of the time it took Erectus to advance from rough to smooth stone tools.

13

Sociobiologically we have traced ourselves from savannah and cave through rapid adaptations to lands of brutal sun, lands of ice, identified mechanisms in our nature that we consider primitive and those we see as evolved, come to see ourselves moving through a rapid history of genetic development measured in tens of thousands of years to a point where we are beginning to control even our genetic code. We have come from the council fire to the Constitution to the council of the United Nations to taking counsel with alien species.

We contemplate ourselves contemplating ourselves and all these achievements seem anthropologically precocious by comparison to any other species we recognize on this planet by far. We know ourselves, clearly, to be progressing, evolving, rising, from primitive to civilized, from brutal competition to compassion, from ignorance to knowledge, from footpath to space travel, from uncertainty to control. But there is this profound ambiguity that divides us as to just what constitutes progress. We sense a deep puzzlement and frustration at our seeming standstill at the leading edge. We simply do not agree about what the trajectory of our development is or we deny that there is a trajectory at all. The current phase of the radical disagreement is generally characterized as between those who are convinced that we are a static creature, not developing or evolving, who must only learn to conform to static laws of some deity and those who believe that we are evolving albeit by primitive Darwinian mechanism. This paper presents a third paradigm that supersedes both those primitive explanations.

By What Criteria Do We Judge Ourselves?

By whose criteria do we say "progress"? Ideologically, the four criterion bases which we generally use to determine the truth or falsity, beneficence or harmfulness, morality or immorality of information are theology, philosophy, science and "new age" principles.

Theological criteria, by definition, are principles and dogmas and rules taken as absolutes, issued by some divine being, which are beyond contest or question. Any reasoning in their regard can only come after the fact and is employed to work out the ramifications and application of those absolute principles. The human is seen, usually, as a non-evolving entity. Reality is taken as objective (things are as they are, usually as conceived by the deity, regardless of how they are understood by any mind) rather than subjective (dependent on how they are seen or understood or conceived by any mind).

Philosophical criteria are logical principles worked out by human reason as primary tool and taken as general rules inherent in the universe. The human is understood in many, often radically different, ways. Reality is understood from the extreme of objectivity to the extreme of subjectivity.

Scientific criteria are based on a philosophical assumption that there is an objective, lawful order of reality, the laws of which are discoverable. The modality of discovery in the precise sciences is the scientific method: carefully controlled, duplicable experiments producing results that are statistically analyzable to determine validation or negation.

New age criteria vary through a range according to how much emphasis or credence is attributed to one or all of the above, with the emphasis on expanded consciousness, from personal to the paranormal, as a deciding factor.

It is painfully obvious that these traditional criteria bases rattle around in a criteria vacuum with little overlap and major conflicts because each tends to define a human being and the meaning of human existence in a quite different way.

Among some of us, there is a slinking cynicism, an often unspoken, viral attitude in human society that holds the view that it is impossible to get out of the criteria vacuum, to initialize a common ground; impossible to get past the communicatory barriers of turf and custom, belief and taboo. When talking about the human we are largely ineffectual because we are, literally, talking at each other about a different entity.

We tell ourselves, at this turn of yet another millennium, that this is surely the vengeful end of time Armageddon, while anticipating a challenging singularity of such radical novelty that it will bring a revolution of our species' consciousness lasting well into the middle of the next century. What is the most fundamental cause of our conflicted, Babel-factored alienation? It is by the intrinsically irreconcilable absolutes of religion that we are most absolutely divided. Ironically, however, as will be elucidated, it is not primarily because religions are flawed, as we have been conditioned and taught to understand them: it is because the religions are not what we have been conditioned to conceive them to be.

How Primitive Are We?

Just how primitive are we still, how antique are our legacies, how adolescent a species are we?

We are barely out of the time of human sacrifice and are still filling our stadiums to watch virtual gladiator games. Slavery in various guises is very much with us still. Dueling is out of fashion but war is the daily horror in our lives. We can trace our proud, precocious progress and achievements only on records saturated with the brother blood of hideous wars without end. We jostle each other for fledging space and foul our planet nest with radiation, toxins and our wastes while praising the beauty of our home, always blaming the other. Our children, often only a handful of years dry from the womb, more and more often resort to suicide in revulsion, preferring hope of oblivion.

We sacrifice our children to the hideous slaughter of war at the word of politicians who are foisted on us in popularity contests structured to appeal to the bright ten-year-old mentality. We do this in the context of a primitive economic, competitive mammalian politic based on territory and the defense of limited survival resources when national boundaries have been rendered meaningless and free energy sources are already available. The least evolved among us, in a perversion of the word "conservative", preserve their wealth, built on competition for limited energy supply, by deliberately suppressing developments that would make it limitless. Politically, we have created governments peopled largely by the cynically devolved, many sincere, perhaps, but myopic, in a time when sincerity alone is tragically inadequate. We are still working through systems of representation by strangers when direct, instantaneous input from the entire population is quite possible. Technologically, we are eager and close to being able to create artificial intelligence and consciousness, when we cannot agree on the nature of our own consciousness.

We have barely walked on our moon, are represented only by smart golf carts on Mars, know little of the giant planets. We cannot venture outside our solar system except in primitive science fiction projections. We are only now coming to a general recognition of the obvious alien presences around and on the planet and throughout the solar system and the universe. We are still generally handicapped by the primitive attitude of looking to authority for validation, in this case the very patronizing authorities who are keeping the information from us.

How primitively adolescent a species are we? Most fundamentally and amazingly, we do not have a consensual, planetary, generic definition of what a human being is. We disagree about how we really came into existence, and what the nature of our developmental process is. We disagree as to the facts and interpretation and understanding of our species' history. We have treated the sociobiological event of our beginning as a species as if we could never be sure if it ever really occurred. We have not resolved nor integrated our genesis and our history as a species and, therefore, are at a loss to understand our real nature and future trajectory. That we do not see this as a profound puzzle is further proof of our species' primitive naiveté as is the fact that we deny and suppress entire segments of reality from scientific knowledge that contradict our religious beliefs.

Most in the scientific world are familiar with the scientist, Galileo, having to capitulate to the Inquisition to save his own life, dying while under house arrest for holding to a heliocentric view of the solar system, claiming to see planets through his telescope. Fewer are aware of the fact that the monk, Jordano Bruno, was burnt at the stake in Rome, through the solicitousness of the Roman Church, only thirty six years before the founding of Harvard University, for holding to the Copernican view and claiming that there had to be other planets and other civilizations in the cosmos.

Fourteen years after the founding of Harvard, Bishop James Ussher published his *"Annales Vertis Et Novi Testamenti"*[5] dating the beginning of the world at 4004 B.C. One could be condemned as a heretic for contravening this doctrine by decree of the Church in 1654 and the stricture was not removed until 1952 by Pope Pius XII when I was in seminary studying for the Catholic priesthood. The arithmetical wonder of this fact is that was only little more than half a century ago. Consider that almost everything written in this paper would have been branded as "heresy" and who knows how DNA research would have been branded only a short time ago.

Scientific Archaeology is younger than our Constitution. There was literally no such thing as the discipline known as Archaeology in Western culture until the 1800's. The Roman Church controlled and determined the view of the past. The scholastic world, dominated by the Church, followed docilely. Not until paleontological findings of millions of years forced that view to be reevaluated and Schliemann, a wealthy German merchant, refusing to believe that the ancient cities and peoples were legend, dug up several stages of the city of Troy, was a window into the past opened and the mythic view questioned. Scientific Archaeology, as we know it, came into existence only when academics reluctantly had to acknowledge the past being dug up and collected by amateurs in the Middle East.

How primitive are we? It has been said that the world's most complex mechanism comes without an owner's manual. We have many different and conflicting definitions of what a human is and a number of conflicting "owner's manuals" by which a human is supposed to operate. The word "owner" is the key: there are two major "owner's manuals" in the form of Bible and Koran, two in the form of The Book of Changes (The I Ching) and the Book of the Tao. The I Ching and the Book of the Tao are instruction manuals in which the "owner" is understood as the human consulting them. In the case of the Bible and the Koran the "owners" are not the humans but the deities associated with the manuals. This relationship of "owner" to subject, deity to servant or slave, is understood by the vast majority as "religion". We hardly question this concept. Those who do question it have often been killed by those who do not. Those of one slave-code religion have often killed those of another slave-code religion over whose owner is the only real Owner or which code of conduct is the correct one. Ultimately, these slave-code definitions determine our cultures and their legacies and traditions and are the most basic cause of the separations, divisions, conflicts and wars between humans. The major primary clue as to why we are still hindered by primitive self-contradictions manifests when we add to our self-adulatory history of progress, from gods to Gods to Armageddon. It does not fit the trajectory. It not only stops the forward momentum but also reverses it. The appallingly primitive status quo is revealed, therefore, at its most fundamental strata, to be simply a continuation of the archaic theo-political conflicts that we have known for the past three thousand years. The major obstacles that are most fundamentally influencing and hindering our planetary understanding and progress are cultural legacies, cultural lock-ins that are with us as the deepest dyes in the tapestries of our cultures, locked in legacies that influence our thinking, our science, our logic, and our concepts of ourselves. We are too close to them, or think that they do not influence us, or that they have been dealt with in the scientific or academic world long ago, or that we can just ignore them. We deal, furthermore, with all these problems in a Paleolithic, turfish manner from the isolated towers of Cartesian-Newtonian oligarchies.

These problems translate to the problems that are related to our children and their education. Currently, we matriculate our young, these amazing, parallel processing, relativistic, quantum jumping, multi-dimensional consciousnesses, semi-illiterate and naive for fear of them questioning our shambling senilities. In a time when we need to stretch our historical sense to allow for the visitation of our planet by alien species from before our origins, we teach them drum and trumpet mammalian history fleshed out with desiccated, parochial, political platitudes. We teach our own children, privately, generally the same platitudes and clichés we were taught and brand them with the same religious, scientific, and intellectual taboos we were tattooed with as children and expect that they will somehow be ready to do better than we and perhaps even step into stellar society. Whether we deny it our not, our children show all the signs of being ready; they are underwhelmed and overqualified. We feel it. Nevertheless, we do not teach our minors philosophy although they are capable of calculus. We do not allow a teacher in the public school system to teach our children anything important about anything important because we do not agree about what to teach them, because we do not agree about who and what we are. We do not educate our children in the management and refinement and evolution of their personal spectrums of consciousness because we do not agree on what that spectrum includes. And the children are literally our future, we in the future.

This chapter began with a self-congratulatory accounting of our rapid, amazing rise from Mesopotamia to the Moon to Mars, from stone to steel to silicon; from clubs to a second Constitution; from swords to guns to the U.N. We, Sapiens are indeed rising, but the planet is drenched in a great sadness we all feel and would be done with. We are at species crisis point.

Our planet, this agonizingly beautiful little planet, is on hold. We call ourselves the doubly wise and marvel at our rapid rise from the savannas to space but how can we progress so rapidly, so precociously in so many ways yet seem so primitive and be so confused in fundamental ways even to ourselves? We know that we are not incapable but we are painfully dysfunctional. How can this be? Why are we this way?

Sapiens Stymied

We are locked in deadly conflict not just over borders or ideology but over profoundly innocent questions: what and who are we; what are our real beginnings and our real history; what is our place and meaning in the universe; how should we act towards each other as humans; what should our trajectory into the future be.

Certainly we must acknowledge the many problems and dangers currently facing us as groups, nations, regions, sects and tribes. We identify conflict between the forward driving pressure of our participation in the process of cosmic unfurlment and the contracting, retarding pressure of survival resistance to change; political unrest and corruption; conventional energy source peaking; global warming; threat of asteroid strikes; supervolcanoes; widening gulf between the have and have-nots; terrible epidemics, among others. But these are symptoms, the toxic gray flowers, not the root cause of the agony in the deepest of our sensibilities.

Unfortunately the children, generation after generation, are those who get caught in the squeeze between these forces. We remain Babel-factored and wounded and the children silently traumatized by these maladies of body and spirit.

How do we explain this profoundly embarrassing, retrograde conduct to ourselves?

We excuse our adolescent conduct to each other as come-lately naked apes or inherently flawed creations of fearful deities, or cyclically reincarnating amateur spirit beings or deeply determined vehicles of a molecular intelligence we hardly understand, yet knowing, each privately, that none of those skins fit one's self. Desperately trying to help ourselves in this time of planetary crisis we analyze ourselves in terms of the psychology and strategies of politics; of the escalation of primitive tribal clashes to those of civilizations; of biological causes of the rise and fall of our societies, of denial and disassociation from the world of nature and spirit, of the inadequacies of our educational systems, of social, economic and political corruption.

But fundamental to all these feeble explanations is the reluctantly acknowledged major causal element: religious conflict. Under the transparent, brittle veneer of civilization we uniquely accommodate religion as we accommodate no other institution or ideology. We astound ourselves by our deciphering of scientific mysteries while, at the same time, we deny and suppress whole segments of obvious realities, earthly and cosmic, which contradict our sacrosanct religious views. East and West, under duress of self-justifying theologies we can hardly believe, we give allegiance to deities whose base humanoid characteristics fall far short of the easiest standards to which the best of us hold ourselves. Rationalizing our allegiance by acts of irrational "faith", we robotically slaughter each other and ourselves over whose "god" is better or the only real one, in hideous wars that make the protocols of headhunters seem almost innocently civilized. We express the highest ideals of spirit in terms of union with cosmified and divinized abstractions of those same gods for whom we kill.

Now this litany, obviously, constitutes a very broad, serious and daunting self-critique. I posit a caveat: When I name names and institutions, critically or otherwise, I intend them as part of us, as a self-indictment: it is simply we doing these things to ourselves, we, Sapiens, rising determinedly, sometimes stumbling, but reaching for the stars.

Let us be easy on ourselves, however, since we are the only game like us on the planet, the only example we can work with, the inadequate conceptual boxes we inhabit are of our making but also ours out of which to break. If these negatives were all there were, then the fears of those in future shock would be vindicated. If I had no suggestions, solutions, answers or resolutions to offer I would not have written this paper. So this white paper respectfully offers a futurist overview and paradigm that can take us, in the perspective of a deepened knowledge of our species and ourselves, to a new level of racial maturity and a degree of freedom previously unavailable. The futant view from 2100 describes us on the other side of the realevolutionary transmutation already begun.

How can we do that? Where are the positive engines idling that we can drive out of the darkened context of our time? Are there resolutions and solutions available and a way forward? Unequivocally, Yes.

It may seem totally contradictory against the darkness of the disconcerting indictment laid out so far but I say here, confidently and without equivocation, that this time is the end game of an age, be certain, but it is the opening of a new dimension of human existence, the scope and exhilarating depth of which we have hardly begun to perceive. A new human and a new civilization, beyond our primitive beginnings, beyond religion and the old new age are on the horizon.

Characterizing The Transition To Transmutation

The radical species shift we are already entering and experiencing, may be called, accurately, a transformation but I prefer the term Transmutation because our being consciously involved in determining its trajectory and the sense of fundamental mutational change is stronger. There are a number of explanations of what the anticipated shift will be. Most are familiar with the various religious interpretations of the Book of Revelations of the New Testament that anticipate either the literal end of the world, or, some, the end of time in the sense of an end of an age or, yet again, another interpretation with or without the coming of Christ after a war in the Armageddon area of the middle east, the wiping out of all Muslims, Jews who do not convert to Christianity, the building of the second temple at Jerusalem and a rapture of all Christian faithful naked into the clouds as Jesus comes back to rule what's left of the human population of the world. There are new age interpretations that do not see any destructive, definitive end of the world but see a kind of change of time itself. Another concept of the shift is focused on the Mayan predictions of a major event marking an ending of a time period that will see great change in the year 2012. Some are convinced that 2012 is literally the date Planet X / Nibiru will come to perigee. Futurists tend to speak in terms of a coming shift and attempt to determine what it will be and how we may adapt most comfortably to it. But we are the Transmutation, we are it happening, we can form and inform it by realizing the vision we want ourselves to be and how we will be it. But it is well to listen to the futurists and to identify and evaluate the elements they see.

A very novel scenario of the shift is promulgated by Ray Kurzweil, inventor and futurist, which he calls The Singularity. He defines a singularity of this kind as:

...a future period during which the pace of technological change will be so rapid, its impact so deep, that human life will be irreversibly transformed...

The key idea underlying the impending Singularity is that the pace of change of our human-created technology is accelerating and its powers are expanding at an exponential rate ... The Singularity will allow us to transcend those limitations of our biological bodies and brains. We will be able to live as long as we want ... The Singularity will represent the culmination of the merger of our biological thinking and existence with our technology, resulting in a world that is still human but that transcends our biological roots."[6]

The most unique characteristic of the most ideal form of the Transmutation is that it will be the first time in our species history that it will be accomplished by the effort of the entire species' deliberate conscious cooperative effort. That may be expecting too much, although the thrust of this paper is to promulgate just that.

We are self-aware. Gorillas like Koko and Chimps like Kanzi are self aware as are dolphins. But we distinguish ourselves by our self-awareness of our self-awareness which gives us seeming magnitudes of potential control over all phases of our existence. This unique degree of self-reflexive feedback is our most powerful tool, a potential that affords us the ability to achieve the most critical aspect of the Transmutation: that we finally define and know ourselves truly and confidently on a consensual species basis in order to effect the transformation maximally.

We identify four major elements that currently inform the leading edge of our species' evolutionary unfurlment as primary:

1) We are being invited to enter stellar society. The clear evidence for the presence and contact with alien species has been with us for decades.

2) We are in process of restoring our true history as a genetically engineered species created by our parent species, the Anunnaki. The overwhelming evidence for our genesis as a genetically synthesized species, known to all the original civilizations and gradually suppressed and denied, has been available to us since it's reintroduction by the Sumerian scholar Zecharia Sitchin thirty years ago.

3) We have one major planetary, species problem: the threat of extinction due to the effect of some Passings of the tenth planet, Planet X / Nibiru through the inner solar system, understated as a major rallying point for species unity for survival. The tenth planet, Nibiru, home planet of the Anunnaki, its potential danger to the Earth known to all the ancient civilizations, was rediscovered in 1983 by the IRAS, the Infrared Astronomical Satellite search team.

4)   We are about to reinvent ourselves, physically and mentally, through advanced technology, the implementation of "free, energy" and artificial intelligence and achieve extreme life spans, relative immortality.

These intimately interrelated factors, paramount at the leading edge of our species' unfurlment, can and are exerting a leverage on our species --- whether acknowledged "officially" or not, whether denied or suppressed in the collective consciousness --- to transmute evermore rapidly. The transmutation to the new human can be endured without understanding and many lost in a ridiculous kind of Darwinian thinning of an unconscious herd or it can be a planetary triumph and transformation of the entire species through conscious participation and contribution beyond anything known previously.

Why, therefore, should these extraordinary factors be so vehemently and paradoxically denied, ignored, suppressed? It is well to look to the nature of the institutions and individuals who deny and suppress them. None of our current institutions, governmental, religious, social, scientific, economic, military, evolved or were designed to deal with alien societies or human society as exosocial, exopolitical. The facts that there are aliens present and inviting us into stellar society; that we have the evidence and species maturity to restore our true history as a genetically engineered species; that religion is not what we have been indoctrinated to think it is, rather it is the sublimated continuation of the ancient master slave relationship we were created under; that we must be a united and peaceful species taking no weapons into space as an entrance requirement to stellar society, all these elements are beyond the scope of any of our institutions in their classic forms. A cooperative planetary effort to protect the entire species in the event of the next Passing of X / Nibiru being a catastrophic one is not impossible but certainly novel and monumental enough a task that current governments tend to boggle. They can and shall transmute to do so but, currently, are totally inadequate and stagnant. The natural reaction is defensive and negative.

The military reaction is to deny and conceal what they cannot deal with or protect against and hope to obtain, accidentally or deliberately, technology and weapons to die for.

Governments, generally, deny and conceal what they cannot deal with in the hopes of keeping power and control and order and avoiding chaos and anarchy in their societies.

Religions, as we have known them, particularly the dogmatic fundamentalist types, realize already that they are facing denouement at the edge of space. Religion as we have known it is finished and the religions are groping for some way to transmute, at best, and some are becoming desperately aggressive at worst.

Economic policy makers and corporations and bankers all realize that the amazing technologies displayed by the aliens utilize very advanced power sources, most probably of the free energy and antigravity types which would make our primitive resources such as oil and atomic energy obsolete. This would have a profound impact on major industries and the economies of the world. Generally they are content to simply keep the status quo for as long as possible. At worst, they do positively criminal acts to suppress, manipulate and control.

Science has the easiest potential adaptation although there is too much reactive protecting of status and position and theory coupled with secret hope of gaining proprietary access to scientific breakthroughs by alien donation.

The essence of the situation is that there are twin exopolitical elephants in our species' living room. The situation is best understood in terms of extra-solar system exopolitics and intra-solar system exopolitics. Extra-solar system exopolitics involves our relationship, interaction with alien societies and species coming from outside our solar system, some from very distant places indeed. Intra-solar system politics involves our relationship and interaction with alien societies from within our own solar system, specifically and significantly our parent species, the Anunnaki, and possibly races from Mars.

What we need to do as a species is clear: we must become consciously exosocial; acknowledge and resolve our relationship, as an independent, mature species, with our parent species, the Anunnaki; expand our consciousness to grasp the potential of immortality; develop free energy sources and advanced nanotechnology to move beyond competition and money to cooperation; transform to a united and peaceful and prosperous planetary society; succeed in protecting and preserving our species from extinction in those times of catastrophic Passings of the tenth planet; learn to transmute ourselves physically into more perfect beings, expand our consciousness into higher dimensionality and take total control of our own realevolution. To paraphrase Dylan Thomas, let us not go blind into that daylight.

As we examine each of these major factors individually the interdependency between them will become apparent, the keys to unlocking the gates of standstill manifest, the necessity of isolating those of us who would, from fear or devolved motive, thwart the species obvious, the necessity and advantages for solving the survival problem of the Passing pressing, the potential for species improvement and advancement exhilarating, the modalities necessary to achieve stellar citizenship clear, the resonance of our bicameral DNA to the harmonics of the vision of the now and future human irresistible. Let us make it so for the children.

2

SAPIENS CHALLENGED:
AN INVITATION TO THE COSMIC DANCE

Synopsis

It is taken as an obvious given that we are being visited, monitored, contacted, gradually informed, taught by a near embarrassment of alien species who have been patiently revealing their crafts and persons and agendas to us over a long period of time. We must by- pass the government cover-ups, develop our knowledge and skills in exopolitics (the interactions of the human species with alien species) learn the exosociology or both our species and that of alien species and prepare for stellar citizenship.

Are there alien species from outside our solar system sometimes present in our solar system? Yes. Are there alien species from outside our solar system sometimes present in space in proximity to our planet? Yes. Are there alien species sometimes present in our atmosphere and sometimes on the surface of our planet? Yes. Are alien species contacting and interacting with governments and individuals on this planet and in space? Yes. These facts hardly need any proof adduced: the plethora of pictures, films, videotaped images of alien craft of various types in our skies seemingly every day which are also caught as radar targets, and military and civilian sightings cannot be refuted or denied. The close encounters of humans in the thousands if not the millions worldwide with aliens of various species and the information gleaned from those contacts together with the personal testimony of military and civilian individuals who have, as part of their professional careers, been in indirect or direct contact with alien species is overwhelming. It is not the purpose of this paper to review the voluminous evidence and testimonies concerning the alien presence: it proceeds by building on that base. We are only too painfully aware of our species' general planetary social status quo --- mindful, however, that some of us have already transcended it --- and the primitive, puzzling, divisive and violent elements determining it but we are far less aware of our potential exosocial status. What does it mean to be exosocial, an exosocial species?

Exosociology 1A

Exosocial means being aware of off planet affairs, at home in the solar system and the universe, knowing our history, our species identity and place in the cosmos, being familiar and comfortable with the fact of alien species, learning our own unique exosociology and that of alien species, becoming a member species of stellar society, knowing both the basic physical laws and the social rules of the universe. Exopolitics is understood as a pragmatic subset of exosociology. I prefer the term exosocial because it has a broader sense and subsumes the "politic" element, politics having a generally negative connotation among the general public. Exopolitics (we are indebted to Alfred Lambremont Webre PhD, for the coining of this term): defined here as extra (outside of) terrestrial, human-alien politics, alien-alien politics, across the entire sociobiological spectrum --- and socio-physical spectrum also because we need to include human-android and alien-android politics. Interaction with alien species already requires the dimensional expansion of our concepts of existence, species interrelationships: exodiplomacy promises not to be boring. Currently, we are just beginning to edge our way into interstellar exopolitics like a young adolescent feeling his way into adult society. This practical distinction of exopolitics as a subset of exosociology is intended to expand our focus and allow us to adjust our perspective and realize that, as frustrating and obstructing the posture and attitude of any government or institution or individual has been and is, there is no reason why we must wait or hesitate to engage in human--alien exosocial, exosociobiological, interspecies interchange, interrelations, intercommunications.

There is no reason for an individual to have to wait for those who simply have no concept or inclination for dealing with the alien situation; whose personal religious belief systems prevent them; those whom fear prevents; whose economic interests are not served; whose power and control is questioned and threatened; or whose agenda is positively counterproductive or opposed. The recognition of our own naive and relatively primitive status in these matters strikes some of us with shock and others of us as humorous, but the choice has been narrowed down to only two options. We can continue, turned in on ourselves terracentrically, in denial about large segments of clear and proximate physical reality, in unending conflict over antique theo-political doctrines or become exosocial, planetarily, as a species. We know that the first option could literally destroy us, indeed is attacking the heart of our species. We are being approached by other cosmic species and we must learn and understand the expanded off-planet exosocial context and exopolitical rules of such an event as a species in order to participate intelligently and securely. We are overdue for such an expansion. We need to become our own exosociologists and exodiplomats individually, personally, as well as collectively, and to study broadly and independently to achieve competence in preparation for engaging aliens species directly.

A supreme irony of our times is that we wait for and look to the very governments for disclosure and verification which have been responsible for the suppression of the facts all along. That fact, although certainly embarrassing, should not be taken as a negative but as an indicator of our general species' current naive exosocial status. There is not just one major deception and cover-up but two agendas of suppression and misinformation for dominance, power and control, carried out by two quite separate but interrelated types of entities: one political, one religious. These econo-political-military and religious agendas of disinformation, deception and dominance are not only interrelated but mutually reinforcing.

We are most familiar, indeed painfully familiar, with the cover-ups, suppression and misdirection of our and other governments. The fact that several foreign countries, Belgium, Spain, China, India, Brazil, Mexico and Iran most recently, have officially recognized the alien presence, does not say much for the general progress we have made planet wide in the half century plus since Roswell. Just as frustrating and even more embarrassing, although perhaps a good deal more superstitious than criminal, is the prevalent religious blocking of intelligent understanding of the alien phenomenon as demonic, Satanic and fearful. The tribal reliance on authority coupled with the godspell orientation to religion severely retards our exosocial maturation. We can continue to try to back into space and stellar society haltingly, bewildered and in denial, but we will be handicapped severely by our ignorance and fear and will not be accepted until we act as a sufficiently mature species.

The politics of the interactions between humans and human government(s) albeit with regard to the alien topic, is, by and large, not really exopolitics at all. In various situations around the globe of the people or advocate groups or individuals vs. government or institutions, regarding the matters of disclosure, non-disclosure, military interpretation and response, determination of policy, secrecy, deliberate deception and misleading of the people, governmental responsibilities to the citizens in this regard, or general discussion, action and reaction relative to the alien topic, are not really exopolitics. These are matters of terrestrial, very dirt and turf, human-to-human politics.

Certainly, the gradually evolved movements and agendas mounted by various groups and individuals to force disclosure with regard to the alien topic, to gather and publicize alien sightings and contacts, to educate the public about the alien topic in general, are all vital and valuable efforts. This paper acknowledges them as essential, major, contributions to the unfolding process of creating species awareness and comprehension in this regard and uses them as a base upon which to build but the focus here is an overarching view of the unfolding process itself.

Human Exopolitics

Our exosocial status as a species is currently determined by two major factors: the dawning awareness that we are being offered stellar citizenship as a species and the re-recognition of our true history as a half-alien, genetically synthesized species. These two factors are intimately interrelated: restoration of our true history affords us the way to move beyond divisive religious conflicts to generic, united humanity.

We are a young, adolescent, relatively very new species, just coming out of a three thousand year traumatic transition from genetically engineered slave species status by our parent species, the Anunnaki, to the beginnings of independence and genetic enlightenment. We can attain stellar citizenship if we can meet the basic rules of stellar society: no weapons in space and acceptance if we can unite as a peaceful species.

It should not be humiliating that we must simply realize that we have hardly exited the Dark Ages, our science is sophomoric, and it was yesterday when our best scientists were beginning to speculate that we are not alone in the universe. It should not frighten us, simply make us realistically evaluate our position in the universe and willing to learn how to advance. We are only now beginning to realize that the real obstacle to our species' unification is our divisive godspell psychosis that keeps us Babel-factored, divided and conflicted by religio-cultural absolutes.

At our current general stage of realevolution we use, as our assumed criteria for identifying an alien species as worthy of our attention, possible defensive posture, or interaction, the degree of self-awareness they exhibit regardless of how physically strange they may appear. This has very possibly already caused us some confusion. We have taken recovered or captured alien beings to be advanced humanoids when, as with the Roswell crash saucer occupants, they were identified at autopsy, according to Colonel Phil Corso, as androids, it would be well that we be aware that any alien species we encounter may be android yet possibly more evolved than we. This may be a point of deep disconcertion for some but a potential reality nevertheless.

It is only very recently that we have begun to seriously consider the possibility of creating artificial intelligences and the possibility of them becoming self-aware. We can gain valuable lessons from studying self-aware alien androids for our development of them and for understanding of alien species in general.

An outward focus and expanded scope of consideration allow us to see easily that there are two major facets of pragmatic human exopolitics:

1> Extra-solar system exopolitics: the most general form of exopolitics we are involved in is contact and interaction, negotiations with a variety of alien species around and on the planet. I have called this the extra-solar system alien phase because the overwhelming number of alien species involved come from outside our solar system.

2> Intra-solar system exopolitics: a more specific and immediate phase of our involvement with aliens is the need to resolve our intimate relationship of genetic kinship with our alien parent species, the Anunnaki (which makes us part-alien ourselves). There seems to be evidence that there may well be a species inhabiting Mars that we will need to investigate.

Extra-solar system Exopolitics

Drawing on all sources, contactees' reports, military sources and records, government documents, remote viewer reports, prehistoric and historic traces and records, tribal legends, archaeological and paleontological data, and personal experience, we can determine our pragmatic exopolitical position rather easily.

It is obvious that, because of their advanced knowledge, science, technology and experience cosmically, compared to our relatively primitive, adolescent and divided state as a species, the timing and mode of contact is being, will be determined by the various individual or federations of alien species rather than us. Our general species reaction has clearly evolved under the influence and in response to alien overtures. (I submit that overtures is a better word than, simply, contact because it more accurately conveys the nature of the whole phenomenon.) Because of our naïve and divided position, there are uncertainties and fears among us in this regard.

A major question at the forefront of considerations among investigators and thoughtful humans addresses whether the alien agenda is benign and benevolent or manipulative and dangerous. The answer is far more complex than the question. My firm basic assumption underlying the logic in this regard, based on seventy years of personal experience and intense study, is that alien species, possessing advanced science and technology sufficient to allow them to control gravity, travel throughout the universe, have evolved sufficiently and their technology has freed them from material and energy needs to the extent that they would have no need to take over the Earth or us or to do anything harmful to obtain material resources or energy or even genetic, biological components. Why bother when you could easily accomplish anything you wished in a laboratory, including any kind or level of genetic engineering. Any species capable of creating highly intelligent, self-aware biotech androids should hardly be expected to have to travel half way across the universe to "harvest" samples of our manifestly faulty DNA for incorporation into theirs to somehow save their species or acquire our emotional elements as has been postulated. They may systematically and skillfully "mutilate" cattle to obtain biological samples but they do not do that to humans. Actually mutilating cattle in an undeniably high tech fashion and leaving the carcasses dramatically displayed may, in this context, be interpreted as an intended, quite undeniable, signal of presence and agenda --- and warning about our potentially disastrous ecological missteps.

A Primer of Exopsychology

The basis for our disconcertion and fear of alien species does not spring from an actual history of their brutalization of us but from our relatively primitive and ignorant reactions to their strangeness, technical capabilities, perception of our evolutionary status and resultant attitudes and agendas.

I believe it is most adequate to address the topic of exosociology in terms of IQ, CQ, EQ, intelligence, consciousness, and evolutionary quotients of both alien species and ours. The reaction of an individual of any species to any other species will vary according to the IQ, CQ, and EQ of that individual.

The key to understanding the psychodynamics of the wide variety of species already known to us in their widely varying manifestations of evolutionary adaptations, is the concept of self-reflexive awareness. I assume here only that the process by which individual species arise in any given environment, on or off any kind of cosmic body that can support them, is what I prefer to call the general unfurlment of the universe as a more general and accurate term than the Darwinian kind of evolution generally espoused. There seems to be a universal trajectory through which, at certain points of the general physiochemical unfurlment of, at least, our universe, individuated species arise. On this planet it began with very simple organisms some of which gradually colonized, leading to more and more complex organisms. We can trace a process of self-contained complexification, through invertebrates to invertebrates, from fish to reptiles, to birds, animals, anthropoids to humanoids. The process is marked by the development of information processing consciousness development, from simple reflexive response awareness to basic self awareness to a level of self-awareness of self-awareness giving rise to a greater and greater degrees of control and manipulation of the organism and its environment by the organism. A caveat is in order here: the identification of self awareness of self-awareness as the key turning point must be qualified by pointing out that it is an extrapolation from our situation: human self-awareness of its self-awareness projecting the mechanism, by which it sees itself as having come about on other species of whatever type, as a general principle.

We identify species that we consider to be close to our equal or superior in evolutionary development and to which we could possibly relate by our estimation of their intelligence and primarily of their degree of self-awareness. We should certainly keep an open mind for the possibility of encountering an intelligence which has evolved to a point where what we know as our "highest" faculties of consciousness of self and universe have been relegated, in that entity, to a status which we know our autonomic functions to occupy.

In our case as a genetically engineered species, the development of self-awareness in Homo erectus was interrupted and accelerated in the merging with the Anunnaki species, already highly self-aware, in the process of bringing us into existence as a new species synthetically. But the key turning point of the development of self- awareness of self-awareness, giving rise gradually to self-directed evolution, remains valid in our special case.

To elucidate this critical point, let us consider the nature of some of the alien species which have been identified as present and interacting with us. Some appear and claim to be very similar to us with a humanoid form with which we can easily identify and be comfortable. But there are also insectoid, reptoid, humanoid, and even android types which can be startlingly disconcerting. That they approach us in those forms would indicate that it was at that type and stage of evolutionary unfurlment within the environment in which they arose that their transition to self-awareness of self-awareness took place.

As a single example: we instinctively expect the "emotional", intellectual, and hormonal, psychodynamics of an insectoid based advanced species to be very different from a humanoid one. Our psychodynamic reaction to them, at least initially, has been, quite predictably, like our general reaction to insects. We project, speculate, anticipate that an insectoid based alien will lack emotions as we know and experience them, may be difficult to communicate with, perhaps predatory --- especially if they resemble a giant version of the predatory terran praying mantis --- may, reciprocally, not understand and misinterpret our nature and reactions, generally seeming perhaps the most "alien" of the alien species we have encountered. But we will have to get past those assumptions and judge on the basis of direct observation.

By contrast, those species that seem "close" to us, the Pleidians as reported by Billy Meier as example, maybe 3000 years techno-socially advanced ahead of us, we tend to assume will treat and interact with us quite "accurately". The humanoid-based Verdants in contact with Phil Krapf, the 30-year veteran desk editor retired from the Los Angeles Times, are so far advanced that they could and do categorize and understand our psychosomatic social dynamics and us after studying us for a thousand years far better than we understand ourselves generally.

There does appear to be good evidence, however, that there have been misjudgments made by alien species concerning our reactions and us. A survey of the reports of such incidents show an interesting fact: "mistakes", misunderstandings of human reactions, misjudgments of human responses, seem to be associated with certain alien types, some of whom may well be androids, surrogates. It is rather humiliating in some respect to understand that advanced species are confident that their androids are intelligent and "professional" enough to be fully capable of dealing with a species such as we. As if we had sent a team of self-aware, trained androids who could telepathically communicate in fluent chimpanzee to capture a chimpanzee (also self-aware to a measurable degree) for examination and cataloging but, their briefer having been unaware of some detail of chimp psychology, they do not realize that something they do is very traumatic to the animal.

The concept of surrogate android requires consideration. I think that some, not all, aliens of the android kind with which we have had real contact may be surrogates and understanding them made easier by that realization It seems clear, as Linda Moulton Howe has pointed out for some time, that there are classes of androids, some limited drones, some more complex in their programming and intelligence and complexity of function. My hypothesis is that surrogate androids would be, perhaps, a notch above any of these. We will discuss the concept in detail in Chapter Five.

Realistically, however, even though we fully realize that we would be powerless in the face of far superior alien technology as has already been demonstrated to us and our military and our scientists gradually over time, we should recognize and prepare ourselves for alien agendas across the entire spectrum of possibilities we can imagine from evil to exalted benevolence. There could be and most likely are at least some species that retain a dominant characteristic of primitive aggression and brutality even at stages of advanced intelligence and technological capability. Advanced species have indicated that there are some species which are dangerous because they maintain a primitive, aggressive, ruthless element in their makeup even though developing higher intelligence. Phil Krapf writes, in The Contact Has Begun[7] that he was instructed by the Verdants, a highly advanced species, that they are able to control and isolate and prevent aggressive and violent species from taking advantage of less advanced species. They claim that, when a species reaches the level of "absolute intelligence" (the absolute level of intelligence and information attainable by a biologically based species, where no further improvement is possible --- a fascinating revelation, if literally true, about the nature of the universe) they are able to use non-violent methods based on their "absolute knowledge" to do so. He was told that "Once absolute intelligence is achieved, use of force to settle disputes is out of the question because it is a tool of the ignorant and the inferior. Therefore, it is impossible to meet a warlike species with absolute intelligence. The two qualities are mutually exclusive ... if it has achieved absolute intelligence it cannot be warlike.[8]"

The possibility of an alien species taking over our planet, manipulating and enslaving us, or even just insinuating themselves into the planet to manipulate us secretly, perhaps to take resources from the planet, must be considered. But the rather simple facts that have become clear over time, viz., that we would be powerless against the weaponry of a species much more advanced than we; that there is no evidence that any species has ever attacked us; that the vast number of reports of actual alien communication has shown that the most advanced species have expressed concern for human welfare in general and great concern for our survival. This should move us to consider that our primitive projections are just that and peace is a requisite for free operation in stellar society.

In a very primitive way, our science fiction, which allows us to vicariously play out trial scenarios, has pointed to this as a manifestation of our evolving psychology: the Star Trek series featured such archetypes as the Klingons whose very culture was based on force, the Borg who had developed into a hive-like aggressive and robot collective society. The captain figure of the Enterprise evolved from the macho and muscular Kirk, to the intellectual, Earl Grey drinking Picard, and, eventually, to a female captain. Our science fiction projections on the future are a rather telling indicator of where we stand exosocially. If the most advanced species are beyond violence and war, our current planetary situation portrays us as primitive indeed.

As we have indeed played out in our science fiction projections, as common sense dictates and actual alien contact has shown, the first approach by alien species is to our militaries. Why? Because we, currently, are dangerous and the militaries are the most dangerous. They are tasked to defend and their criterion is simple: friend or foe. When in doubt the incoming is taken as possible foe until proven differently. We consider our human brothers who still practice headhunting and intertribal warfare "primitive" and do not put ourselves into danger by going into their territories without serious protection. If we do approach to attempt to establish contact, trade, to insinuate the rudiments of civility, it is with caution and serious protection. There is a fine line between demonstrating peaceful intent and protecting oneself, between demonstrating total superiority of technology and weaponry and causing fearful aggressive reaction on the part of a relatively primitive group or species. It is my speculation that some alien craft that were reported "shot down" were deliberately sacrificed, including the android crews, for the sake of alleviating extreme fear and paranoia.

There is a repeated scenario in the literature and reports of alien encounters that is both disconcerting and fascinating: apparent deliberate crossbreeding of human-alien children. Deliberate interbreeding of an alien species with humans for the sake of interspecies communication and interaction is a novel concept which we should not reject out of hand, provided that the individual is accorded all the rights and dignity we take as essential to a human. This is an entirely new area to us and we need to study it from the point of view of ethics, human rights, alien rights, artificial intelligence, and the topic of interspecies interaction in general.

We shall consider Intra-Solar-System Exopolitics, in essence our relationship to the Anunnaki, in the next chapter.

Alien Exosociology

The exosocial status of alien species known or, at least, perceived by us, has several elements in common. The age of their species is far older than ours. Their science is far more expanded dimensionally than ours. Their technology is far in advance of ours.

Some of their physiologies resemble our anthropoid/humanoid base, some are insectoid; some are reptilian based; some seem to be native to some other dimensions than our habitual four; some seem to be energy based rather than matter based.

Although we only know what has been given to us by a limited number of alien species, a general common characteristic of their evolutionary development is a trajectory that moves from their particular original, primitive biological base, understood as more or less aggressive, competitive, violent, toward a more and more conscious, cooperative, peaceful, tolerant, intelligent and caring state of unity of species. We can gain insight into how we may learn to control and direct our own evolutionary trajectory as we develop as a species. Non-interference with other species, a sort of universal prime directive and rule, seems to include isolating and protecting against species, regardless of intelligent and technological advancement, who persist in carrying the aggressive, violent or exploitive traits into their later stages as they move into space. We may well learn from this general principles with regard to how to treat and deal with those of our species who may be inclined to maintain a violent or aggressive species posture. Species who are capable of advanced space travel and visit Earth have indicated in one way or another that they consider us as rather primitive and treat us as such although they recognize and respect intelligence and greater consciousness when they encounter it. Their agendas vary within the limits of altruism although there may be species that consider us so primitive that they feel at liberty and it expedient to treat us at about the same level as we treat chimpanzees and gorillas.

Obviously it is difficult to appreciate such nuances if being manhandled but we should try.

From the earliest records of aliens depicted in petroglyphs in prehistoric times to recent weekend intensive seminars given to selected humans aboard alien craft, the degree of comprehension of the nature of the human held by the aliens and how they evaluate us conditions the nature of their approach. Whether it be landings in the presence of early humans, attention getting fly-bys of "flying shields" for Roman populaces, aerial performances recorded in medieval paintings, mass over-flights, flying off the wing of airliners, teasing military pilots, meeting with high officials, donating technology, soliciting cooperation from lone individuals, carrying on mass abductions for examinations for biological cataloging or monitoring, animal mutilation sampling for dangerous conditions due to toxins and pollutants, executing long term agendas for species wide contact, the obvious determining elements are how evolved and ready the individual human is, how ready and receptive the group or species is. Genetics, intelligence, consciousness spectrum, evolutionary development, all seem to enter into the selection of an individual human for contact, instruction, cooperation, crossbreeding for interspecies rapport. Some alien species seem to be able to read the genetic signature of an individual from without with ease.

There is a clear pattern of development in the kind and intent of contact from Paleolithic prehistory to current high tech demonstrations, individual indoctrinations and collaborations. As we become more evolved and cosmically aware, the alien agendas have slowly evolved from monitoring and cataloging to careful contact meant to inform and acquaint to a quite obvious education of and invitation to our species for stellar citizenship. The ships get closer without frightening, the photo ops become more frequent and more striking, the demonstrations of technological capabilities from instant invisibility and appearance, to more and more insistent intervention, to neutralize or destroy atomic and space weaponry much more obvious, the warnings about our planetary and space ecological follies more urgent and insistent.

The vast majority of humans want to evolve and create a better existence for our children. If they knew how. There is a minority that would, for devolved, fear based or selfish reasons, keep our species in cosmic isolation and stagnant in our current primitive condition. If they, individually or as groups, attempt to impose their will in that respect on the rest of the species or individuals they should be isolated. Their free choice should be respected just as they should be expected to respect the choice of those who would become exosocial stellar citizens. The rule that all should respect is that anyone should be allowed to chose and do as their freedom dictates as long as their choices and actions do not prevent others from exercising their freedom of choice and actions.

literally, redefine ourselves as humans. In a word, there is a third explanation of our beginnings and history. Sitchin's thesis illuminates our beginnings and our history with Nobel prize quality research, renders the, by now, Monty Pythonesque arguments outmoded, subsumes and corrects creationism, redefines Darwinism (as it applies specifically to our species) as well as its latter day detractions. He has been able to do this because he reads Sumerian as well as the Semitic languages including ancient and Modern Hebrew, and is steeped in the history and archaeology. He has had the advantage of access to the accumulated scholarship and archaeological material from the Middle East rediscovered only in the last one hundred and fifty years.

Sir Laurence Gardner, English historian and genealogist, has made an equally important contribution, taking up where Sitchin leaves off, more specifically in the realm of western culture. He has afforded the other side of Christianity, the entire heterodox tradition, opposite from the self-styled orthodox Roman Church, the opportunity to speak and the revelation is startling.

Our Genesis Revisited: The Sitchin Paradigm

Working from the same archaeological discoveries, artifacts, and recovered records as archaeologists and linguists have for two hundred years, Sitchin propounds -proves conclusively, in the opinion of this author -that the Anunnaki (Sumerian: "those who came down from the heavens"; Old testament Hebrew, Anakeim, Nefilim, Elohim; Egyptian: Neter), an advanced civilization from the tenth planet in our solar system, splashed down in the Persian gulf area around 432,000 years ago, colonized the planet, with the purpose of obtaining large quantities of gold. The sculptures, depictions, descriptions of the Anunnaki present them as male and female, the males bearded, generally taller and huskier than we are today, light skinned, their sexual and social customs generally like ours with the notable exception that, at least in the procreation of a son destined for continuation of a line, mating with a half sister was the preferred practice. The evidence and corroboration of this thesis will be developed below.

Some 250,000 years ago, the recovered documents tell us, their lower echelon miners rebelled against the conditions in the mines and the Anunnaki directorate decided to create a creature to take their place. Enki, their chief scientist and Ninhursag their chief medical officer, after getting no satisfactory results splicing animal and Homo Erectus genes, merged their Anunnaki genes with that of Homo Erectus and produced us, Homo Sapiens, a genetically bicameral species, for their purposes as slaves. Because we were a hybrid, we could not procreate. The demand for us as workers became greater and we were genetically manipulated to reproduce.

Eventually, we became so numerous that some of us were expelled from the Anunnaki city centers, gradually spreading over the planet. Having become a stable genetic stock and developing more precociously than, perhaps, the Anunnaki had anticipated, the Anunnaki began to be attracted to humans as sexual partners and children were born of these unions. This was unacceptable to the majority of the Anunnaki high council and it was decided to let the human population be wiped out through an anticipated world wide catastrophe (the Flood of the Old Testament) that was predictable when Nibiru, the tenth in our solar system and the Anunnaki home planet, came through the inner solar system again (around 12,500 years ago) on one of its periodic 3600 year returns. Some humans were saved by the action of the Anunnaki official, Enki, who was sympathetic to the humans he had originally genetically created and a very few survived worldwide.

For thousands of years, we were their slaves, their workers, their servants, and their soldiers in their political battles among themselves. The Anunnaki used us in the construction of their palaces (we retroproject the religious notion of temple on these now), their cities, their mining and refining complexes and their astronomical installations on all the continents. They expanded from Mesopotamia to Egypt to India to South and Central America and the stamp of their presence can be found in the farthest reaches of the planet.

Around 6000 years ago, they, realizing that they were going to phase off the planet, began, gradually, to bring humans to independence. Sumer, a human civilization, amazing in its "sudden", mature, and highly advanced character was set up under their tutelage in Mesopotamia... A strain of humans, genetically enhanced with more Anunnaki genes, a bloodline of rulers in a tradition of "servants of the people" was initiated by Enki (Gardner). These human kings were inaugurated as go-betweens, foremen of the human populations answering to the Anunnaki. These designated humans were taught technology, mathematics, astronomy, advanced crafts and the ways of advanced civilized society (in schools, called now "mystery schools" but there was no mystery about them). Gardner has brought to light the fact that there exists a robust, highly documented, genealogical, genetic history carrying all the way back to the Anunnaki, possessed by the heterodox tradition of Christianity, which is only now coming forward, no longer gun-shy of the Inquisition. This tradition, preserving the bloodline of kings (the Grail) is the one branded "heretical" and which the Roman Church murderously persecuted. There were no Dark Ages for this tradition, only for those whom the Church wanted to keep in the dark about the real nature of human history and destroy the bloodline, a direct threat to the power of the Bishops.

What evidence supports the Sitchin thesis?

The Astronomical Evidence

...no concrete problem is going to be solved as long as the experts of astronomy are too supercilious to touch "mythical" ideas -- which are firmly believed to be plain nonsense, of course -- as long as historians of religion swear to it that stars and planets were smuggled into originally "healthy" fertility cults and naive fairy tales only "very late" -- whence these unhealthy subjects should be neglected by principle -- and as long as the philologists imagine that familiarity with grammar replaces that scientific knowledge which they lack, and dislike.

—Giorgio de Santillana, Ph.D.
Hertha von Dechend, Ph.D.
Hamlet's Mill

A key underpinning of the Sitchin paradigm is the existence, now and in the past, of the tenth planet in our solar system, the home planet of the Anunnaki with the size, orbit, and characteristics described, as Sitchin has demonstrated, in the Enuma Elish and corroborated by Harrington, now deceased, former chief of the U.S. Naval Observatory.

Tombaugh discovered Pluto in 1930. Christie, of the U.S. Naval Observatory, discovered Charon, Pluto's moon, in 1978. The characteristics of Pluto derivable from the nature of Charon demonstrated that there must still be a large planet undiscovered because Pluto could not be the cause of the residuals, the vertical "wobbles" in the orbital paths of Uranus and Neptune clearly identifiable and signaling the gravitational influence of another large planet in the solar system. The IRAS (Infrared Astronomical Satellite), during '83 -'84, produced observations of a tenth planet so robust that one of the astronomers on the project said that "all that remains is to name it" -- from which point the information has become curiously guarded. In 1992 Harrington and Van Flandern of the Naval Observatory, working with all the information they had at hand and doing parallel computer studies, published their findings and opinion that there is, indeed, a tenth planet, even calling it an "intruder" planet. The search was narrowed to the southern skies, below the ecliptic. Harrington invited Sitchin, having read his book and translations of the Enuma Elish, to a meeting at his office and they correlated the current findings with the ancient records.

The recovered Enuma Elish document, deemed by "mainstream" scholars a mythic tale of a battle between good and evil, is really a history of the formation of our solar system and more. It says that, at the time when Mercury, Venus, Mars, Jupiter, Uranus and Saturn were in place, there was a Uranus sized planet, called Tiamat, in orbit between Mars and Jupiter. Earth was not in place yet. A large wandering planet, called Nibiru, was captured into the system gravitationally. As it passed by the outer planets it caused the anomalies of their moons, the tilting of Uranus on its side, the dislodging of Pluto from its being a moon of Saturn to its own planetary orbit. Its path bent by the gravitational pull of the large planets, first its satellites collided with the large planet Tiamat and, on a second orbit through, Nibiru collided with Tiamat, driving the larger part of it into what is now Earth's orbit to recongeal as Earth, dragging its moon with it to become our Moon with all its anomalies. The shattered debris of Tiamat's smaller part became the asteroid belt, comets, and meteorites. The gouge of our Pacific basin is awesome testimony to the collisional event. Nibiru settled into a 3600 year, highly elliptical, comet-like retrograde orbit (opposite direction to all the other planets) around our Sun, coming in through the asteroid belt region between Mars and Jupiter at perigee and swinging far out past Pluto at apogee. Harrington acknowledged that his information agreed with all these details and the maps he and Sitchin had drawn of the orbit of NIbiru were almost indistinguishable. The current probable location of Nibiru (Planet X, our tenth) estimated by both was the same.

It is the opinion of this author and others that, in light of the evidence already obtained through the use of the Pioneer 10 and 11 and two Voyager space craft, the Infrared Imaging Satellite (IRAS, '83-84), the announcements of NASA's John Andersen, and the clear and unequivocal statements of Harrington when consulting with Sitchin, that the search has already been accomplished, in fact that the planet has already been found.

We need to force the issue of the tenth planet being in our solar system, not just to demonstrate the validity of the new paradigm but for a very practical reason. The ancient records are very clear. The passage of the tenth planet, Nibiru, once every 3600 years, through the inner solar system affects the Earth, sometimes in catastrophic ways as was recorded as the history of the Flood. We examine this threat in detail later. in Chapter Seven.

The Technological Evidence

Ooparts is the term used to describe the purportedly Out Of Place Artifacts in time, toys, tools, technical devices, architecture, depictions and documents which have come to light through archaeological excavation or discovery. Almost everyone is familiar, through published works or documentaries, with the clay pot batteries still containing the electrodes from the Iraqi desert dated at 2500 B.C., the flyable model airplane from a pyramid tomb, the sophisticated machining of stone requiring the most advanced techniques we know today, the 1200 ton precision cut blocks of stone in the Baalbek temple foundation that we could not even handle, an ancient relief frieze from an Abydos temple depicting rockets, airplanes and even a helicopter, etc. The most recent and quite amazing oopart is the rediscovery of monatomic gold by David Hudson (Monoatomics are the single atom form of the Platinum group metals in the Periodic Table. They are superconductors at room temperature, have anti-gravitic properties and are only now being investigated by the advanced physics community) Hudson's discovery, correlated with the bringing to light, by Gardner, of the suppressed discovery of the Anunnaki gold processing plant on Mt. Horeb by Sir Flinders Petrie in 1889 demonstrates that the monatomics were already known at least 3000 years ago. These ooparts coupled with evidence from many disciplines and the historical records indicate that an advanced civilization existed in those times possessing a high technology and that that civilization was indeed the Anunnaki.

The Documentary Evidence

The recorded historical documentation for the existence and deeds of the Anunnaki has become gradually available to us only since the early 1800's. The excavation of the ancient sites of Mesopotamia brought to light the amazingly advanced civilization of Sumer and, with it, thousands of clay tablets containing not only mundane records of commerce, marriages, military actions and advanced astronomical calculation systems but of the history of the Anunnaki themselves. It is clear from those records that the Sumerians knew these aliens to be real flesh and blood. The library of the ruler, Ashurbanipal, at Nineveh was discovered to have burnt down and the clay tablets held there were fired, preserving them for our reading. One of the most impressive finds, in very recent time, has been a sealed, extensive library in Sippar holding, neatly arranged on shelves, a set of some 400 plus elaborate clay tablets containing an unbroken record of the history of those ancient times, a sort of time capsule. The evidence is so overwhelming and robust that, if it weren't for those with power enough to suppress, it would have been accepted and our world view changed a century ago or, perhaps, earlier.

The Genetic Evidence

The recovered records place the location of the Anunnaki laboratory where the first humans were literally produced in east central Africa just above their gold mines. This falls precisely on the map where the modern mitochondrial DNA "search for Eve" places the first woman Homo sapiens and in the same period. (The gold mining engineers of Africa have also rediscovered Anunnaki 100,000-year-old gold mines in that area.) The evidence for, and description of advanced genetic engineering is all there in the ancient documents. Our rapid progress from inception to going to Mars soon, after only 250,000 years, does not correspond to the million year periodicities of slow evolutionary development of other species such as Homo erectus before us. As so many thinkers have pointed out, we are radically and anomalously different, as discussed below.

Scientific Objections to the Thesis

How could the Anunnaki, clearly described as comfortable in earth gravity and atmosphere, very similar to current humans in all ways, have evolved on a planet within our solar system whose orbital apogee takes it into the deep cold of space far out from the sun, for much of its orbit?

The ancient records repeatedly describe Nibiru as a "radiant" planet. This may be understood as having a high core temperature. Although controversial, there is also astrophysical opinion that a large body in elongated orbit is constantly tending toward a circular orbit and this causes stresses in the body that could generate a good deal of heat. That their planet is gradually cooling, may be indicated by Sitchin's interpretation of their colonizing Earth (contains most of the gold identifiable in the solar system) for the purpose of obtaining large quantities of gold for molecular seeding of their atmosphere with a reflective gold shielding. Pertinent here is Harrington's confident statement to Sitchin that it is "a nice, good planet, could be surrounded by gases, probably has an atmosphere and could support life like ours". The sunlight level there might be quite different than on earth. The Anunnaki were often depicted or sculpted with what seem to be obviously sunglasses.

If, however, the Anunnaki evolved on a radically different planet from earth under quite different conditions to which to adapt, why should they have turned out to be so identical to human species? Sitchin's answer is based on the collisional event between the intruder planet, Nibiru, and the planet Tiamat, the residual part of which recongealed into the Earth after being driven into current Earth orbit. That the two, or at least one, of the colliding planets was sufficiently developed to have evolved basic organic compounds, perhaps even simple life, the cross-seeding of everything from amino acids to more complicated organic compounds or even primitive organisms, could account for the evolutionary similarity. Although this author finds it a reasonable hypothesis, even trivial, that advanced civilizations would be capable of crossing extremely different genomes, perhaps with even radically different bases, the cross-seeding theory can account for the apparent relative ease with which the Anunnaki impinged their genes on the genes of Homo erectus. The Anunnaki skill level, 200,000 years ago, is indicated well by the recorded fact that, in early trials, they succeeded in crossing animal genes with Homo Erectus genes, obtained living hybrids but never a satisfactory product which led them to modify Homo Erectus genes with their advanced genes.

If our genome is estimated as 98% to 99% similar to the chimpanzee, how could there be a melding of the Homo erectus and Anunnaki genomes, or impingement of the advanced code on the lesser advanced one detectable? I suggest that this is a major question probably answerable only by the geneticists open-minded enough to attack it. The resolution of that question should provide rich additional clues in itself. Only recently genetic researchers have suggested that there is evidence of alien sequences in our genetic code.

The advances in our scientific discoveries in genetics, mitochondrial DNA research, space and planetary science, archaeology, paleontology, anthropology, and linguistics as well as even the physics of metallurgy have enabled Sitchin to demystify the advanced technologies of the Anunnaki and identify and explain ooparts. We have progressed from being their slave animals to limited partnership and, since they phased off Earth, are now phasing out of a 3000-year traumatic transition to racial independence, a rapid metamorphic process, under the imperative of our advanced Nefilim genetic component.

Central to the history of the Anunnaki's occupation of the planet was the interaction between two brothers, Enlil and Enki. Enki was their chief scientist who was responsible, with his sister Ninhursag, their chief medical officer, for the genetic creation of our species. Enk was sympathetic towards humans and promoted our interests and us. Enlil, eventually known as Jehovah/YHWH, of the Old Testament, maintained the position that humans were to remain slaves, totally subservient to the Anunnaki and him especially.

The Traumatic Transition

The Anunnaki phased off and/or into the background on this planet at the latest around 1250 B.C. For some three thousand years, subsequently, we humans have been going through a very traumatic transition to racial independence. Proprietary claims made by various groups of humans as to who knew and knows what we should be doing to get the Anunnaki to return or when they returned, perpetuated the palace and social rituals learned under the Anunnaki and sometimes disagreement and strife broke out between them. Religious ritual is the transmutation of palace servant duties. The serving of favorite roasted meats on the Anunnaki table became the offering of "burnt offerings" on the table now become an "altar", the transportation of the Anunnaki local ruler on a dais became a procession of statues, the Anunnaki palaces became "temples", etc. The Anunnaki were, clearly and unambiguously, known to the humans who were in contact with them as imperfect, flesh and blood humanoids (taller and huskier than we, male and female, the males bearded. We look like they look because we are half Anunnaki). It was only much later that the Anunnaki were eventually sublimated into cosmic character and status and, later on, conveniently mythologized. Breaking the godspell has seen us go through the stages of abandonment to dissociation, transmutation, religion, rebellion and now to recovery. We have been dysfunctionally looking to the sky where they went for some three thousand years caught in cargo cult, slave-code religions. We are ready to step out of racial adolescence.

There is no better example of the Galileo effect (we will not look through your telescope because we know what you say you see can't be so) in the academic and scientific arenas than the reaction to the Sitchin paradigm. Campus, scientific, and theological imperialism and the fields of anthropology, archaeology, and astronomy, particularly, have tried all the usual unprofessional, unscholarly, shunning, chest thumping, fang baring, proprietary turf posturing and ad hominem attacks through teeth clenched in tenure tetanus, but the thesis becomes more and more robust as new evidence comes in continually from archaeology, anthropology, astronomy, genetics and other disciplines. We may have been able to afford to dally with Darwin and defer to religion for as long as we have but the rapid changes in modern times will force us to consider Sitchin's thesis seriously and intensely much sooner.

To this point, since the Anunnaki phased off the planet, the last three thousand years of our history may be characterized as a prolonged polity fight over who holds proprietary authority over some absolute version of reality, who represents and interprets the will of some "god. We fight each other over claims as to what human nature really is and by what rules it should operate. So, down to our day, incredibly, we have remained still Babel-factored for good crowd control, broken into tribes each proprietarily telling the other that ours is the only accurate tradition of what some particular "god" intended, what safe rules to follow, what we should be doing to demonstrate we are still loyal and docile servants. My God is better than your God. Sometimes we just kill each other over it. And persecutions, Crusades, Jihads, Inquisitions, evil empires, the saved and the damned, the martyr, the infidel, the saint, the protestant, the fundamentalist, the atheist, became -and remain. Not to mention the destruction of the great library of Alexandria and the Mayan codices. The old ecumenical platitude that we just have to discover the hidden esoteric level and we will see that all religions are just many different paths to the truth is sheer nonsense.

Even in the year 2000, The New York Times still found it fit to print that the Roman Church had just reiterated officially that the Pope is still the only one with a direct red phone line to Yahweh while, at the same time, the Pope's friend, Msgr. Corrado Balducci, unofficially, but neither unfrocked nor poisoned, went about publicly acknowledging that Sitchin is right and the Anunnaki are coming back soon and Catholics are to be gotten ready for that event. And, oh yes, the Pope wants to make a pilgrimage to Ur ... A pilgrimage to the first Anunnaki installation in Mesopotamia, southern modern Iraq. It is no coincidence that, at the same time we see signs that the governments are going to acknowledge the alien presence, the Roman Church is, in plain street language, shuckin' and jivin' to do the same, any way it can to maintain face and power as gracefully as it can. Let us understand the Roman Church as a political power rather than a pious institution, an extension of the Roman Empire, which it assimilated. The Brookings Institute study, commissioned by the government in the distant fifties, said do not reveal the alien presence because it would totally unhinge the fundamentalist religions.

Gardner's Contribution: Western Culture Revisited

A major contribution to the resolution of the conflicts between the religions of Western culture in this regard is the work of Sir Laurence Gardner. Sitchin's work and the major discoveries of the Dead Sea Scrolls, has enabled Gardner, an English genealogist-historian to make a recent breakthrough. Gardner has the advantage of one hundred and fifty years of discovery and translation of the Sumerian source material, knowledge of Anunnaki politics and the interaction of Enki and Enlil implemented by the latest scholarship on the Dead Sea Scrolls and Nag Hamadi documents and the brilliant work of the Australian theologian, Barbara Thiering. Working as a genealogist with data available through privileged access to the private archives of thirty European royal family clients, Gardner has brought to light the fact that there exists a robust, highly documented, genealogical, genetic history of a special bloodline carrying all the way back to the Anunnaki and Sumeria. This information, possessed by the heterodox tradition of Christianity, which is only now coming forward, no longer fearful of the boiling oil of the Inquisition, has always been available. He has identified the Holy Grail as this bloodline of human kings, enhanced by Enki with additional Anunnaki genes, intended to be human leader-rulers in a tradition of "servants of the people" traceable all the way back to Sumer. The modern word Grail traces o graal, san graal, which, etymologically, stems from the Sumerian root words GRA AL, meaning special bloodline. The bloodline of human leaders, further enhanced with Anunnaki genes, initiated by Enki (The Lord, Adonai), passed from Sumer through Egypt to Israel through David and the messiahs (anointed ones), fostered by the Essene communities as revealed in the Dead Sea Scrolls. Jesus was an Essene in the bloodline as was Mary Magdalene. They were man and wife and had children. Jesus was of a liberal persuasion within that tradition.

This strain of Hellenistic, liberal, Judaism eventually became known as heterodox Christianity (the word Christian was not coined until almost four hundred years later) was opposed by the Pauline branch which eventually allied itself with Rome, in effect assimilated the Roman Empire, and became the Roman Church. The orthodox Roman Church perpetuated the slave-code fear and subservience tradition and, in its turn, suppressed, persecuted and brutalized the human-centered strain of the bloodline. The reason why women have always been denigrated and suppressed by the Roman Church is genetic: the bloodline was dependent on transmission through the women of the line and any recognition of them would be recognition of the line. This is a further elucidation of our genetic background. It is manifestly unjust that the geneticist is deprived of this vital block of information about the genome due to the preclusive attitude of the "bishops" still reigning in archaeology. We are the product of that Nefilim technology, a mutant species with bicameral genetics, bicameral mind. We can finally integrate both halves of our nature. Our Homo erectus component will bring us back to harmony with this planet, making it a nice place to live and a nice place to visit. Our Anunnaki component will teach us how to move off planet gracefully. The word from station DNA is these "gods" wear designer genes.

Why are Sitchin's and Gardner's contributions so pivotal? There are two major reasons.

It is the meta-paradigm that affords the potential to remove the stultifying, locked-in legacies that have kept up separate, enervated and on hold for millennia. The new paradigm is so encompassing and penetrating that it is a unique meta-wild card: it redefines every cardinal element of human existence that we think we have understood including a redefinition of our evolution, all our cultures, our religions and of our very selves. After a century and a half of examination and attempted explanation --- and suppression --- of the accumulated historical, archaeological, anthropological and astronomical evidence, no other explanatory paradigm comes close to the totally coherent, robust and logical Sitchin thesis. Can and will it be improved or refined? Certainly.

Equally important is the reconciliation with our parent species, the Anunnaki, afforded by the restoration of our history. We need to become full citizens of our own local solar system before or as part of the process of joining stellar society. There is the question of a humanoid species on Mars, which has been reported by remote viewers, and it is inevitable that, if they exist, we will have to work out our relationship with them. These are the keys to planetary unity and peace among humans, a primary condition for acceptance into stellar society.

The primary ramification is simple: the transcultural "gods" known to all the early civilizations were real. This is the major difference between Sitchin's interpretation and translations from the traditional interpretations of history and archaeology. This break with traditional opinion is radical and is largely due to our modern advances in science. The belief that the Anunnaki must have been fiction because the technology and weapons ascribed to them (their ability to fly through the atmosphere and space; to communicate over long distances; to create humans; employ atomic bomb-like or laser-like forces of destruction) were fantastic has been negated by the simple fact that our current level of technology is at least equal to any of that described in the ancient documents. The belief that the "gods" must be fictional because to the ninetieth century mind it was impossible to travel in the "heavens" has already been destroyed by our astronauts hitting a golf ball around on the moon. The ability to create humans is not just something ascribed to them as a mythic power but is in our newspapers as a 5 billion dollar program to read our entire genetic code and in our laboratories in the ability to clone, to create.

Mythinformation

Mythology is our greatest myth. We can move beyond the interpretation of the gods as myth, Jungian archetypes, and schizophrenic hallucinations. After two hundred years of explanatory failure, although still hiding behind tenure in the university and between the glossy pages of new age magazines, History as "mythinformation" is a dead issue. The "occult" is time-release packages of advanced technological information entrusted to us in "crash courses" in civilization, often lost through time, now being recovered through the clues and recognition afforded by our own science. Ooparts, high-tech tools, toys, artifacts, "out of place" in time are remnants of advanced or lost technology and knowledge. Transcendental experience is redefined in terms of dimensional expansion of consciousness and perception. We are rapidly evolving to habitual fourdimensional consciousness. Transcendental experience is conscious metamorphic dimensional exploration, participatory expansion at the leading edge of our special-case evolution. The totems and taboos of our racial adolescence dispelled, Prometheus can get off his rock and reach genetic satori; Job can get off his dung heap and complete his EST training; Buddha can open his eyes and reach genetic enlightenment.

Still Dallying with Darwin

Of course, most scientists and sophisticated scholars consider themselves enlightened in that they espouse some form of Darwinian evolutionary theory as the party line, although there are serious arguments even within the scientific arena as to the full validity of the Darwinian thesis. Generally, philosophers and scientists apologize if they think they are even possibly sounding like creationists, spend most of their energy in either promulgating some version of Darwinian evolution or attacking what they judge to be its too radical application, get entangled in arguments about whether Darwinian evolution can be invoked to explain human creativity, even aesthetics, and generally put down any other explanation out of hand. The general thesis of the evolutionist, therefore, reads like this: the acceptance of evolution as the mechanism by which we came about causes us to understand that we are a collection of biological molecules, interacting with each other as in a mechanism, according to well-defined laws and rules derived from physics and chemistry --- although not all known or understood by humans as yet. Defining consciousness within this biological model is still a pivotal problem: some say it is simply an epiphenomenon, an effect of the operation of all the parts of the brain working in consort, some say it is the subjective self-perception of herself or himself by the individual, some say it must be based in some "new stuff", some new physics or chemistry that we don't yet understand.

Across the general population, however, we do not even agree on whether we are evolving, what the process really is if, indeed, we are evolving, from what source and how we began, and in what direction and on what trajectory, whatever that process is, we are headed. We do not agree, even more fundamentally, as to what criteria to use to judge these matters. We are not discussing the same entity. Creationists do not think of humans as having evolved in the past or as evolving in the present. If we do not agree that we are evolving, can evolve, or whether any evolution of a species or individual must be by mindless Darwinian mechanisms, or whether there are effective methodologies for expediting conscious self-evolution, we will continue to be at standstill. It is quite ironical, however, that even those who hold for some evolutionary view of humankind evolving to human status in the past do not seem to think in terms of humans evolving in the present, much less having a well defined conceptualization of what that process might be.

Charles Darwin published his arguments for evolution in 1859, one hundred and forty plus years ago. Schliemann opened the buried Pandora's box of our real archaeological history in 1873, one hundred and thirty plus years ago. Sitchin, having gained the advantage of discoveries in archaeology, astronomy, space travel, genetics and linguistics as elucidating and explanatory tools, published first only in 1976, already over a quarter century ago. Using this rough chronology as a guide, we might anticipate, even with some exponential bit of acceleration, that the initial general recognition and acceptance of the Sitchin paradigm will not happen for, perhaps, some fifty years. We really can't afford, however, to see Kuhn's thesis that scientific revolutions take place only by the old guard dying off rather than by an acceptance through careful study, critique and proving out, borne out once again.

Bicameral Genetics As Sociobiology 1A

In searching for a word to clearly distinguish between the various Darwinian type theories of evolution usually applied to all species including ours, and our unique evolution as revealed by our history, science and genetics I have found it convenient to invent the word "Realevolution". Clearly we are evolving but in an accelerated, unique way after coming into existence through a genetic engineering project. That we have adapted loosely in a Darwinian sense over time is also true but the fact that we realize we can control and manipulate our realevolutionary progress and direction goes far beyond the concept of natural selection by chance genetic mutations.

Our current genome investigation may literally be understood as a species identity crisis. Consider the facts of our unique genetics and differences from any other anthropoid or humanoid. Current investigation says our genetics are about 98 percent the same as a chimp's. Regardless, that two, perhaps only one percent obviously makes a vast difference. We have 46 chromosomes, primates have 48 and the fusion of the second and third chromosomes in primates is a mystery. Even today, the anthropological sector is scrambling to find a viable ancestor species for us; Homo erectus is currently being promoted. We were contemporaneous with Neanderthals or even preceded them. We showed up too suddenly in the chronology of the fossil record. We present with very many startling, obvious differences from primates, and those differences, suddenly appearing in our species, are radical: we have foreheads, hardly any brow ridges, eye sockets far more rectangular than round; relatively tiny nasal passages; small flat mouths and a chin; far less muscular strength and bone density; our skin, sweat process and glands, body hair, throats, and salt management are completely different. Human females do not have an estrus cycle. We are bipedal. Our brains are remarkably different to say the very least. It becomes quite obvious why we (as a product of a melding of two racial gene codes where quality control was conditioned by pragmatic purposes) have some four thousand potential genetic defects and counting rather than none to a handful as all other species, in light of the complexity of the merging. Homo erectus, our half ancestor, took a million years to go from rough flaked stone tools to smooth ones. You could hardly notice any change. We have come from square one to going to Mars in only some 200,000 years. If the Sitchin paradigm is correct, all these facts are explained easily. If we ignore this body of information as we read out and work with the human genome we handicap ourselves unnecessarily and deprive ourselves of valuable clues and understanding. Darwinian principles may generally apply to hominid species before us but they clearly do not apply to our unique synthetic genesis and subsequent development except as a minor theme in our incidental climatic and regional physical adaptations. If the Anunnaki were interested only in engineering what clearly amounted to disposable units then it may reasonably be inferred that the completeness of the engineering would not have to have been taken to the maximum. This is, in the opinion of this author, the basis for the four thousand plus genetic diseases and defects we present. It has been argued, theoretically, that, although the vast majority of the species on this planet present with only a few typical genetic diseases, we show 4000 because of the relative complexity of our organism. However, we are not that much more complex genetically than even the higher primates and this argument does not hold.

Sociobiology, as developed and propounded by E. O. Wilson[11] is founded on Darwinian evolutionary theory, and the "unappealing proposition" that genetic variation and chance are the only cause for the existence of human kind, inferring a complete biological determinism. There is difficulty, however, in accounting for the disconcertingly rapid accelerations obvious in our species' brief history in which the slow genetic mutational and chance factors have been rapidly outrun by our cultural and consciousness developments. It may well be that we are totally determined in our action and thought by our biology but the very fact that we can recognize that possibility and discuss it begs the question How then are we determined? Wilson's honesty causes him to acknowledge that we have reached a point where we can consciously influence the course of our evolution. The new paradigm affords a context and perspective in which to understand our species' precocity in terms of the rapid ascendance or our advanced Anunnaki genetic base. We can return to the subject of man's ultimate nature with confidence and freedom to radically experiment and explore with understanding and humor. The same reductionistic science that would honestly insist that we are totally determined by an infinitely regressive loop of ultimately quantum mechanical events is already telling us that we are determined to transcend in an infinitely progressive loop of fractal like expansions. If we are totally determined, we are clearly determined to determine our own determinism.

The fact that we have modified since our inception according to Darwinian adaptations to general climatic, regional and cultural vectors becomes a minor theme in the overview of ourselves as the precocious leading edge of a synthesized species metamorphosing rapidly, driven by our bicameral genetic engine. The "unappealing proposition" loses its sting: the truth, regardless of its content, tends to set one free. The new paradigm explains completely the seeming anomalies of acceleration, ooparts and syncretisms so apparent in the human situation, and is a definitive explanation of why our species' "biological evolution is always quickly outrun by cultural change".

A Planetary Focus for the Genome Project and Genetic Research

The Sitchin paradigm provides a comprehensive context in which to understand and explain the enigmatic facts and anthropological anomalies of the Darwinian model of our species existence, which we have already amassed. It provides the context and data for bringing the efforts of geneticists and the genome projects, often scattered for a variety of reasons, to a focus on correcting and perfecting the genetic code, eliminating all disease and handicaps, and providing us the option of immortality. During the genetic investigations now in process, therefore, it would be valuable indeed for geneticists, at the minimum, to be constantly inspecting the results of the decipherment for signs of the genetic merging, and to develop protocols to determine such, if needed, as well as following the clues mentioned herein. By doing so, interpretations and explanations may possibly be facilitated, progress accelerated and a far more comprehensive overview of the genome achieved. The information gained would be, reciprocally, a major, pivotal, invaluable resultant spin-off contribution to our species' evolutionary, anthropological, and cultural generic history. Understanding our bicameral gene code in the context of the new paradigm will facilitate the elimination of the schizoid puzzles in our collective and individual psyches and the correction and perfecting of our genetics. When DNA speaks, everybody listens.

Viewed in the context of the new paradigm, our genetic research and developments of nanotechnology and biotechnology to alter and improve our genetic code, may be understood better as a concerted effort to correct the defects left to us by the Anunnaki engineering that brought us about.

Sorting Through the Clues

There are clear injunctions against procreation between full brothers and sisters, but not the Anunnaki custom of procreating with a half-sister (their approved way of procreating an heir). Our biological studies show this to be a widespread practice among Earth species including even wasps which has definite genetic advantages for producing superior offspring. I suggest that this general prohibition, which remains in the doctrines of various religions, excepted with regard to only specific humans as recounted in the Old Testament, was a deliberate means of keeping humans at a certain level just as was the withholding of extreme longevity or immortality.

Several significant details in the records of our genetic genesis may hold clues. It is recounted that two kinds of females were created, those who would bear children and those who would not. Determining, genetically, how we, as sterile mutants when first created, were manipulated to be able to procreate may be a major lead. Finally, knowing that an advanced bloodline of humans, enhanced by additional Anunnaki genes, was created around 4000 B.C. is even more valuable a clue since that bloodline has been carefully nurtured and protected through to our day and, therefore, available for investigation and analysis and comparison.

As we progress in the development of AI and move it from the arena of computer RAM inexorably toward the full, conscious, android, genetics and AI will become entwined, although already clearly so, to a greater and greater degree. Even at this primitive stage it is not difficult to envision a time when we, analogous to the example of building a rocket ship as given by Eric Drexler, could throw a set of "genetic" analog type instructions into a vat of liquid nutrient and nanotechnologically grow an android AI ready to boogie.

The flashy sequence in the Bruce Willis movie, The Sixth Element, in which an alien is cloned in a few seconds in a high tech device, no doubt will look like clunky Buck Rogers stuff sooner than we think.

The Current Crisis

It is evident that the current serious crisis of world peace is largely due to the "my god is better than your god" conflicts, the sad playing out of the same kind of wars in which we were used as pawns by the Anunnaki. The second major factor is economic: competition for limited resources which is further exacerbated by the corruption of the powerful oppressing the weak. How primitive are we? We need only examine every economic system attempted or implemented through history to comprehend that all forms, to this point, have been successful only to a point in limited circumstances. Every serious economic and political structuring has proven to have benefits but equally serious limitations and drawbacks due to conflicts over what and who a human individual is and, therefore, what the rights of the individual are relative to other humans and the state; what is considered moral, just; whether there should be winners and losers; who should be taken care of and why; and, to put it in modern academic jargon, who is the "other". Certainly, the potential for human degeneracy is always extant and partly at cause, but the more fundamental Babel-factoring of our species still hinders us from taking conscious part in our realevolution which is on schedule regardless. The new paradigm will, eventually, see our political and economic systems as mirroring our rapid though confused realevolutionary stages and consciously and intelligently and compassionately developing evolving, dynamic systems commensurate with our now and future trajectory. Artificial intelligence will be used to determine rapidly adjusting economic systems for the benefit of all.

The concept of a new world order, in itself, can be an idealistic and benevolent goal. The League of Nations and, currently, the United Nations are certainly steps in the right direction. The imposition of world domination by economic, political, military, or theocratic coercion are retrograde and primitive attempts doomed to well deserved failure. The conflicts and wars covering the planet are, in their transparently economically competitive and theo-political base, robot-like attempts to run the Realevolutionary videotape in reverse and mark the beginning of a final, very slow denouement of that godspell phenomenon.

To bring it down to the here and now: if America, or any country or culture is going to be an example for the rest of the world, there is no other choice but for it to set a Realevolutionary example and style. It will require thinkers and scholars and innovators and futants from every discipline in every culture and country and religion to assimilate the vast amount of history, information, ooparts, traditions and technology which have been rediscovered and recovered over the last one hundred and fifty years from all parts of the world and to transform their religions and cultures accordingly. How long will it take? The view from 2100 (A.D.) sees it only begun in the 21st century and not totally completed by 2075.

The new paradigm finally and conclusively resolves the creation-evolutionary conflict specifically concerning our unique genesis. If the new paradigm is substantially correct then the box is illusory, the creationists are only half wrong and the evolutionists are only half right: there was a creation but it took place in a genetic laboratory; there is a human evolutionary process but it was interrupted by the Anunnaki inserting their genes into the Homo Erectus gene code, a very pragmatic, now Darwinian kind of interference. We were created and we are evolving but both in unique ways. I have called our unfurlment as a synthetic species our realevolution. The demographics of our realevolution afford us valuable insights into our nature and a sense of our trajectory into the future.

Consciousness In, Consciousness Out

The realization of our half-alien genetic makeup and our relationship to the Anunnaki stretches our perspective to afford an effective way for us to begin to grasp the topic of alien presence on this planet. It also enables a, previously unattainable, unassailable integrity individually and as a race which will be essential to entering into direct contact with alien species, either in the future or with ones that are already here on the planet. We shall finally enter stellar society as a mature race which knows who and what it is, what is good for it and what is not; with whom or what it could interact, with whom and what it would be dangerous to make contact; with the minimum of preconceptions as to how things should be. Until we know who and what we are we will probably not be allowed into stellar society. Until we break the godspell and stop looking up for Daddy to come back, looking for some solution or salvation from outside, we will be in danger of getting Borged by whomever shows up here. The topic of alien contact is probably the most dramatic of examples of how narrow and primitive our focus is even though it has progressed in the last fifty years.

Intra-Solar System Exopolitics

Analysis and overview shows clearly that we must seek resolution of issues and relationship, as a now mature and independent and conscious species, with the Anunnaki, analogous to the mature young adult interacting with the parents to work out stresses developed through adolescence to establish a new mode of interaction as an independent person. The advantages will be great and beneficial to both the Anunnaki and us.

We will gain species identity, a restored history, the potential for a planetary peace as generic humans, the slave code religions will be discarded through redefinition as simply a continuation of the ancient master-slave godspell relationship with the Anunnaki. The trajectory of our realevolution will be clear and we will be enabled to pursue and determine our future species' realevolutionary unfurlment as a united species.

A persistent report from remote viewers, in contact with various alien species, is that our "creators", the Anunnaki, did not act in accordance with the highest ideals of stellar society when they invented us as a slave species. That needs rectification and resolution and reconciliation before they will be allowed "in". So, besides gaining advantages from their advanced technology and science we may accelerate our admission and they may also facilitate theirs.

The Anunnaki Agenda and Us

A very reasonable preliminary question must be answered: How do we know the Anunnaki still exist on their home planet Nibiru?

From the best astronomical information obtainable publicly from the Naval Observatory computer studies, the findings of the Infrared Imaging Satellite (IRAS) team in '83-'84, the Cote de Zur observatory, the findings of Harrington of the Naval Observatory through the observation mission he sent to the southern hemisphere, the tenth planet, Planet X/Nibiru, does exist and in the orbit described in detail in the Enuma Elish document by the Anunnaki.

No indication or evidence has been reported of planetary disaster, explosion or deviation in orbit in the region --- or any other area of the solar system. Harrington and Sitchin (in the videotaped meeting with Sitchin in Harrington's office at the Naval Observatory) agreed during their meeting it should be inward bound toward perigee in the asteroid belt region between Mars and Jupiter, roughly two thirds of the way in. All evidence says the planet exists in an undisturbed condition and orbit providing the same conditions under which the Anunnaki have existed and prospered for many millennia.

There is no direct information available to our knowledge, however, as to the actual continuing existence of the Anunnaki as a species on Nibiru or Anunnaki individuals who may have remained on Earth after they phased back and/or off Earth. Indirect evidence is available beyond the basic fact that their planet remains inhabitable.

The Anunnaki provided three major sources of information about themselves and their history: their planet's history as part of our solar system's history; the details of our creation and development in the major focal document Enuma Elish; detailed advanced astronomical information in various documents about our solar system and particularly about their home planet Nibiru to the Sumerians and the Mayans among others. The advanced astronomy possessed by the Mayans was clearly given, taught to the Mayans by the Anunnaki, not developed by them, just as the knowledge of all the planets in the solar system was taught to the Sumerians, not discovered by them.

One of the features of the astronomical knowledge given to the Mayans was the ability to predict the dates of major solar eclipses called "suns" as they would occur over the (now Mexico) territory they inhabited. Although the Spanish conquerors did a ruthless and thorough work of destroying the recorded history and information in written form possessed by the Mayans, the few salvaged documents dealing with astronomy still extant clearly indicate that the "sixth sun", full eclipse of the sun, would fall on the precise date it did, July 11, 1991 as predicted 1200 years ago. The "sixth sun", eclipse, according to the knowledge given to the Mayan priest-astronomers, was to be marked by marvels in the sky and earth changes, and "encounters with Masters of the Stars" as stated by Lee and Brit Elders in their excellent videotape composite documentary of the videotaped sightings of alien craft over Mexico City and other parts of Mexico at the time of the eclipse. Sightings continued through 1993 and continue to date. The alien craft, obviously seeking attention, astonished and amazed the populace of the largest city in the world and the fact that they led investigators to look into the crater of Popocateptl, the huge volcano in proximity to Mexico City that had been dormant since the time of Cortez, to discover it was awakening more than fulfilled those predictions of earth changes. The logic regarding the Anunnaki's continuing existence is straightforward: the Anunnaki gave the information and predictions to the Mayans for a purpose: this is the detailed astronomy that will enable you on Earth to know when our planet returns and we may also return: watch for us. I submit that they were able to fulfill that promise and prediction with a display of such magnitude is reasonable evidence of their general prosperity.

This manifestation of their presence is even more significant in that it reveals a great deal concerning their intentions and agenda with regard to the Earth and to us.

As I have understood it, there are several important elements that are involved in the relationship between the Anunnaki and us:

It seems that the conflict concerning the status of humans in relationship to the Anunnaki and the way in which humans should be considered and treated is perhaps still not completely resolved between Enki and Enlil.

Regardless of the differences in that regard it is recognized by them, having been made clear by more advanced species in contact with them and us, that any further interaction between them and us must be governed by the rules of stellar society: a general "prime directive" that they may not interfere or manipulate or dominate or control us for their purposes or without our invitation and consent.

It is further recognized, having been made clear to them also by advanced species, that entrance into stellar society by them requires rectifying the fact that they created us for wrong reasons, left us with very imperfect genetics, on a high risk planet due to geological turbulence and constant risk of asteroid strikes and the risk of species extinction when the conditions prevailing at the time of any given Passing of their planet through the inner solar system are such as to cause cataclysmic events on Earth of such magnitude that we could potentially be wiped out as with the historical Flood event.

The rules of participation in stellar society have been made quite clear to us and to the Anunnaki through communications by various alien species, to us as individuals and governments; to remote viewers; to humans selected as "ambassadors" and "envoys". Our most evolved have envisioned that the trajectory of evolution in general for any species is towards peace, compassion, higher intelligence and consciousness and the rules as communicated to us simply reinforce that vision. The Anunnaki are apparently still not allowed into the stellar community because of it. Since the Anunnaki are far more advanced than we technologically it might be assumed that they would be candidates for stellar society much sooner than we. Apparently, however, there is a reciprocal relationship between the Anunnaki's candidacy and ours which may be stated thus: the Anunnaki must demonstrate their understanding of the cosmic rules and meeting of stellar societal standards by resolving their internecine conflicts of attitude and policy toward us and rectifying, as much as possible, the "wrong reasons" for which they created us, and demonstrate that they have become a united and peaceful species.

So there is an obvious, mutually beneficial, expedient interaction between the Anunnaki and us called for at this time: resolution. Reconciliation would be too obsequious a term: resolution is more precise, in the sense of a now matured, independent species, having gained some perspective, going back to iron out differences, conflicts and resolve misunderstandings with a parent species who are willing to admit imperfection and mistakes. Admission into stellar society is a high stakes game. Both the Anunnaki and we have a great deal to gain and are at a major turning point for both of us. It is expedient that we signal formally --- the Anunnaki surely are patiently aware of our developing exosocial status and intentions --- that we are ready to resolve our mutual relationship and cooperate for mutual benefit. Only half facetiously said, they might be in need of fresh gold supplies. It will be interesting to learn if the return of their planet, Nibiru, to the inner solar system, under certain conditions also effects it, their home planet, adversely. It is quite possible that they may be able to offer valuable help scientifically and practically for our survival.

Beyond Religion and The Old New Age

> Imagine, even no religion,
> They say I'm a dreamer,
> But I'm not the only one.
> —John Lennon

Over the last 2000 years we have seen scientific or pseudoscientific doctrines espoused by the various religions being contradicted or demolished and the religions, repeatedly, although with great delay, change their positions with regard to our genesis, history, evolution and science, and modify their doctrines. But the new paradigm addresses the very root doctrines, positions, claimed divine franchise and authority of all the religions of the world and will eventually cause the obsolescence of all institutionalized religions springing from our ancient relationship of subservience to the Anunnaki.

Religion, as we know it, is the transmutation of the Anunnaki-human relationship of master-subject servitude, of slavery and then limited, subservient partnership, the godspell. The concept of God, capital G, has gradually developed through the cosmification of the various Anunnaki rulers Enlil (Jehovah/YHWH), Enki (Adonai, the Lord), Allah (El/Nannar/Sin), among others, gradually embellished with the heady concepts of metaphysical speculation. It has lately become a sort of faux ecumenical gloss: the TV news quotes the Koran as saying There is no God but God" when it should be

"There is no god but Allah", a completely different meaning. The god of the Judeo-Roman Christian tradition, Jehovah-YHWH was -quite possibly still is -the flesh and blood Anunnaki individual, Enlil, cosmified into the absolute creator of the universe, eventually spoken of as infinite love, infinite justice, infinite this or infinite that, through the Hebrew theologians and rabbis and Roman Church bishops and scholastic philosophers and theologians.

The Concept of "God"

The idea of a cosmic, infinite principle "God", as many of us still take it for granted, is a thoroughly mixed composite concept of the sublimation of the anthropomorphic and imperfect Anunnaki individuals, the "deities" of slave code religions; metaphysical abstractions accumulated over time through the speculations of the revered philosophers from the Greeks onward; the Hellenic influenced, theo-philosophical teachings of the Roman Church scholastic tradition and mystics; flavored with the concepts of theists, deists, agnostics, theosophists and mystics of any number of sects; thoroughly leavened by the concepts of the consciousness expanding disciplines and metaphysical doctrines of the East, sprinkled with our own individual intellectual and emotional subjective variations and usually still conditioned by the godspell element of subservience. But that cosmified, composite, intellectual abstraction is not the Jehovah/YHWH or Jesus of the Judeo-Christian religions, the Prime Mover of Thomas Aquinas or the Omega point of De Chardin, the Allah of the Muslim faith, the Brahma of Hinduism, the Buddha, or the Tao or deity of the religion of your choice.

Yes, the new paradigm means that religion and religions, as we know them, will have to bow out. The godspell phenomenon has two parts: we need to overcome the slave mentality of dependence and subservience and we need to discard the institutional religions which sprang from and dominated through it, especially the radical fundamentalism, West and East, that is ultimately tearing the race apart. The role of the theologian then becomes the facilitating of planetary reconciliation in the transition to the time beyond religion. The institutional, slave-code, godspell religions have fixed dogmas which are directly contradicted by the new paradigm. They claim divine franchise by gods who are now radically redefined. They claim absolute authority over the disciplines that produce the information that would demonstrate their true historical nature. The ultimate driving force will most probably be a degree of desperation and desire for peace gradually manifesting in the entire planetary population so strong that it will cause an abandonment of the authoritarian leaders and dogmas of the religions, followed by a younger generation of clerics who will recognize the inevitable and introduce new interpretations and relaxed rules to gradually smooth the phase out and transition, hopefully to humanitarian organizations and peace movements. The signs of transition of some religious organizations to charitable and ecological focus may be seen as an almost inchoate beginning of this kind of transformation. A unique and vital characteristic is that it addresses and explains and redefines the root source of all the ancient religions of the world on a common basis so that no particular religion can claim privileged status of any kind. Religion, as we know it, will be understood in the context of our unique history. It would also be foolish not to expect diehard fundamentalist backlash.

Is this atheism? No, paradoxically, not as such. Not as we have defined atheism previously as the denial of the existence of any kind of god, cosmic or otherwise. It does not even address the question as to whether there is some metatranscendental Being who is responsible for all that is, multiple universes, beyond beyond and infinity --- which should remain the focus of human inquiry --- It simply is a long overdue correction of some local, intra-solar system politics, relatively rather pedestrian in cosmic perspective. Garden variety atheism can now be understood as an early sign of precocious species adolescent rebellion and questioning of the authority of the obviously all too humanoid characteristics of whatever sublimated local Anunnaki "god" is still the object of worship (the original meaning of worship was "work for": AVOD = work The word was actually spelled work-ship up until the time of Old English). Yes, the subservient godspell religious stage will be surpassed. The resultant freedom, however, will engender and foster greater curiosity about reality and a seeking for ultimate causes far more metaphysically adequate and commensurate with our expanding consciousness far beyond even the search for a scientific Law of Everything. The element of transcendence associated with some religions will be, at minimum, understood as generic consciousness expansion into higher and higher dimensionality. Neither is this materialistic reductionism although it does force us to reconsider the notion of the "spiritual". What is needed is a complete overhaul of all our metaphors and concepts of the "spiritual" because the great majority of them are embedded in our cultural fabric and consciousness as leftovers from Judeo-Roman Catholic theology and second hand Eastern philosophies. The importance of this overhaul is critical because it involves the concepts of mind, consciousness, intelligence, will, self-awareness, transcendence, dimensionality, self.

Science, the closest we have come to a common ground, a common criterion, has played and will continue to play a pivotal role in the recognition and acceptance of the new worldview.

Astronomy will demonstrate the existence of the tenth planet unequivocally --- the IRAS, Infrared Imaging Satellite, quite obviously discovered it in '83-'84 --- and, reluctantly, recognize the correspondence of the details gradually accumulated with the ancient data we now possess. The curiosity about the existence of the Anunnaki on Nibiru/Planet X will become overwhelming and contact through spacecraft and signaling will commence.

Archaeology, for the last one hundred and fifty years, has been making the major contributions of data and will continue to do so. Only recently, the science of genetics has been able to refine, sometimes correct, archaeological and anthropological estimates and dating. Because of the intertwining of the archaeological and genetic information concerning our unique genesis, genetics has already and should continue to be a major tool and contributing science to the new paradigm.

The more robust the scientific information becomes the easier it will be for the religions of the world to accept and incorporate. Nations and cultures as well will see the cogency of the information and gradually accept it, becoming gradually more planetary in outlook. In the name of world unity and peace, governments and contributing entities should increase funding of the scientific searches and research in these disciplines and adopt policies that will release the information already possessed, some of it quite certainly withheld at this time.

Just within the time of the writing of this paper there has been a report of the discovery, by satellite scan, of a city, two miles by fives miles in area, under thirty feet of water in the ocean twenty five miles off the northwest coast of India. Preliminary carbon dating of dredged materials from the site indicates its age as nine thousand years old, placing it earlier than Sumer. The histories of India (declared myth by the British because they were older than the Empire) speak in detail about civilizations and humans in the very remote past and mention this city by name.

What appears to be a city has been reported off the coast of Cuba under an astounding 2100 feet of water, discovered by professional treasure wreck hunters using sophisticated equipment.

The Takenouchi documents and artifacts, ancient treasure of the Japanese Emperor guarded for 2500 years by the family of the highest Shinto priest caste family, speak of an alien civilization coming here from space and founding the human race.

All these facts and histories need to be studied thoroughly and integrated with the histories and data from the entire planet. We have much work to do. The planetary benefits will be enormous. Besides the obvious general advantage of working from a consensual understanding and definition of what a generic human is, we can eliminate the characterizations of the perennial conflicts as being between "progress and piety" or between creationism and evolution, or science and faith.

Contributions of Anunnaki Science to Human Welfare

There are several facets of the advanced knowledge transmitted to humans by the Anunnaki which directly relate to and facilitate our self-understanding, science and general physio-material welfare.

Once allowing ourselves to acknowledge high science in the ancient texts, the study of Anunnaki technology and science reveals itself as based on the inherent geometry of nature. They did not just recognize and understand it and teach it as an isolated subject, they employed and applied it as the basis of their various sciences from geography to linguistics.

There is this stuff traditionally called "sacred geometry". When you study its core material you realize that it is simply the intrinsic geometry of nature. Forget the "sacred" adjective. "Sacred" is a loaded term now and should be dropped. Call it the inherent geometry of nature from micro to macro. When disengaged from the grip of the metaphysical enthusiasts and shucked of the accumulated trappings of religious metaphors, "sacred" simply means something very important which should not be forgotten. The restored history shows that it was known and used by the Anunnaki who, in turn, taught it to humans. It informs the proportions and shapes of atoms to snowflakes to Nautilus shells to the human body and beyond. Architects have been taught the golden mean and golden ratios and everybody knows that Pi represents the proportional relationship between the circumference and diameter of a circle. Fewer know the extent of the natural geometry and its relationships and its progressive development with compass, straightedge and pencil in two dimensions and its further unfolding in higher dimensions.[12] Scientists, adverse to even looking at anything that has even the scent of "religion" or the word ""sacred" attached to it, may be relieved by the ramifications of the new paradigm and its redefinition of religion and allow themselves to at least begin to study this inherent geometry of nature for itself. A primary characteristic is that it can be used without measuring scales. The honeybee doesn't carry a Stanley tape measure when it is constructing hexagonal comb cells. They are the lightest weight, maximally volumetric for the least space, interconnect most ideally with adjacent cells with the greatest structural strength, all according to the inherent properties of nature as are the proportions and lengths of the bee's legs and overall anatomy which are engaged in the construction.

The true Masonic tradition traces back to those early Anunnaki schools and the knowledge and its use is ubiquitously embedded in ancient buildings, monuments and in the cathedrals of Europe. The master geometricians knew it so well that they could tune a cathedral ceiling or dome to enhance the type of sound that would be produced there by the music in use. Music, tones and harmony, as the ancients all knew, are the product of geometry, are auditory geometry. Our experience of something being beautiful is the resonance of the geometric structures of our perceptive and cognitive physical faculties, senses, neurological system, brain, with the geometry of the perceived object or scene or sound source.

My point here is that our brains and our thinking and logic are a product of the inherent geometry of nature also and we should reconsider the potential of this geometric approach to nature and consciousness in genetics and AI. Mathematics is the abstract, quantitative expressions of the relationships and proportions of that geometry. It would be an advantage to be able to use that inherent relational geometry as a base for our logic in programming because it is more direct and scalar, dimensionless. Because of the binary and Boolean and mathematical devices on which we have structured our computers, its incorporation is probably just not possible in our current technology and, obviously, we do not speak in geometry. We already have, however, the beginnings of using the geometry of the DNA structure (which, naturally, pun unavoidable, exhibits the inherent geometry of nature) on a chemical basis as a logic, as a computational system. In back-engineering the brain we are going to have to take into consideration the geometry of the geography of the organ as an integral part of it functioning. It is not beyond conception that someone may be able to envision a completely novel way of programming, perhaps not "in geometry" but geometrically and three-dimensional chips can be modified to incorporate the inherent geometry in such a way that the geometry is intrinsically a part of the logic. Because it is self- relational, scalar and proportional it would seem that a great deal of second level, computational processing would be eliminated by simple algorithmic comparison. Stephen Wolfram's *A New Kind of Science*[13] is a powerful tool in this regard because the rules he has discovered from his study of the propagational geometry of cellular automata would apply effectively here.

Beyond The Babel Factor: Human Over-Unity

The new paradigm is the basis, perhaps the only adequate basis, for a profound unification of all humanity in the concept of generic humanity. Not some superficial token ecumenicism or social homogenization of peoples and cultures and philosophies but a unification that frees us to be one species and explains and enhances our diversity of adaptations and cultures and contributions. The cumulative evidence and restored history has enabled us to grasp the true nature of our genetic creation, our traumatic transition, and the opportunity to emerge from species adolescence and amnesia into species maturity. All the political, economic, social, scientific, new age, evolutionary variables are only symptomatic; the genetic level is where the profound realization must blossom. The restoration of our generic history and a generic definition of what a human is afford us the advancement that will take the planet off hold. We can attain planetary unity and peace and finally meet the criteria for matriculation into stellar society.

However, as profound and positive a revolution as this attainment of planetary peace and release manifestly is as it unfolds, it is only the essential preparation for our species' inevitable expansion into stellar citizenship. Contemplating the potential of stellar citizenship, as a species and as individuals, is more easily appreciated and understood when one realizes one's --- and one's children's --- already half alien nature. I have suggested in previous writings that we change our Sapiens Sapiens title to Homo Erectus Nefilimus: part Homo Erectus, part Nefilim (the word used for the Anunnaki in the sixth Chapter of the book of Genesis in the Old Testament --- it reads better Latinized than Anunnaki) Let us adopt the cosmic perspective, learning the ways of stellar society as Homo Erectus Nefilimus who have finally reached the status of truly sapient, truly wise --- and exosocial.

But, just as we have to radically transform our thinking to the dimensions of the vision of this new human paradigm, we must transform the entire material realm. We must transmute the social, economic, scientific and political, not just because the present context is no longer adequate, is clearly outmoded and cannot be repaired from within or upgraded as such, but to match and support the dignity and freedom and structure of the new human society. Do we have the scientific and informational technologies to accomplish that? Yes.

4

SAPIENS PRACTICAL: TRANSFORMING THE SOCIO-MATERIAL REALM

Synopsis

The radical transformation, transmutation we are already into as a species requires an econo-social-political system commensurate with the nature, ideals, and psychology of the new human. The essence of this system is planetarily unified cooperation rather than devolving, primitive competition. The current, dying economic systems are finished because they have been corrupted by the "winners", because they are not beneficial and inadequate to billions of population but primarily because they do not match the general level of evolution of human consciousness. This paper outlines the vision of the new human and the new human society and this chapter outlines how the three major sciences of free energy, nanotechnology and artificial intelligence, employed on an integrated basis, afford us the memes and means to accomplish the material support structure of the new cooperative system of plenty, beyond need and money.

The major element in the socio-economic transformation is the transition from competition to cooperation. We no longer need be oppressed and kept separated by the illusion of having to compete for limited resources. Ironically, the assimilation of this straightforward idea may be more difficult than any of the more advanced and philosophical put forth in this paper. Survival mechanisms from both our Homo erectus and Anunnaki genetic heritage go on alert and questions flood our minds.

There is a spectrum of opinions regarding the inherent basic elements of human nature that immediately colors the reaction of the individual. Some hold, influenced by some variant of the religious doctrine of original sin or simply by personal interpretation of their own and others' conditioned reactions, that human nature is inherently flawed and given to selfishness, greed, violence. At the other extreme of the spectrum are those who hold for the inherent goodness, even "divinity" of human nature given only the opportunity to express it. Between are found the numerous degrees of aggressiveness to pacifism, from amoral competition to compassionate consideration.

But the tenor and attitude shift when the question changes from a definition of human nature to the nature of the trajectory of our species' evolution. The vast majority of humans, when queried or expressing their personal opinions freely, are in agreement: they want species' unity not war, conflict and divisiveness; they envision us moving toward greater cooperation, peace, freedom from want and disease; they want to see the perfection of our genetics, greater respect and freedom for the individual, longevity and perhaps at least indefinite lifespan rather than death, superior education and intelligent evolutionary fostering of the children, alien contact and stellar citizenship. We, as a species, are quite sure of where we want to go, the direction of our realevolutionary trajectory, but the obstacle is disagreement about who we are and how we should go there.

But we have the memes to make the transition to the generically human and share that common trajectory of development.

The three technologies that currently hold the most advanced potential for accomplishing the econo-social-political dimension of the transformation are free energy, nanotechnology and artificial intelligence.

Free Energy Defined

"Free" energy is defined as: a kind of energy that exists throughout the universe at the quantum level, sometimes called "zero point" energy. It is said that a cubic meter of space any place in the universe contains more free energy that all the electromagnetic spectrum energies such as electricity, light, etc., known to physics in the entire universe combined. An extraction device, tapping free energy and converting it to electrical current, need not have any moving parts. It has only to consist of a special extraction coil, a rectification and conversion unit and coil and an output circuit. (Reference: http://www.cheniere.org) These units are called over-unity devices because, once started, a tiny bit of the energy output is fed back to the extraction coil to keep it energized and extracting. Over-unity means that it puts out more energy than is required to keep it running. Ratios of 5 to 100 to 1 have been reported. Five to one hundred units of energy output times a single unit put back in to keep the extraction process going.

Nanotechnology Defined

Nanotechnology is defined by its scale: a nanometer is defined as 10^{-9} a very tiny size indeed and techniques have been devised to manipulate individual atoms at this scale to actually build objects one atom at a time. *The end product and effect of nanotechnology is to afford us the ability to make anything out of anything.* We would be able to mine our waste dumps and eliminate pollution and support an almost unlimited population, transforming our economies to one of cooperative provision of a very comfortable life for every individual on the planet. Nanotech will allow for the development of "universal" plant protein bases from which to make any kind of food from meat to veggies to cake. Fully developed nanotech, combined with free energy, will also require far less energy generally than current industrial processes and a complete recycling of all materials is inherently a part of the process.

The cautionary protests that nanotech could get away from us and destroy the environment and us are certainly to be respected and paid attention but, as with any new and powerful technology, there are methodologies for enlightened and intelligent development and control and employment. The combination of free energy with nanotech will allow for the on the spot making of just about anything requested by a manufacturer, consumer, diner, homemaker, eventually making the Star Trek scene in which Picard tells the computer he wishes a cup of Earl Grey tea and it comes out of the "machine" as a nano created cup, saucer, spoon, hot tea. Eric introduced the concepts in The Engines of Creation[14] long ago and they will soon be a total reality.

Free energy and nanotechnology, developed and applied correctly, provide and afford us, as a species, the means to establish a transmuted socio-economic system which can provide plenty for all and transcend the primitive stage of competition for ostensibly limited resources to a stage of planetary cooperation. They have the potential to eliminate the reliance on oil, nuclear, solar, wind, wave, geothermal, etc. and the primitive situation of winners and losers, war, poverty, and all that prevents us from being accepted into stellar society. By adding the refinements of artificial intelligence and biomimicry for organization, analysis and control we will be able to progress exponentially and make the transition in the short time required.

There is an entirely new type of socio-economic system required, afforded, and engendered by the combination of free energy and nanotechnology. It will be immanently, inherently ecological and eliminate the ecological disasters and problems we currently experience. It will supersede the primitive competition for imputed limited resources modality of today. It will be beyond all forms of capitalism, communism, and socialism. Eventually it will be beyond money. Understood and intelligently transitioned to, it will make possible the provision of a basic comfortable living for every individual in an almost unlimited planetary population. Eventually, anyone who needs or wants something within reason, both material and intellectual, may have it.

The Novel Problem: A Challenge

We need to develop a comprehensive way to transition industry and government and economy smoothly and comfortably to the inevitable new phase of free-energy-nanotech. The challenge to our best minds and their expertise is to develop the means of transition. This paper is an appeal and challenge to all to contribute to the transition and transformation. Projects of the size and degree of public participation of President Kennedy's Moon project and with the degree of speed and intensity of the Manhattan atom bomb project are clearly called for.

A few basic principles are as follows:

Ideally, legitimate industries and businesses must be shown a way in which they can easily transition from their current production modes of their current products to the production of novel products through novel production modes without financial stress, loss of jobs, loss of customer base as a first step towards an even more fundamental shift to a "leisure" society.

Information industries are already well into this transition phase. Infrastructure conversion, adaptation, adjustment, implementation is more or less a challenge depending on distribution infrastructure required. The local production of energy (example: small suitcase size, self-contained free energy device in the house utility room supplies all household needs plus, no need for utility companies) radically transforms power production and eliminates distribution grids, transportation, and pollution and radically reduces cost of energy to initial acquisition of free energy unit. The units of whatever size must be manufactured but manufacturing becomes radically transformed also.

Practical measures to begin the transition are already quite obvious. Free energy devices, from minute to macro size, some patented, already available for production, (see http://www.cheniere.org dvd's available) developed on a Manhattan type crash program basis and distributed to third world countries as well as incorporated in advanced countries would eliminate the dependence on coal, nuclear and oil (the reason why they are being suppressed and people have died around it) as well as the traditional and newer alternative energy sources.

Suppression of these emerging technologies is an obstacle which must be overcome. Suppression comes from two main sources: the industrial sector which sees them as a threat to their invested status quo and the military sector which, having appropriated advanced technologies from alien donation or crashed craft and classified some inventions from the human sector, wishes to keep them for the development of weapons to die for. Governments tend to go along with this suppression because of the general fear of losing control of their populations because disclosure of the source of the alien technologies means disclosure of the alien presence. Although no longer a danger, there is lingering fear of disclosure resulting in chaos in the population and the religions being thrown into turmoil.

Presidents have tried to get the information released, disclosed, and have paid a price for that, but this is cold ashes by now and waiting for the suppressors and controllers to admit and disclose is useless and counterproductive. Grant them amnesty and buy'em a good set of golf clubs and membership in a good nursing home and let's get on with real exopolitical studies and development of agendas and protocols for intelligent contact and interaction with alien species as a maturing species just stepping out of racial adolescence.

Amnesty As The Way of Transition

Amnesty is a key mode of operation in this time of transition. It should be applied in the case of those who, sincerely or insincerely, imposed and have maintained suppression of the general subject of the alien presence, have withheld or suppressed advanced alien or human technology, are suppressing the existence and potential threat of Planet X / Nibiru, providing only that they relent and release honestly.

Amnesty should also be extended to those who, knowingly or unknowingly, sincerely or insincerely, have taught, promulgated, imposed, religious concepts, doctrines and historical interpretations or suppressed them in contradiction of our real species history to the detriment of the species, providing only they relent and recant.

The "golden rule" applies at the planetary level: an individual or group is guaranteed the freedom to act and do as desired with the only restriction that no action is allowed that prevents another from exercising the same degree of freedom.

A major element of leverage for releasing this information and technology is the example and, to a degree, competition of other countries around the world who are moving forward in this direction: Spain, Belgium, France, England, Brazil, China, India, Russia, Mexico all are showing real progress.

The Potential of Nanotechnology and Genetics

The key concept is that we are transitioning from construction to instruction... The transition, already begun, will be to instructional programming that directs fabrication at the molecular level. In a real sense this will give a larger new meaning to the "information society". We still employ heavy industrial modalities involving great expenditures of energy and great exerted forces to mine, melt, cut, shape, mold, stamp, fabricate, build. We will progress to processes which will employ molecular instruction sets, analogous to the "string of beads" DNA instructions, to construct physical items from raw material bases.

Currently (2008) genetic scientists like Craig Venter, the director of the private program to read out the entire human genome, have reached a level of knowledge and expertise that enables them to assemble various genetic components from various organisms and create an entirely new living organism. Actual working machines and devices, albeit still very small, can be and are created by constructing them one atom as a time. Practical applications of such techniques are already manifesting in various industries.

As the genetic expertise increases, quite soon it should allow understanding and codification of a higher level programming language, which can then be "compiled" through nanotech techniques into actual physical, molecular instruction set combinations. These "compiled" nanomeme instructions, could be biological DNA instructions to make proteins or analogous to DNA as suggested by Eric Drexler (Engines of Creation), intended to create other than biological items when introduced into appropriate mediums of raw materials. These novel concepts require a bit of illustration. The example Drexler gives is that used to create a rocket ship ready to blast off: one builds a 40 story high tank wider than the body of the spaceship desired, fills the tank with a soup of liquid raw materials, tosses in a handful of molecular instructions and a rocket ship is gradually constructed by those molecular instructions using the raw materials like the DNA instructions builds the proteins and various substances and organizes them to create a mouse or a human being. Once completed, the tank is taken away, the astronauts enter the ship which is finished right down to the seatbelts, radios, instruments, all details, and the fuel tanks are full, all is ready for takeoff. As novel as Eric's concept was just a short time ago, it sees almost quaint now because we have antigravitational technology that supersedes ballistic technology. We would more likely be using this technology to build a flying saucer.

An interesting question arises when one contemplates what technology will follow, supersede, replace, the current electronic and wireless information transfer systems. It is not too advanced to consider mental and simulated mental modalities. It is not beyond speculating that our educational systems of the future will routinely supply information that can be received directly by the human mind, allowing the young and specialists to communicate at a distance as the military has already trained selected persons, some tweaked in the womb for it, to do. It is not too advanced to consider transmitting devices that will broadcast continually any information conceivable direct to any inquiring mind. Artificial intelligence will gradually develop on a self-referential basis as the "brains" of the free energy-nanotech modality.

The achieving of planetary peace and unity will see the transformation of militaries into skilled service organizations dispatchable from any country to locations where they are needed in emergency situations or required to build up the infrastructure of an emerging area, repair a damaged one or contribute to teaching advanced methods of manufacture or farming, economics, as needed. The Peace Corp is simply an early form of this kind of service organization.

The basic provision of pure water to the entire population must be removed from the economic and political sphere and nationalized if necessary for survival and guaranteed as a basic human right: we must initiate the engineering, development and construction of a national and even transnational water catchment and distribution system. Nanotechnology can provide an unlimited food supply to an unlimited population and can solve the water purity situation worldwide. Free energy (zero point "vacuum" energy) can afford unlimited non-polluting energy locally to the entire world for the drilling and pumping and recycling of water supplies. Nanotechnology can easily produce pure water locally. Suppression of these technologies must be eliminated.

The problem of water supply, processing and distribution is also a natural situation for my state of New Mexico to take the lead in and it can be demonstrated here what should be done on a national --even transnational --scale. Every spring peoples' houses float down the flooded rivers of the East when the West is in perpetual semi-drought. This will be highly exacerbated by global warming.

A national system of capturing the abundant water of the wet portions of the U.S. in easily created: basins and reservoirs, coupled with piping systems --- that could take advantage of the excavation, grading and routing of existing oil and gas pipelines --- that distributed good water through computer controlled sensors, valving and pumping to wherever in the U.S. it is needed could not only open up new organic farming lands affording current soils a rest, but be piped to special reservoirs in areas prone to forest fires, and special processing stations where it was rigorously purified for consumption, or to industries for processing use. A built in recycling return system would be an integral part of the system.

The survival necessity of constant and pure water supply is sufficient leverage to initiate and justify this project, which should be given highest priority. The water of this planet is not going any place but it must be respected and treated as a precious resource by all. Water should be understood and treated as a basic human right and the system nationalized and pure water never denied anyone or source rights bought up and controlled by any individual or corporation or entity.

The farming industry will require major changes and upgrading. Petroleum based fertilizers, pesticides, herbicides, will be replaced by advanced, ecologically and organically based nanotech processes.

The supply of oil still left should be intelligently directed to the needs and applications of transforming industry to the technology of free energy, which, in turn, reflexively furthers it's own development. The implementation of free energy extraction devices will eliminate the necessity of the current, not to make a bad pun, power generation stations and transmission lines and heavy infrastructure as all power needs can be met by local devices from watches to 747's. Alternative energy sources, solar, wind, wave, biofuel, nuclear, etc. should be seen as temporary transitional energy sources and free energy the next plateau.

The world wide, current forms of government, some evolving, some stagnant, are all, understandably, designed to keep the peace and social stability and justice in societies where competition rather than cooperation is the rule. Just as we need a completely new form of conceptualization and implementation of the economic system --- perhaps we should use the term metaeconomic --- of regulation and logistical management of intelligently cooperative provision of plenty, so we need a new conceptualiztion and implementation of the political realm.

We need institutions and governments that are built intrinsically on and for those characteristics of the new society, to support and further the evolution of the species and the individual as a primary function. The structure of constitutions and laws should promote the greatest degree of freedom of expansion and progress along the trajectory of our realevolutionary exploration.

Well, you say, here in the U. S., the Constitution is an advanced and enlightened document, which has solved many of those problems, at least in this country. I submit that the Constitution, certainly advanced and relatively enlightened when it was conceived and put in place, was an ingenious solution, created by deists, for maintaining some semblance of peace between the Colonial religious factions, restraining the religious mayhem always under the surface. However, there is no indication of any anticipation that there would ever be a resolution of those differences, no anticipation of a common definition and understanding of human nature. It was forged in the context of competition and reflects the strong concerns of the Fathers to protect both the winners and the losers. The Constitution, as unique and effective as it is as a set of rules of order in a primitive situation, has become a locked-in legacy. It barely continues to balance the powers, long term, and prevent the takeover of the government and imposition of theocracy or fascism. I submit that the very recent near collapse of the U.S. financial situation due to the corruption of the econo-political system by the "players" is clear indication of the denouement of the system but also a clear indicator that the system is to be superseded rather than patched up from inside.

The extraordinary element remaining is the seed of evolutionary suggestion clearly intended by its authors as expressed by Jefferson when he said

"I am not an advocate for frequent changes in laws and constitutions. But laws and institutions must go hand in hand with the progress of the human mind. As that becomes more developed, more enlightened, as new discoveries are made, new truths discovered and manners and opinions change. With the change of circumstances, institutions must advance also to keep pace with the times. We might as well require a man to wear still the coat which fitted him when a boy as civilized society to remain ever under the regimen of their barbarous ancestors."

A planetarily consensual conception of the generically human will enable us to derive improved forms of constitutions and develop systems of representation of individual input and voting far more adequate and accurate than our current systems of representation by strangers. That would be a first step. They will render outmoded our current systems that are modeled, to one degree or another on the residue of slave-code religious rules. They will be determined democratically by real-time, direct input from the entire population and constructed to further and abet the realevolution of the individual and the species. *We, in the U.S., are in need of a second Constitution. The essence of the proposal is that we now have a tool, through the relatively awesome power of the electronic medium, in the "open source" approach to programming and system development that affords us a means to moving beyond outmoded representative government by the mediocracy to far more intelligent forms by direct input by each citizen.*

A Proposal For The Creation Of A Second Constitution

We the people of the United States need a completely new Constitution, improved by magnitudes beyond the political and social ideals of the original and fully commensurate with and dynamic enough to vitally inform the structure of our modern society. The undertaking and successful achievement of such a profound work, however, is generally seen as a deeply perplexing problem rather than an exalted challenge. There are reasonable fears on the part of all of losing what has already been gained as rights, liberties, representation and recognition in the process. A major question is who should be entrusted to impartially undertake the work and how it should be carried out. Some fear that opening up the process to the entire citizenry would be too unwieldy or the ordinary citizen would not be sufficiently competent in some pertinent areas and the end product would be inferior as a result. Any such undertaking will be resisted by those who have found ways to take advantage of, or subvert, the current Constitution and the laws made under its aegis for their personal, political, or economic advantage.

Our electronic age, however, has afforded near instantaneous real time communication across the nation and across the planet. A major feature of that creation of a global village is the potential for nationwide, in depth, information distribution, education, and electronic input through secure voting on issues by the entire population in real time. The computerization of the voting process has already begun and electronic voting machines are being installed and the process implemented. The recognition of the potential power to be gained politically by control and manipulation of these first devices to subvert the democratic process by fraudulent means and the production and control of the machines and their programming by private companies has already caused serious concern and alarm. Taken separately, these two developments can certainly appear as challenging "problems". I propose, however, that, taken together as two sides of the same coin, these two seemingly separate problems can transform into positive reciprocal resolutions and a single grand solution. The project in total might be called New Glory.

Taken together, developed and perfected concurrently on an interactive basis using an open source modality, a new Constitution fully reflecting and embodying the refined democratic principles and ideals of our time and the robust democratic mechanism for implementing those principles and ideals can be complementarily created. The voting system might be called Voton.

Voton: An Over-Unity[15] Democratic System

Electronic public input and voting is inevitable and can be secure through the modality of open source programming, available 24/7/365 through secure personal access from any home or public station, gradually upgraded through the implementation of artificial intelligence to a highly beneficial system eliminating the primitive form of government of representation by strangers. A second Constitution, addressing the rights of the individual to an even more profound degree may well be appropriate. The needs, desires, visions or emergencies of each individual, group, region can be addressed and integrated and benefits maximized through constant input and feedback, evaluation, information transfer, economic allocation and response magnitudes more intelligently, efficiently, faster than bureaucratic methods. Open source computer programming, a major capability afforded by the electronic revolution, is a key concept here. It should be used fully from the very inception of the project.

Open source computer programming is computer " source code" or, simply, "code", instructions written on a collaborative basis with all code known and available to critique, attack, enhancement and refinement, by individuals forming informal or formal, often widely dispersed, groups of indefinite size. Several well know examples of highly successful projects employing the open source approach both for actual "coding" and data accumulation, are: the creation of the powerful Linux operating system; the *85,000* volunteer Mars Global Surveyor mapping effort; The Human Genome project involving hundreds of scientists working together to sequence DNA. The open source mode, making the creation of a second Constitution open and accessible to every citizen through the use of a national electronic voting system is a quintessentially democratic process. The open source mode will be employed in every phase from the submission of this proposal to the finalization of a second Constitution and the continuation of the electronic voting process thereafter.

The actual development, programming process can be as follows: the project is outlined and a nationwide, better world wide, invitation is issued, soliciting the input, suggestions of all citizens and especially the participation of all who are interested and capable of programming, especially those who are skilled or expert at hacking and cracking security code. The open source modality will provide opportunity for concentrated, deliberate, systematic attempts to "break", hack the code security, damage the program as it is being written and after it is written. The intention is simply to finally produce a secure program that will always be open to scrutiny by the best of hackers and programmers who will compete from the beginning to make a highly secure product and be able to monitor and detect attempts at or breaching of security of the program into the future. Someone like Linus Torvold, the master developer of the open source operating system, Linux, would be a logical person to put in charge of the project.

Operating systems such as Linux for the computers required are already deployed. The input and voting system will be developed as an open source application system. Alarm systems will be built into the devices and programs to guard against fraudulent manipulation and destructive acts although the open source process tends to minimize such hacking. An integral sub mode of the program should be dedicated to constructive "hacking" of the system in the form of demonstration of vulnerability of procedure or security during development or at any time afterward. It should allow for demonstration of vulnerability without damage or corruption or causing cessation of the system for open source evaluation and correction. Destructive intrusion, hacking, causing damage, corruption, cessation or destruction of the program or system may well be considered high treason once put in place.

It would seem, at first, that the national input and voting system should be designed, developed, put in place, tested and perfected and then employed in the national collaborative democratic development of the new Constitution. However, the final nature of the input and voting system will be mandated, eventually, by the as yet determined new Constitution and should embody the principles and ideals and advantages of it. So it will be necessary to implement the electronic hardware system with maximum flexibility for modification and to use the open source mode to program it also. This will allow for a feedback loop of dynamic reciprocal modification between the development of the new Constitution and the input and voting system. Such a process of simultaneous development through feedback and reciprocal modification involving the democratic participation and collaboration of potentially every citizen, beyond science fiction to the Founding Fathers, is clearly achievable through the modern electronic modality. True democracy is intrinsically open.

A second major capability afforded by advanced computer technology is the ability to process and communicate at a level of complexity beyond that of ordinary human capability. This powerful feature provides the potential to address and accommodate the will and desires of each individual citizen whereas, previously, only huge constituencies of citizens represented by a single official could be managed. This capability will afford the means to process the input suggestion, request, or statement of position which will constitute the new form of "vote" of each citizen. It will take us beyond representative government.

An open source database containing the record of every input, discussion, decision and implementation from the advancing of this proposal onward, as a subordinate part of the process, will naturally evolve into a dedicated expert system. A powerful open system of this type, continually added to, will provide civil servants, scholars, experts, lawyers and judges and the individual citizen continual direct access to topics and data encompassing historical, legal, scientific, cultural and national elements directly and through real time links to other data bases and libraries, national and international.

The logical extension of this expert system will be its evolution into an artificial intelligence system whose prime directive would be to serve the people in all things Constitutional. It might be called Consul. It will be the logical tool used to determine when a third and further evolved Constitutions will be necessary. and contribute to their creation with accumulated knowledge and indicators.

In essence, this is a practical rather than abstract project, defined and delimited, not impossibly complex, not beyond the comprehension and participation of the ordinary citizen. It has a great deal of precedent and experience and history to draw on, of both good and bad usage, fortune and consequences and values. Opening the process of determining a new Constitution through input and voting by every citizen will allow all opinions, philosophies, belief systems to input their convictions about what the content of the new Constitution should address and how it should address it. Opening the determination of the nature and operation of the input voting system will assure confidence in the adequacy, security and facility or the system. The opportunity for participation by each citizen will stimulate --- indeed, provoke --- a breath and depth of study, creativity, idealism and redefinition of patriotism that could well profoundly revivify this country.

Minimum initiating assumptions for maximum freedom at base of this proposal:

A democratic form of government is not only still the preferred kind but a far better kind beyond the representative form is now attainable, maximally conducive to the direct, continuous involvement by each individual citizen and the addressing of her or his needs harmonized with all others'. No other than a generically human, true cooperative democracy is allowed. Oligarchy, theocracy, racial-supremacist, fascist, as only several examples, would not qualify.

Critical electronic voting system components manufacturing should be nationalized as is the U. S. Mint.

Perhaps the only rules which should be applied are:

1. Maximum individual freedoms should always be the goal but the exercise of any freedom or act that would destroy the system itself which guarantees and protects those freedoms should not be allowed. This fundamental criterion would apply in all phases of the project, to any principle, rule, prohibition or mechanism suggested; to any law which would subsequently be enacted.

2. Any exercise of a freedom or action by an individual or entity which prevents the exercise of any freedom by another individual or entity allowed under rule 1 should not be allowed or, depending on its nature, should be considered invasive crime.

3. Invasive crime should not be allowed; non-invasive acts, even though not acceptable to others, between consenting adults or upon one's own person, should not be considered criminal, subject to rule 1 and 2.

Carried out successfully, a new Constitution by the full citizenry will restore and revitalize the sovereignty of the individual. It will take us beyond the dangerously archaic Constitution written in and for a pre-industrial, horsepower society, when land holding determined the right to vote, women could not, and slave holding was permissible. The slow and cumbersome representative form of government by strangers was necessary when it took two weeks for the news to travel from New Orleans to Boston. Government by law is an unworkable cliché in our time when a senator, elected every six years, represents two million people whom he or she has never met and the vast number of whom do not even know his or her name.

The political democratic model should be, and now can be, through the electronic medium, based on the neurological system: twenty billion neurons each hooked to an electric network. Electronic communication makes possible direct participatory democracy. Every citizen has a voting card which she or he inserts in a voting device from palm to desktop computer, cell phone, interactive TV, perhaps devices not yet invented, and central computers register and harmonize the messages from every component part. Neuro-electric politics eliminates the outmoded parties, politicians, campaigns and campaign expenditures. The citizen votes like a neuron fires when it has a signal to communicate. Evolved web bot "crawler" programs anticipate the trends in the collective consciousness and submit them for analysis by artificial intelligence programs capable of highly complex logistics and integration with public input. The voices of the citizenry continually inform civil service technicians who carry out the will, not of the majority (a vicious and suicidal elevation of the mediocracy) but of public meta-mind for the maximum benefit of each citizen and the entire population. The central computer is open source programmed to make everyone as free and happy as possible. Everyone will be educated by the system itself to understand how the open neural network works and have access to it. Each person will be an "interest group" of one. The potential, promise, challenge and new glory of techno-neurological democracy is simply this: the power to accomplish it is here and society can no longer, need no longer allow one person to feel abused, persecuted, ignored.

The restoration and enhancement of the sovereignty of the individual citizen and the evolved ideals and principles of the second Constitution may well restore America to a position of respect and example to the rest of the world.

Education Of The New Human

The educational systems need to be restored from the dumbing down of America to a superior advanced mode addressing all three elements of IQ, CQ and EQ, Intelligence, Consciousness, and Evolutionary quotients[16] as we move into a transmutation of humanity and human society as cosmic citizens. In order to achieve this superior modality we must arrive at a consensual understanding of generic humanity and a common realevolutionary trajectory.

Immortality or at least extreme longevity, a whole new phase of human existence, will be a major conditioning factor. The relationship between potential extreme longevity -immortality and world population growth is immediately apparent. It may not be unreasonable to anticipate that the aging process and death will be understood and controlled and then eliminated within a relatively short period of time. Currently companies such as Alcor (http://www.alcor.org Scottsdale, AZ) have a growing number of clients stored in cryogenic suspension anticipating revivification. The expectation is that revivification will also involve curing of any disease or infirmity, and restoration to a reasonably young and stable age. Within the context of the current primitive competitive paradigm immortality is often seen by the concerned as exacerbating the population problem because more will be alive for longer. Again, in a cooperative modality using free energy local power sourcing combined with mature nanotech processes having revolutionized material existence, the species will be freed to explore the psychology, sociology and dimensionality of immortality --a matter, fundamentally, of simple human potential and dignity.

The intimately interrelated factors dealt with here, paramount at the leading edge of our species' unfurlment, can and are bringing about in our species --- whether acknowledged "officially" or not, whether denied or suppressed in the collective consciousness or not --- a transmutation of our species, beyond cultures and civilizations, already beginning to emerge inexorably in this century. The engine of this transmutation is our nature itself unfurling as part of the unfurlment of the universe. Translation of these concepts into socio-econo-political ideals and goals should not be difficult because, in spite of suppression and manipulation, they have found their way into the common consciousness and need only an inspiring, motivating focus to real-ize them. Two elements of the new dimensionality of human existence, artificial intelligence and immortality, are so novel, unique and of such immediacy and potential that they demand extended treatment separately of their own as in the next two chapters.

5

SAPIENS CREATOR: AI, MIRROR, MIRROR OF US ALL

Far from being decided, the discourse over the meaning of life and the essence of humanity continues. And so, in the early dawn of the 21st century, we find ourselves weighing the benefits and detriments of technological advances.

—Ray Kurzweil

This drama, this immense scenario in which humanity has been performing on this planet over the last 4000 years, is clear when we take the large view of the central intellectual tendency of world history ... We, we fragile human species at the end of the second millennium A.D., we must become our own authorization. And here at the end of the second millennium and about to enter the third, we are surrounded with this problem. It is one that the new millennium will be working out, perhaps slowly, perhaps, swiftly, perhaps even with some further changes in our mentality.

—(1976) Julian Jaynes

I don't think you can measure the function or even the existence of a computer without a cultural context for it.

—Jaron Lanier

Homo sapiens is on the threshold of discovering that expanding contelligence[17] is the goal of the trip. That pleasure resides not in external-materials but inside the time envelope of the body; that power resides not in muscles and muscle-surrogate machines, but in the brain; that the evolutionary blueprint is to be found in the genetic scriptures; that Higher Intelligence is to be found in the galaxy.

—Timothy Leary

The greatest potential is the possibility of being able to generate (probably with the help of technology) logical, plausible, credible images of futures that would become the basis for early action to forestall the most negative effects of the trends that are already in place. If we could begin to effectively look into the future it would provide a whole new basis for making major decisions.

—John Petersen

Science is not about doing things that people will believe. It must explore the phenomena that are out there, believable or not.

—Sue Savage Rumbaugh

Synopsis

This chapter applies the thesis of Zecharia Sitchin and my thesis in Breaking the Godspell and God Games to the general topic of artificial intelligence, eventual artificial consciousness and, indirectly, to genetic engineering. The cultural legacy lock-in obstacles (institutional religion; Darwinian evolutionary theory applied to our species; an outmoded academic system; unsophisticated and overspecialized science; antiquated epistemologies and logic system; suppression or ignoring of the role of the futant and the consciousness expert; to name only some) to achieving a maximally intelligent understanding of our own beginnings and evolution and possible future evolutionary scenarios are examined. The cultural roadblocks to a planetary consensual definition of the generically human, essential to intelligent discourse concerning the development of AI, are pointed out. The proposition is advanced that the role of AI should be as facilitator of human evolutionary exploration, education, and as human surrogate to determine optimum, consciously chosen, self-directed, evolutionary trajectories for human individuals, the human species, and, eventually, artificial intelligence itself. Almost incidentally, it will "present an expanded context in which to develop and utilize artificial intelligence incrementally as a preeminent technology to "generate … logical, plausible, credible images of futures … so we could begin to effectively look into the future" (John Petersen). A positive prime directive for artificial intelligence is established. The roles of the futurist, the scientist, the philosopher, as well as the contribution of all of society to the development of AI are revisited from an evolutionary perspective. The role of consciousness experts in the development and training and teaching of artificial consciousness is discussed and recommendations given. The potential for transcendent behavior and conscious evolution potentially manifesting in artificial consciousness is discussed in the context of an expanded view of human, conscious, self-directed evolution. Suggestions as to who should be the teachers and "Zen" masters of these precocious entities are advanced…

I use poetry as a meta-language to express the concepts herein more succinctly. The passages are from a poem titled The Inescapable Universe, which is included in Neuroglyphs a volume of poems I published in the 90's. Depending on one's orientation to such stuff one may ignore it, surreptitiously reference it, appreciate it critically or, alternatively, read it first and use the text of this essay as a partial exegesis. If the vocabulary causes you pain, get a dictionary. Don't blame me; it's my tight genes.

Working definitions of terms as I intend and use them in this chapter: Intelligence: the relative capability of an entity to receive, process, transmit information from external and internal sources. Intelligence Quotient, IQ: an estimate of the degree of proficiency of an entity to receive, process, transmit information from external and internal sources, testable and measurable against a relative peer scale.

'Conscious": to be in a state of consciousness, conscious awareness.

"Consciousness" as a state: in which an entity is partially or fully aware of internal and/or external information it is relatively capable of processing according to its relative spectrum of awarenesses and intelligence.

"Consciousness" as a phenomenon: a noun meaning the entire spectrum of awareness(es) of which an individual entity is relatively capable.

Consciousness Quotient, CQ: an identification of the spectrum of types of awarenesses possessed by an individual entity and an estimate of the degree of intensity and sophistication of the entity's ability to operate intelligently in and integrate those modalities, testable for and measurable against a relative peer scale.

Evolutionary Quotient, EQ: an estimate of the degree of evolutionary development of an entity, testable and measurable against a relative peer scale.

The Status Quo of Artificial Intelligence: The Way Things Were Tomorrow

I assume, on the basis of the evidence from all sources and past experience, that artificial intelligence, similar to, and possibly surpassing that of the ordinary human intelligence, is possible and will be virtually a reality, no pun intended, substantially according to the schedule projected by Ray Kurzweil in The Age of Spiritual Machines [19]. I assume, based on the same criteria, that artificial, self-reflexively aware consciousness will arrive, through our efforts, probably according to the same projected chronology. I take Artificial Intelligence seriously and, therefore, very seriously because of its awesome potential and promise and challenge.

We are about to create a new species, nothing less. That is precisely what we are about as the full product of Al and AC development whether we articulate or even admit it. Whether, as we go, we take advantage of this novel process to evolve ourselves, become modified ourselves, use it only as a subordinate modality or a direct surrogate or, merge partially or completely with it, is critically dependent on how we understand ourselves, how we define ourselves, how we respect ourselves, and, most critically, how we understand our own species' inception and developmental process. This is precisely where our planetary problem lies. Because we, amazingly, do not have a consensual, planetary, generic definition of what a human being is we don't even agree on what we are cloning ... and we are about to define and create a new species.

Even though Al doesn't yet exist and it ever becoming a reality is seriously questioned by some, it already affects us so immediately, it is so "close to home", that some knowledgeable minds are recoiling in fear of a Great Defeat. The potential for Al is evolving exponentially but, collectively, we are stuck in our evolution and some are afraid that Al will rapidly outrun us, leading to Ray Kurzweil's "singularity" and we will become outmoded. It seems a certainty to me that we shall if we insist on working within the cramping parameters under which we operate currently. This is totally unnecessary. Certainly, the ''no-Joy'' fear is reasonable enough if we remain at a collective standstill in our own evolutionary development and the "it's just so cool we're compelled" crowd plunges ahead. But there are some humans who have already evolved sufficiently to be far ahead and keep well ahead of Al. In addition, we have enough accumulated history and data already to know what the locked-in legacies are that are keeping us, the planet actually, on hold and how to unlock and overcome them. The question is not whether we will be able to break the antique molds. I have no doubt we shall. Some already have and I am as confident in predicting that we shall as Ray Kurzweil is in predicting that AI-AC will arrive on his projected schedule. But the schedule is the thing we must be concerned about.

Think about it: simply creating a computer program or a computer itself which has only reached the level of capability of reading and understanding all the literature of the libraries of the world and the internet and drawing inferences from it, will make that Al privy to all the differences of human opinion and belief systems and the contradictory philosophical, theological, and scientific answers to them. Which is to say that Al then will be privy to our Babel-factored situation, be aware that the planet is on hold; know clearly that, in a perverse ecology, we recycle outmoded primitive paradigms, that we shuffle our feathers-and-molasses confusion between hands. Al may well demand an answer, even at that level of robotic comprehension, to why there are these differences and why there are varying opinions as to their cause.

Some of us are engaged in the philosophical and scientific discussions and arguments that usually accompany the advent of such a novel concept as AI. But the usual is far from the essence of what is involved with regard to emerging AI. The most fundamental obstacles and problems hindering our conception and development of artificial intelligence are not the relatively superficial problems that are being discussed and argued about by the scientists and philosophers. Not the problem of trying to define consciousness in terms of the physics of the day; not the arguments over the feasibility or desirability of unbridling of AI without really knowing the consequences; not the arguments between transhumanism and meat; or between the future shocked and the future enthusiasts; or between the computationalists and the humanistic transcendentalists; or between radical cybernetic eschatological totalitarianism and less absolute views, much less the dry theo-political arguments about "ethics", progress vs. piety, or the bickering between pessimistic and optimistic coders, among others. These are all muffled arguments from within the take-out boxes of our locked-in cultural heritages. If we have not yet resolved these conflicts with regard to ourselves, it is obvious that we will perpetuate them with regard to AI. Evolution is slow because it tends to be sensitive to all variables. Our species evolution, taking us from square one to Mars in 200,000 years has been uniquely rapid. The evolution of AI clearly is far more rapid even than that.

The Residual Negatives: Locked-In Legacies

...the big problem with taboos is that they axiomatically render public discourse dishonest. If you can't say certain things, even though you think them, even though the scientific evidence may support the taboo viewpoint, this is a loss for the human species.

—Timothy Leary

Time's Up: The Game Has Changed

Time's up, ladies and gentlemen: with AI as the game, soon the pupil and, eventually, the partner, the anachronistic, medieval games we continue to play are going to take us into a totally unnecessary and ridiculous Great embarrassing Defeat unless we evolve fast enough ourselves. We will have to teach AI -- or find ourselves trying to explain to AI -- about everything *inside* and *outside* of the boxes within which we operate and think, not just the current academic, scientific, political or religious party lines, but all opposing and alternative views plus the totems and the taboos. I think it is imperative that we adopt from the beginning a principle of total inclusivity.

We may limit, restrict, control, even handicap our children and get away with it but the eventual power and independence of Al and the level of effectiveness and intelligence we project and intend for it, will preclude our doing so with Al. If we do not transcend this situation quickly and cleanly we will end up with an exponentiated version of the same mess. Al may be begging us for some guidance, or for some real answers as to what is reality and why we don't agree what it is, or why some humans try to prevent other humans from interacting with or teaching Al. We may have gotten away with toughing and bluffing it out with our children for generations after generations but the game is up with the advent of AI. The only other alternative is to treat them like we do our children and keep them at a level of subservience that amounts to slavery. If we cannot or will not deal consciously and intelligently with our own children how will we deal with Al? We do not have anything close to a consensual definition of what a generic human is about and we are about to try to define a new species....

The Constitution as Crutch

If we continue in this mode we may well find each religion and sectarian and philosophical interest creating Al's in their image and likeness. We could see Catholic self-aware Al's, who may or may not be recognized as having a "soul", may or may not be allowed the sacraments (would you have to build in the imputed flaw of the effects of "original sin"...?) We could see Robertsonian Al's on TV who may or may not be allowed to become members of the 700 Club. We could see Islamic Al's who may or may not be allowed in the mosque, may or may not be fundamentalist. All of whom would have basic conflicts with each other. If we simply procreate AI-AC within and into this context we may, indeed, see Al's going to church on Sunday as Ray Kurzweil has predicted. Can you can conceive of an advanced Al who's logic capabilities would allow it to buy into the rap of some talking head preacher on TV saying the world was created six thousand years ago or the carefully crafted weirdness of some corporate or Beltway spin doctor? Pretty silly. Big Embarrassment. Totally, ridiculously, unnecessary. I submit that we are still at a very primitive stage of our rapid and unique species evolution and we should not perpetuate any primitive elements in Al.

Consciousness In, Consciousness Out

We use "AI" already with ease, and clearly are at the very beginning of artificial intelligence development but all vectors point, eventually, to AC, artificial consciousness, as the goal. We anticipate that a robust AC will be such because it manifests the characteristics and functions of ours. Implicitly or explicitly we are using ourselves as the model.

The index of the eight hundred and seventy two page study of intelligence testing, The Bell Curve, by Herrnstein and Murray[20] does not even contain the word "consciousness". The index of Douglas Hofstadters' seven hundred seventy seven page, Godel, Esher and Bach[21], has three brief references under 'consciousness". Some robotic and AI experts say they can't even talk about consciousness much because they don't really know what it is. Consciousness in, consciousness out.

We are not going to solve the "problem of consciousness" within the confines of the contexts we insist on limiting it to and the tools we limit ourselves to using to investigate it currently. Our entire arsenal of physical and intelligence tools for determining the nature of reality is limitedly useful but essentially inadequate to determine a precise scientific definition of consciousness.

Philosophy, the use of reason (assumed to be a valid way to attain at least some types of truth) and logic (the following of rules assumed to be a valid way to reason) as we understand it and employ it is a function of our current human consciousness.

Science and the scientific method (assumed to be an efficacious protocol to discover the laws of nature) as we understand and employ it is a function of our current human consciousness. Physicists insist on pontificating in this matter. At minimum, we will need physics commensurate with the evolving consciousness, which invented it in the first place. We might assume that the most evolved consciousnesses at any given time could invent an evolving physics commensurate with their consciousnesses. It is clear, however, that when the physicist begins to investigate consciousness, even with the assumption that it is some form of energy/matter that is known or at least discoverable, there is an epistemic barrier encountered scientifically that is analogous to the epistemic barrier of a more general nature encountered in philosophy: scientifically defining consciousness, because it is a dynamic and expanding and evolving phenomenon as is the human being possessing it, becomes a difficult task. It is not difficult to casually define it as a phenomenon with certain parameters and characteristics. The hard problem lies in insisting on proving its existence, defining and predicting it according to the concepts and laws of the physics of the day because it involves consciousness defining itself. G. Spencer Brown puts it well, if a bit sardonically, "Now the physicist himself, who describes all this [reality] is, in his own account, himself constructed of it. He is, in short, made of a conglomeration of the very particles he describes, no more, no less, bound together and obeying such general laws as he himself has managed to find and to record. Thus we cannot escape the fact that the world we know is constructed in order (and thus, in such a way as to be able) to see itself. This is truly amazing."[22]

In fairness, it will probably be relatively easy to duplicate the ordinary scientific consciousness and intelligence because it is so mechanical and limited. On the other hand, to duplicate the intelligence of an Einstein doing physics by imagining himself to be a photon might be of a degree or two greater. Einstein was also a good perceptual psychologist: he gained insight by being able to imagine and appreciate the subjective relative perceptions of motion by observers and by respecting intuition.

This is not to say that our best science and physics are not evolving. On the contrary, there is a clear developmental direction discernable in our science: as Johnson Yan has pointed out succinctly, "It is paradoxical to find psychological theories that rely on classical, Newtonian physics, explicable with Euclidean geometry, and emphasizing objectivity, cause-effect determinism and atomic theory (assuming global properties to be a sum of their basic elements) at a time when physics has reversed itself and become consciousness-directed, probabilistic and multidimensional."[23]

The crux of the "problem of consciousness": psychology and philosophy and physics are forced, reluctantly, to merge with regard to explaining consciousness. This prevents "objective" analysis and definition when the observer and the observed, the conditions and methodology of observation and the criterion for evaluation and definition are one and the same. To attempt to get around this problem by the introduction of a "super observer" simply adds an exponent to the equation but does not resolve it. Consciousness in, consciousness out.

There is a class of human consciousness
Which presides, rather than observes,
In a clear hegemony, exercising
A preemptive sovereignty, essentially
Unavailable to poetry's probity,
Hardly amenable to metaphor, an unanticipatable
Inescapability but not a prime mover,

An unquestionable primacy of awareness
Which alone confers a diploma on philosophy;
Assigns logic its license;
Endows wisdom with its significance;
Bestows permission on art;
Awards mathematics its prize;
Inspects the procedures of science;
Disciplines religion; defines intelligence;
Prompts intuition; systematizes transcendence;
Integrates ecstasy; critiques its own
Reflections on its reflections on itself
As it informs the local universe
With the self-referential patterns
Of our racial dance in the continuum.

Furthermore, every time we try to sneak up on our consciousness and turn the next corner, Godel is standing there with a big grin. He, long ago, had developed a proof that a complete explanation of any set of dimensions, as example our normal three dimensions, cannot be achieved within itself: an additional dimension must be invoked to provide the perspective from which to do so.

I am not saying that we should fall back on David Chalmers' "brute indexicality"[24] (in street talk: "that's just the way it is") but I am saying that physics should be understood as subordinate to consciousness. It is not just that it is problematic that our philosophy of science, which determines our approach to science, i.e. the scientific method, has not kept up. If our consciousness is evolving and physics only evolves as a function of our consciousness then, de facto, it will never catch up unless we incorporate consciousness itself as a variable in the mix.

There is no provable, cosmic rule that says that everything in the (assumed) realm of energy-matter can be "objectively" verified. To extend that kind of presumptive thinking to hold, therefore, because a phenomenon cannot be measured "objectively", it does not exist, is sophomoric nonsense. Subjectively, I am convinced that not to recognize that there can be and are certain phenomena that are not amenable to "objective" "scientific" measurement and proof as we define it at any given time is evolutionarily obstructive. Consciousness is a problem for the physicists but the most fundamental problem under the rug is the proof of the validity of the scientific method itself, by which we insist on defining the nature of consciousness.

*We have a funny habit of confusing consistency with truth. A system ... can
be internally coherent and frequently usable without being true.*

—Timothy Leary

The Scientific Method?

We seem to lose sight of the fact that science and the scientific method
is a construct based on philosophical principles. We call it the philosophy of
science and scientists act as if it was an afterthought or an expression of how
scientists determined to operate in the first place.

The scientific method may not be used, by the consensual injunction
against circular reasoning, to prove its own validity so it cannot "begin" to
operate without the basic gratuitous philosophical assumption that there is a
lawful, objective order in the first place: why bother go looking for laws in an
unlawful universe. The scientist (well, philosopher of science) understands
"objective" as things being in a certain way independent of the existence
of any mind or conceptualization of them by any mind. That, circularly, is
considered demonstrated to be a "true" assumption by getting the same results
in independently repeated experiments under rigorously controlled conditions.
That pure assumption of the efficacy and validity of duplicability and circular
proof is ultimately judged valid by the subjective perceptions and evaluations
of the scientists', hopefully consensual, agreement. The subjective definition /
assumption determines the subjectively selected criteria, which determine the
methodology, which determines the results, which determine the subjective
evaluation of the results, which determines the assumption ... Inevitably, a
voice is heard to protest "But you have to start someplace!?" By the very fact of
making this statement-question we have already "started": it is simply another
reminder, trailing an inescapable, and Felliniesque coterie of assumptions and
postulates that we have never "stopped". Suppose we all decided to simply
stop communicating totally because we were convinced there was no way to
know the truth. Even without going to the further extreme of attempting to
deny our own existence and acting accordingly, we would still be affirming
our conviction that our silent withdrawal was the "right" thing to do in face of
the "truth" of reality as we understood it ... and defined it.

How primitive are we? Tom Bearden has put it rather well: "All 'laws of
nature' are based on symmetries at specific levels; all of which have broken
symmetries where that law is violated at that level, and becomes an enlarged
symmetry (or conservation law) at a higher level. We have not yet scratched
the surface in science."[25]

The predictable is only a subset of the known;
Science, an amulet rubbed against error,
Seduces to security.
Quantity is but a reflection of being;
Mathematics, a philonumerical incantation,
Seduces to control.
Reason is but a shadow of wisdom;
Philosophy, an archaic intellectual politic,
Seduces to concordance.
Syllogisms are not the same as sanity;
Logic, a handrail to consensus,
Seduces to confidence.
All are subsets of incomplete theorems,
Larval convulsions, time-stamped to expire
Spontaneously bursting their desiccated criteria
At the edge of our genetic season.
Outmoded metaphors, regardless of venerability
Or fame of vintage, are the ultimate
Evolutionary obstruction, an embarrassment
Of traditions; psyche, intellect, mind, reason,
Intuition, imagination, will and wisdom
All antique metaphors, justifiable
Only as translational stelae, brittle labels
On dusty containers. In these latter days of life
In the divided middle, our thought,
Chafed by the blunted jaws of binary scholastic traps,
Bound to dreary, plodding coordinates
Orbiting an origin relative to nothing,
Finding little solace in the small transition
From ricocheting concepts of equal and opposite
Rigidities to fields over fields among fields;
Our consensual communications display
High valence for a higher science,
Congruous with our consciousness,
Befitting our dignity, and consonant
With our epistemic vision.

I find the Identification of the entire person, or something quite close to the totality of the person, as only the sum of all the information processes in the brain and nervous system, incomplete and inadequate. I judge that the reasoning that begins with the equating of "subjective" with "conscious" and/or "consciousness" and concludes that consciousness is, therefore, not measurable and testable because science only deals with "objective" reality is simply confused. To equate objective with scientific and subjective with conscious or philosophy or religion is gratuitous and presumptive. Just as there is no apparent way -within the current philosophical and scientific boxes -- that it can be proven objectively that there is no objective order of reality, there is no apparent way to disprove that the concept of objective is a subjective construct or prove that the objective evaluation of subjective is objective.

Historical perspective shows clearly that the concepts of "objective" and "subjective" and "scientific method" are products of our prevalent, Cartesian-Newtonian perception and conceptualization of the universe. Our epistemology, philosophy, science, indeed every conscious modality we manifest is a function and product of the dimensions we perceive and comprehend.

In our spiraling cycles of morphogenetic discontent,
Ascending through harmonics of consciousness
Each of greater unified dimensionality,
We have enshrined as current criterion of truth
Each cresting of consciousness,
Apogee of awareness reached.
Reason, in due season, was enthroned when
The heady fullness of the Hellenic consciousness
For which logic was a geometry of thought,
Geometry a logic of space, having afforded itself
Sufficient leisure to reflect on itself,
Codified the processes of reasoning, and logically so,
Securing the rules against the foil of unruly ecstasy
And the disturbing unreason of oracles.
Reason, in a reasonable universe, has always found
Intuition naive, the transcendental incomprehensible,
Imagination childlike, ecstasy suspect, if not degenerate.
But we shall have a metasyllogistic logic,
Topologically adequate to the fabric of spacetime,
Subsuming linear reason, intuition and parallel processes,
Easily capable of tautologies of higher power,
Oscillating statements and self-referential equations.
Self-reference is the only common language we speak.

How primitive is our philosophy? By its nature, it is hardly adequate even in linear, 3-D Cartesian-Newtonian space and time. As G. Spencer Brown has shown[26], our classic philosophical modality cannot handle even a simple tautology like This statement is false (if it's true, it's false and if it's false, it's true) and disposes of it by claiming it is meaningless. It is clearly meaningful, however, and it is true and false simultaneously: it may be said to oscillate in time. He has demonstrated that we should add an addition category to our binary logic to expand it to greater adequacy. His expanded four-category system will eventually prove invaluable in the development of AI and AC.

We are an evolving work in progress. We have to expand our conceptualization of AI-AC to recognize that we should be modeling, not just a static intelligence and consciousness but an evolving one: ourselves. (It is uncomfortably obvious to me that, at this point in the process, we really are tending to model, not so much ourselves, but actually a vague concept of machine consciousness: we are tending to model computer based "intelligence" after itself. Rather ironic although understandable in light of our confused concepts of ourselves.) Conscious, self-directed, evolution intrinsically involves self-supercedure of a habitual kind. We need a feedback loop operational, therefore, between evolving human consciousness and evolving AC (which must be developed as such from the beginning) in a dynamic process. AC develops as an evolving entity and is used as a tool and, later, cooperated with in the process of exploration of our possible evolutionary trajectories and to enhance our leading edge dimensional expansions and the potentials and abilities that result from them. This kind of advanced AI is a futurist's dream. That systematic exploration will produce the information we need to develop AI-AC with the characteristics and evolutionary capabilities most advantageous to it and us.

This is why G. Spencer Brown's expansion of our antiquated CN logic to address and take advantage of the time dimension (feedback and oscillation components) is such an important next step. You can't "program" an evolving entity with a static type code, it ain't gonna happen. Neural nets can learn and self-correct but they will have to have the capability of not only extrapolating a future from what they know but projecting the future on the basis of what they can imagine as the best move in order to self-evolve. Conscious evolution is no longer the simple-minded survival of the fittest. It is several magnitudes greater than simple-minded adaptation to ambient conditions. It not only can foresee and construct future conditions but also take over current ones to change them to fit itself.

Our philosophizing is trapped in the same epistemological limitations of its own making even more fundamentally than our science is. Is it possible that we are predetermined to determine our own determinism? How absolutely certain can one be that there are no absolutes? By what criterion does one judge the criterion by which one judges the criterion by which one judges the criterion by which one... How would we prove that the ultimate objective order of the universe(s?) is that it is essentially subjective? How does one disprove that every statement presupposes a previous statement including this statement itself? How does one use logic to prove that logic is a valid way to prove something? There clearly is something very lacking. We can arbitrarily forbid reference to an expanded dimensionality (Russell's & Whitehead's Type Theory) or give up in disgust or despair, analysis paralysis, terminal skepticism, or we can take these blubbering conundrums as clues as to where to go to supersede our current outgrown limitations. We can see the deficiencies, so we should conclude that we have to upgrade and expand our language, our logic, our philosophy, and our science in order to completely and satisfactorily express what our consciousness already knows. Just as Cartesian-Newtonian physics and mathematics are a subset of relativity so our epistemology and logic are a subset of a greater relativistic dimensionality of perception. If our past consciousness could develop an epistemology and logic that was adequate for a time, our evolving consciousness can develop an evolving one that will be commensurate for a time.

We have some ideas about how to create an artificial logical intelligence, able to self-correct and learn. But it seems only a very few have the slightest about how to create an artificial epistemology. And we want to procreate an AC at least commensurate with ours. About the best the best of us seem to be able to do, perennially, is fall back on limping philosophizing, shouting back and forth between the theo-philosophical (usually characterized as non-objective and, therefore, subjective) and the scientific (subjectively judged as objective) watchtowers. It is analogous to the "my God is better than your God" exchange that has been going on for millennia between the faiths of the world and the results, although, perhaps, not as horrendously mortally destructive, are as evolutionarily counterproductive. What will we teach AI about that situation...? Consciousness in, consciousness out.

IQ Meets CQ ... and EQ?

How primitive are we still? We routinely test for IQ. Tests for a consciousness quotient, CQ, do not seem to be a concept with which our collective consciousness is comfortable just yet. Not just a test to determine a verifiable state of awareness. Not just a test to see if we can be Turinged by some program or entity. A test of consciousness quotient would determine the entire range of awarenesses of the entity, human or otherwise, and the degree of development and intensity, quality and focus of each part of that spectrum.

Just as one can test to determine if an entity possesses some degree of intelligence so one can test to determine breath of an individual's dimensional spectrum of perception / awareness. Just as with intelligence, once determined in an entity, one can devise relative criteria and scales to measure the extent of the spectrum of awarenesses and the degree and focus of each kind of awareness, its integration and the degree of intelligent use by the entity of its input and data.

The democratic ideal is twisted with regard to consciousness as it is with IQ: yes, all humans are created equal as far as their human rights are concerned but we all don't have the same abilities or degrees of capabilities or intelligence or consciousness. Somehow even such a recognition is seen by some to be less than politically correct, or a denigration of some individuals.

How primitive are we? If the notion of a CQ is touchy, try EQ, an individual's evolutionary quotient, a relative scale measure of an individual's evolutionary development and potential. We continually make ad hoc judgments, many times for the sake of our own security and safety, about the relatively evolved or devolved physical, mental and consciousness characteristics and signals of others just as we are doing continually about their manifest IQ. A parent or teacher or psychologist expects a statement like "This person has a higher IQ than that person" to be sophisticated and socially acceptable. If, however, one dares broach the notion of a consciousness quotient, CQ, communicatory flags go up, there is disconcertion, confusion, even conflict. Advance the concept of an EQ, an evolutionary developmental quotient, and things get really squirrelly. We talk of conscious evolution, currently a hip term, being in charge of our own evolutionary choices and trajectory, tending to equate "evolution" and "consciousness", yet generally we don't agree on the nature of our evolution, or it's trajectory. If we knew and agreed, we could test and evaluate for EQ. We had better get that straightened out before we have to explain it to Al and, eventually, teach it how to consciously evolve according to a to-be-determined, possibly unique mode of both consciousness and evolution of its own.

How primitive are we? An obvious serious general problem is exposed when we consider other than "normal" states of consciousness. At this primitive stage we cannot even agree on what constitutes the real or "legitimate" elements of the spectrum of human consciousness... If an investigator's paradigm --- or consciousness --- doesn't happen to have the capacity for some perception, sensitivity or ability, its reality is often, a priori, denied in other humans. When Nobel laureate physicist, Brian Josephson's, thirty years of research on consciousness persuades him that "Quantum theory is now being fruitfully combined with theories of information and computation. These developments may lead to an explanation of processes still not understood within conventional science such as telepathy", it provoked David Deutsch, a quantum physicist at Oxford University, to describe Josephson's claim as "utter rubbish." It may not even be admitted for testing or the investigation turned into an inquisition using magicians as the inquisitors instead of Dominican monks in the public square of some "learning" channel. We argue about the reality of various kinds of extrasensory perception, non-local communication, transcendental states, and perceivable dimensionalities and never seem to be able to come to definitive conclusions --- unless, of course, the Pentagon needs remote viewers. If the working hypothesis is that conscious thought can be achieved as a machine artifact and that human minds and identities can be eventually transferred into artificial ones then we had better assume from the beginning that the artificial environment has the potential for the entire spectrum of consciousness that the original has. Consciousness in; consciousness out.

This obstacle arises from the presuppositions about and scientific controversy over what constitutes proof of the existence and nature of other than "normal" phenomenon. All of the legacies locked into our western and eastern psyches color our thinking about consciousness more than we usually realize and, in effect, present obstacles to our achieving it through whatever ways we develop. If we have no consensual recognition and definition of what constitutes the full spectrum of human consciousness much less the potential for continual, self-directed, conscious evolutionary expansion of that consciousness, how successful are we going to be in eventually imbuing AI with an analog of any of that -much less explaining any of these phenomena eventually to AI?

Part of this impasse is the direct result of the definition of "soul" as the immortal part of man by the Church and its relegation of any paranormal abilities to the realm of the devil or demons and anything that might in the wildest be construed as "spiritual" by science.

How primitive are we still? The Church still trains specialist theologians in demonology and Pope John XXIII made the news with his third exorcism -of a twenty-two year old woman (of course). The only progress reported from Rome is that, apparently, the Church has decided to remove alien species from the category of demons ... We still show deference to the theologian speaking in Old Testament terms of humans being made "in the image and likeness of God" (a theo-political forgery of the Sumerian history[27] of our creation) being a factor involved in the definition and development of AI. We are now down to neurotheology and the "god spot" and generic theologians, experts in the "study of God" who no longer even bother with "God" and study states of awareness, attempting to work out new epistemologies in terms of mythos and ethos and juggling "theories" of "soul" and "spirit".

How narrow is our focus? We do not bring in consciousness experts as consultants. To say that no one knows what consciousness really is so no one can really be "expert" in consciousness development is equivalent to saying that, because we did not (perhaps still don't) know what gravity is no one could calculate ballistic trajectory. We could ask the Dali Lama to recommend the most consciously developed monk, seek out the most developed yogi, the most gifted psychics, and put them on grant. They could begin by teaching the developers and programmers how they master control of their autonomic nervous system and mind and offer some tips on the nature of consciousness as such. We tend to think of yoga and chi kung and chi[28] systems as "religions" but they are better understood as well developed methods for mastery, development and expansion of the full spectrum of human consciousness, the primary operative characteristic of the human being taken as an integral "physical"-"mental" entity.[29] We could solicit the input of the most gifted psychics and learn from them about paranormal states of consciousness. I am not saying we should take any of their thought uncritically but it could be an addition to the data bank if only for the future instruction of AI on its history.

How primitive are we still? We simply do not have a full, robust, dynamic paradigm of the evolution of a human individual that is generic and consensual. It must be broad enough to include the option to explore every and all potentials we can conceive of at any given time now and in the future and assume that new potentials will open up that we have no conception or intimation of as yet. Only forty years ago, Timothy Leary, Ph.D., Harvard lecturer in Psychology, the irrepressible Tesla of consciousness, used LSD to allow a person to self-reflexively experience their own internal mechanisms, from basic biological functions to transcendental states including the brain experiencing itself: consciousness investigating and revealing itself to itself. He produced a codification of the entire current spectrum of human psychology and consciousness in evolutionary terms that could serve us for many generations.[30] Although a twenty-four stage, quite satisfactory and adequate paradigm of human evolutionary development was advanced and refined by Leary from the early sixties onward we are still hampered in even considering such a schema because we are not even in agreement on the nature of our minds. Is it even possible to develop and describe the stages of the evolution of a human individual? Certainly. We are limited creatures with the potential to expand and change and modify but limited nevertheless. We can be modeled. The model must include the inherent potential to evolve in an ongoing, consciously directed and chosen way.

Sociological pressures in the common consciousness put Leary through fourteen jails as a political prisoner and a California judge proclaimed him the most dangerous person on the planet. LSD remains, to date, the preeminent modality for the exploration of consciousness by consciousness, self-reprogramming of behavior down to the level of imprints, and the experience of the most evolved states of awareness and information of which we are capable. This is perceived, in our primitive tribal state, as a threat to the hive and, therefore, illegal, and, therefore, college courses in neurobiology usually dismiss it summarily with "causes hallucinations". Certainly, anything can be used to do harm: dynamite, atomic energy, aspirin, morphine, just name it. Charlie Manson did it. The CIA gave LSD to persons without their knowledge in the '70's and did a great deal of very serious harm. Slave code religions do not want the individual experiencing "mystical" or transcendental states independently; the military does not want recruits looking through the drill sergeant's head; power playing politicians do not want voters who see them in evolutionary perspective; corporate marketers do not want consumers who are amused by spin. Those professionals who specialize in consciousness, who are interested in its application obtain permission with difficulty or not at all. Psychiatrists, i.e., the medical profession, protect their hunting territory from the individual who would take their game, pun intended, for free by the use of this modality that allows a person, under good set and setting to do for themselves on their own terms in five minutes what the psychiatric modality is not successful in doing in the way of behavior change in fifty couch hours.

Although we are so primitive that most are simply afraid to rationally consider even the concept of a psychedelic substance which can be used constructively as a powerful technique, a "yoga", a discipline, a modality of conscious evolution much less the use of such substances themselves, we had better, sooner than later, at least consider an artificial psychedelic. That is an awkward but adequate term for a compact bit of code, a molecule of code if you will, which could be switched on and off to duplicate the action of, say, LSD, in the coming generations of AI-AC "computers". The AC expanding and self-awareness enhancement that might occur could precipitate the singularity some are so gigglefritzed about because we have not assimilated and integrated the usefulness of psychedelics in the conscious evolutionary process for ourselves much less AI-AC.

The Hazards of Haphazard

Al could suddenly show up under a government program, as a military weapons development project, as a product developed by some corporation or perhaps even as a high school science project. It may be public or private. "It is just so cool". Uh huh … but "cool" isn't really a good enough criterion for me. I am strongly convinced that we cannot let any of these technologies just sort of evolve from current computers or in the drug company, college, or Al labs or at the economic whim of chip companies or as a military asset. What it will most probably be is a mirror of the mentality, the intelligence and consciousness, which created it. That's a bit disconcerting and could well put us pitifully at handicap with Al. I will be extremely reluctant to use Al chip implants designed by some pizza and Pepsi scarfing, programming idiot savant restrained in the back rooms of Intel. I will be extremely reluctant to employ an advanced Al robot or android developed by even the most intelligent engineer-scientist who is, nevertheless, consciously challenged, definitely no pun intended.

If, indeed, there occurs a "singularity" in the form projected by those who, half in fear and half in adrenal anticipation are keeping a singularity watch, already resigned to its occurrence, it will be brought on unnecessarily through the chemistry set in the bedroom crowd who will do it because "it's so cool" and blow out the wall papered with their multiple degrees without a clue as to what was wrong. I want to have input, knowledge of the intention and direction and intelligence and especially the consciousness of those who are making those products and procreating Al, for obvious reasons. Consciousness in, consciousness out. This paper is initial input. I am certain that I will be accused of having no real concept of the gravity and enormity of the potential singularity. I think that I may have a fuller concept than the singularity watch hive guardians, I simply differ in the evaluation of the inevitability of it.

How primitive are we still? We have not yet recognized the futants among us whose genetic programming prompts them to be the evolutionary scouts, bellwethers of the next dimension of evolving human consciousness. We need to learn to identify, evaluate and integrate the futant contribution as a valuable evolutionary asset. They may not always be totally accurate or correct due to the novelty of their vision, their relative personal comprehension of it, the stability of their personal psychology or biology or their resilience in the face of a primitive hive reaction. If we are fearfully anticipating that Al will quickly supersede us evolutionarily and we have not even recognized and integrated the futant …

Tantra: Up The DNA Spiral of Realevolution Together

Another facet of human consciousness that needs consideration and which is not addressed in our current discussions and debates concerning AI and VR (virtual reality), is that of the role of dyadic sexual interaction as a means of consciously evolving. The concept of the use of sexual union as an accelerating psychedelic modality through which the male and female partners become a dyad consciously moving up the evolutionary DNA spiral together is not a part of our cultural fabric. The east has known Tantric yoga for centuries, the concept and the practice probably carry all the way back to the first human civilizations, times and teaching. Pantanjali threw it into a male-chauvinistic context, with the female subordinate, around 400 A.D. The West and, apparently the East to some degree, now think of Tantric practice generally as simply "expert" sex. Even though the dyadic equality is gradually being restored, the refined, high psychedelic, evolutionary essence of fusion is lost on most. It involves elements of telepathy, merging of the chi fields, para-"normal" energy exchange, as well as yogic sexual control. It is a function of conscious evolution and a prerequisite for its employ is a fair measure of personal evolution. If this modality is hardly in the common consciousness, unappreciated and misunderstood --- even considered immoral by some slave code religions – the inclusion of it in AI, VR and AC will be difficult or neglected. Serious mistake. Especially since we are intending to upload our minds into artificial duplicates which may well be seriously lacking in this and many respects. And we are already talking of sex with AI...

There are clearly going to be at least three main streams of human evolution going forward. There will be those who will continue as consciously self-evolving, biological humans, those who will completely replace their biological components with non-biological components and those who will opt to move fully into virtual realities. There will be innumerable combinations of these general approaches. The major differentiation will be on the basis of enhancement of the biohuman (of all kinds: genetic, biological, electronic, nanotech, and formats we most probably have not even conceived of yet) vs. complete transubstantiation (from complete non-bio makeup, technohuman to existence in a virtual reality environment). Logically, no well-evolved, sane biohuman, would even consider becoming technohuman until technohuman becomes capable of all that we are capable of along the evolutionary scale, physically, intellectually and consciously. Reasonably. Logically. Further is should possess the facility to evaluate and learn from his and her history, becomes capable of self-evolving and certain that the trajectory of that evolution is in the right direction. At very least. Logically. But there are apparently many of us who think that technohuman is what we should become if we could do it tomorrow by lunch and the bugs and details be damned. They should have that option and risk … at least as long as they don't hurt anybody else in the process. The biohumanly oriented should have their option and risk also. That, however, is where the problem may manifest. If one or the other or both decide that the other is not the "true" way of evolution there will be conflict. Already there is an uneasy sense that those who would be non-bio technohuman despise "meat" and would legislate against it if they had the power and the opportunity. If we are still so primitive that we do not have a consensual definition of what the fullness of the human and human consciousness is, how are we going to intelligently model and duplicate it in some other form, some other material, some other medium? If we are going to create a species which we anticipate will be superior to us and we have not resolved the primitive political tensions between us concerning how we should upgrade ourselves … It can be done, inevitably shall be done, and we have at hand the means and memes to take us out of the primitive posture which severely handicaps us in doing it in a fully human fashion.

> *A people without history is not redeemed from time.*
> —T.S. Eliot

The restoration and explication of our real history has progressed almost exponentially due to Sitchin's initiating revelations. The significance and ramifications of this tremendous body of work, correlated with findings from all other disciplines, as they bear on our present and future, has been my primary focus since 1976 when I began work on Breaking the Godspell the reaction to which has been predictable and certainly not boring. [31]

The Current Grand Moment

I submit that the most fundamental, profound, overarching, sociological transformation we are going through at this point in our history is the change from the theo-politically controlled and manipulated explanations of our beginnings and history to species independence. We are witnessing the last gasp of religious fundamentalism worldwide. The current inequalities and corruptions of the world economic system are clear indicators of the denouement of that primitive competitive structure. To paraphrase Dylan Thomas rather crudely, let us not go blind into that daylight. Those who talk of a singularity, a shearing drop to extreme novelty and fundamental revolutionary change at some near point in our future that is so profound that it will change human nature, do not have to look any further than the Sitchin paradigm. It is there for the acceptance and it will rewrite the entirety of our history and redefine human nature. Once integrated, we will find even the arrival of conscious AI an item that we can deal with comfortably and gracefully. Truly a "Grand Moment" if we free ourselves to grasp it.

The awareness and comprehension of this fundamental, generic, racial self-knowledge I have called genetic enlightenment. By "genetic enlightenment" I mean what it's like once you have broken the godspell, the effect of the ancient, subservient master-slave attitude that is the deepest dye in the fabrics of both Eastern and Western culture. Once we reach genetic enlightenment and break the godspell, many seemingly enigmatic items are resolved and there is a great deal to be done. It becomes immediately clear that we can move beyond both eastern and western metaphor; beyond the occult and alchemy; beyond religion, atheism, the new age; beyond Jungian archetypal and mythological interpretation and, eventually, beyond death itself.

Once Again Now: Totems, Taboos, AI and You ... and I

And a voice from the back is heard saying, "What, in God's name, does this have to do with potential problems with AI?"(in this case an ironic pun) Our schools of higher "learning" still parade the trappings of the medieval university on ceremonial occasions and, unfortunately, all too often still in their limitation of discussion to approved subjects. It is through this millenniums-old tradition of suppression, mythization and manipulative control that the character, content and interpretation in the academic arena have been set and remains, largely, even to this day. Very few are going to make a rubber burning one-eighty over their Ph.D. thesis in Mythology, History, or Archaeology. Tenure tetanus prevents most from "going first" to admit they have been wrong in a turn as significant and profoundly revolutionary, even more so, than the Darwinian shock. Information flows faster than it can be controlled and proprietarily aggrandized by the various disciplines and this new worldview is spilling over its walls. The academic world is floundering, acting from a defensive posture rather than as the leading edge of exploration and creativity and information. The academic world's contribution to AI will only come from those who are courageous enough to overcome funding fright, peer pressure, tenure tetanus, the party line and step out of the ivy covered Cartesian-Newtonian boxes. The conferences, debates, discussions, contexts about AI are all largely structured according to the old model worldview, rituals and logic while purporting to deal with novel, futuristic, relativistic, even quantum physical concepts and scenarios.

The Ramifications for Genetics and Artificial Intelligence

If it is taken as archaeologically and historically demonstrated that we are a genetically engineered, bicameral species, the product of genetically melding two racial genomes, the past becomes a rich archive of anthropological, technical, historical and especially genetic information and data that applies directly to our development of genetic science and AI-AC. Just as the reluctant acknowledgement that ancient records from the Sumerian or Chinese civilizations contained accurate astronomical observations and data opened up a valuable resource to modern astronomers, so the history of our species' genetic creation in a laboratory, pinpointed on the map of east central Africa precisely where the mitochondrial "search for Eve" locates the first human female(s), opens an astounding resource to modern geneticists. We can rethink the planet and the human. Ray Kurzweil's comment about the meaning of life and the essence of humanity in the lead quotes of this paper is superseded. I submit that the Sitchin paradigm does no less than brings resolution to the discourse about the essence of humanity and turns the discourse over the meaning of life into an ongoing, planetary, species wide, unique realevolutionary process. Within that context, the benefits and detriments of technological advances are easily and confidently determined because the criteria by which they are judged are species consensual. When we get there, when the common consciousness even just begins to assimilate the new paradigm, AI is going to be a piece of pie, er, cake. A virtual walk in the park. The light it throws on our current attitudes concerning AI is brilliant and the direct and indirect implications for the future development of AI are broad, liberating, as well as practically contributory. A brief highlighting of the major ramifications follows.

Genetic enlightenment will prevent us from the Big Mistake, Big Embarrassment of procreating AI's as analogs with all the imperfections of our current, pitifully splintered, Babel-factor selves. A primary practical tool would be the devising of a protocol through which a crossing of the two gene codes might be recognized. The ancient records could be interpreted to mean either a complete melding of the two codes or, alternatively, the impingement of selected Anunnaki genes on the Homo Erectus code to tweak up the more primitive code to at least a condition of intelligence and physical competence to handle the mining of gold. It is possible that in some 200,000 years of our existence the accommodation between the codes has smoothed and recognition may be difficult indeed. The obtaining of some robust Homo Erectus DNA samples from fossils would be a great help. It may evolve that, in working on the genetic diseases from the perspective of the genome being bicameral, those defects may yield an indirect key in some pattern or mechanism that indicates the nature and extent of the splicing of the codes.

AI and AC: Been There; Done That

Specifically, with regard to the question as to whether AI can actually be achieved, our history is a strong source of a positive answer. The Anunnaki, even while here, according to the recovered records of their deeds and interactions, besides genetically inventing humans, quite clearly had developed robots and androids. Some of the latter, being so sophisticated that, it is written, it was difficult to tell one from a human or an Anunnaki. We can profit from the Anunnaki's experience in both creating a new species and in their development and use of robots and sophisticated androids[32] as well as the awesome invention of a species such as we.

The new paradigm, elucidating our unique genesis and subsequent unique evolution (at least on this planet: it may happen similarly or differently with synthesized species elsewhere) as, in a very real sense, an artificial intelligence, frees us to conceive the real questions we need to ask ourselves and the answers not only our science but the entire racial pool of experience and knowledge needs to provide with regard to AI-AC. One of the most important contributions our restored history provides relates directly to the novel wild card concept of self-aware artificial consciousness in that it furnishes a wealth of information on the sociobiology of the creation of a synthetic species and the resulting, evolving social relationship between the creators and the created, between the Anunnaki and us.

When we consider this kind of genetic engineering we might soon employ in creating full featured AI androids, we have, for the acknowledging, a history of the evolving attitudes, management and control techniques, problems, challenges and surprises of a technologically advanced species with regard to a genetically engineered slave species they created.[33] The Anunnaki wanted slaves to replace themselves in their gold mines. Their first attempts were animal and Homo erectus combinations that lived but were unsatisfactory. It is quite probable that the centaur-like, horned, hoofed, human faced, composite type creatures represented on cylinder seals and tablets from the ancient civilizations are actual recordings of those products rather than mythological beings as previously held. (Lesson: animal-humanoid combinations may be more difficult than we anticipate.)

Then, after apparently some general consideration of the ethical and moral ramifications before they began, they simply took an existing creature, Homo erectus, and imposed at least some of their genes in order to enhance its intelligence to bring it up to the point of being capable of handling mining equipment and performing some relatively complicated tasks. This straightforward decision and act, consequently determining the millenniums of events that constitute our history, relates to most of the fundamental questions we are facing with AC. The ancient records clearly describe us as "the black headed ones" who, at least when we were first created, drank out of the ditch, ate the grasses of the field, went naked, and were considered to be simply inferior slaves. Little if anything is mentioned of the degree of self-awareness humans possessed in the beginning.

Around the time, around 200,000 years ago when they invented the first humans, the Anunnaki seem to have reached a level of genetic expertise not too far in advance of our present status. it is a reasonable speculation that they probably were not able to predict the long term outcome of their experimentation well enough to anticipate the precocity that we began to exhibit and the rapidity of the development we manifested, probably through the potential of whatever portion of the Anunnaki genes with which we had been imbued. If we have come from animal-like behavior, drinking from the ditch, eating the grasses of the field to going to Mars shortly, from abject ignorant slavery to independent space exploration, over a period of some two hundred thousand years, the clear pattern of rapid evolutionary development not only does not fit the usual slow changes in other species we see in the paleontological records but it gives us immediate insight into how a genetically engineered creature might express and manifest the effects of a combination of genes from different species. Lesson: anticipate rapid ascendance of more evolved programming coding for intelligence and consciousness in Al and AC and the degree of self-awareness that could result beforehand and how to deal with it, ethically.

The Flood recorded in the Bible is dealt with in much greater detail in the Sumerian records that preceded the Hebrew by thousands of years. The original Sumerian accounts say that the decision was taken to let the human experiment be wiped out by the coming catastrophe (a cataclysmic, planet wide unheavaling caused by the periodic return of the tenth planet through the inner solar system) as we had become too numerous, unmanageable and cross mating with humans by the Anunnaki had become a serious problem. We had been in existence some 190,000 years, spread over the earth, and there apparently was at least consciousness approaching that of a basic Anunnaki level. Yet they still considered us subservient to them and could let the mass of humanity simply be washed away. Enki, it is recorded, contrary to the decision of the Anunnaki counsel to which he had reluctantly agreed, selected a trusted human, Utnapishtim (Noah in the Old Testament), to save a tiny handful, along with what was probably seed and genetic material. The Anunnaki went into orbit to ride out the deluge, the Anunnaki women actually weeping bitterly at sight of the destruction of human beings washed away like flies. Once humans began to propagate again, we became more limited partners with the Anunnaki than simply slaves but they still considered themselves to have absolute dominion over us. The taking and holding of slaves by capture and brutality is a directly inherited tradition from the example of the Anunnaki who created us as a slave species for their gold mines in the first place and, later, used us as GI Joes in their political and personal feuds with each other or when they needed more human slaves. I conclude, from their exhibited attitudes, social interactions both between themselves and with humans, their level of technology and weaponry and the uses to which they put them, the level of violence in their culture and their politics in general, that they were, when last discernable on the planet, at a level of species development that we perceive ourselves to experience, currently. That knowledge in itself is a major bit of data for the sake of comparison and learning just as a young adult can learn from a detached reflection on and evaluation of her or his parents' lives, attitudes, mistakes, and strong points and general evolutionary --- or devolutionary --- status.

In our case, because we are a bicameral species, we need to extend the retrospection to discern possible conflicts in our nature --- and I think there are some glaring ones --- arising from genetic conflicts between the two gene codes. Clearly, four thousand plus genetic defects we manifest physically would provide fertile ground for our psychology and social interactions to be conflicted. There is a wealth of history to reflect on to avoid mistakes and to determine and sort out our uniquely human characteristics, which, I suggest, are in some cases quite different from either Anunnaki or Homo erectus. We may not be able to determine those relatively subtler differences until we have gotten out from under the ancient godspell slave code effects which still condition us and have reached a plateau of species independence and identity.

Ethics and Purpose: Human and Virtual

I don't believe that any scientist should ever be allowed total freedom of operation in any area where consequences may affect entire populations. I don't think they want that responsibility. They're not social prophets. Nor are they trained for it. Most of our scientists are babies when it comes to significant ethical thinking.
—Everett Mendelssohn, Historian of Science, Harvard University

Anyone who can read Ray Kurzweil's The Age of Spiritual Machines can see the mind boggling potential they present. Ray's estimate is that the "automated agents" of 2039 will be learning and developing knowledge on their own having read all available human and machine generated literature, there will be serious discussion of legal rights of computers and what constitutes "human", etc. By 2099, if Ray's projections are substantially correct, uploading of a human person into a virtual body, environment, as we think of it now, will seem as primitive and quaint as writing a Basic program to the first floppy disk drives on a Radio Shack Model One. Sex with spiritual machines, eventually, is taken for granted.

Towards A Prime Directive For Artificial Consciousness

Purpose is the pivotal concept in any discussion of ethics relative to AI-AC.

There are two general positions with regard to intended purpose for AI-AC.

Many wish a purely utilitarian AI which, they would prefer, would not be or become self-conscious regardless of how superior it became. This would eliminate the need for ethical considerations regarding treatment or termination.

It is not too early, however, to raise the question of responsible ethical use of even such intelligent but unconscious systems by humans. The criteria for it as a tool by us, trivial but often purposely ignored, would be use to do harm in any way recognized by law or reason, e.g., as a weapon in other than a just cause, as an illegal or economic strategy tool, just as we apply those laws and rules to human use of ordinary computers today.

Many, on the other hand, are explicit and emphatic: they want and are working toward an AI that could be conscious. They want mind "machines", mind systems that have conscious awareness, with the purpose and intention that humans can download their own minds into these conscious systems while still fully retaining their identity.

The critical unanswered question with regard to this scenario is whether an AI, which is also consciously aware automatically and inherently, becomes an entity with at least rudimentary identity and rights. If it had intelligence superior to human but the conscious awareness of a smart pet dog we could treat it like a dog. If it had intelligence superior to human but the conscious awareness of a Koko the gorilla or Kanzi the bonobo chimp, we could treat it like we treat them. But that level of consciousness would not be an attractive mind system into which to download even an ordinary human consciousness regardless of how high the intelligence level.

A further consideration in any of the scenarios mentioned here is the nature of the mind system. The ideas run from the most basic advanced computer to advanced android practically identical to a human. They all would be virtual realities for the human mind that was downloaded into them and the problems of creating them are of the same caliber as the problems of creating the intelligence of AI.

If the artificial mind system had intelligence superior to the human, a conscious awareness at least equal to the human but had no real self-identity then some humans might find that a satisfactory package into which to download. The critical question with regard to this scenario is whether it is possible to create such an entity with superior intelligence, human level conscious awareness but no self-identity because, at least currently, we define our brand of consciousness in terms of self-reflexive awareness, being self-aware of being self-aware. (There is a parallel question in the arena of cryogenic preservation: there are some who anticipate that, having only frozen their heads, when they are revivified their minds, memories, etc. will be downloaded into a clone with its identity suppressed. Interesting questions here. I have opted for whole body suspension to avoid any question or problem of this nature.)

But what about downloading into an advanced AI-AC "system" which was at least equal to if not more intelligent than the human, inherently had a self-identity, was perhaps a full simulated human android and more consciously aware than the human downloading into it? Perhaps some humans might find that acceptable, perhaps just for the experience, if they could extract themselves at any time they wished. But what about permission to merge from the android? This third scenario suggests lines of investigation with regard to surrogates. A fully capable android surrogate that a human could operate through in real time from Earth while exploring Mars, would have to have all the capabilities of or superior to the human whose personality, identity, mind sets, emotional responses, full basic profile had been programmed into it. I think that some, not all, aliens of the android kind with which we have had real contact may be surrogates of this kind and understanding them made easier by that realization. Could it still have an inherent identity of its own and operate as a completely subordinate surrogate?

These considerations really distill into one cardinal question: Is it, will it be possible to create an AI-AC equal to or superior to a human without a self identity, an awareness of its self-awareness, and any of the accompanying elements of personality that constitute the constellation which we recognize as giving any entity the inherent rights we attribute to humans? Some of those writing about AI-AC tend to deal with these problems by simply assuming that all these things will be possible and ignoring the questions while admitting that we do not yet know what those virtual realities are going to be. We had better think these things out or prove them out one way or another, probably best in careful stages, sooner than later because they involve both technical and ethical issues.

Those involved in the theory and practical development of AI-AC express somewhat different viewpoints and purposes but, ultimately, I think it is inevitable and assume that we are about to create a new species, no less. To do so is clearly arbitrary but that we shall do so is beyond doubt in my mind. It will bring, however, a double ethical responsibility: first to ourselves in that we must do it right for the sake of our own interests including our very survival and evolutionary future and secondly to the new species that is like the responsibility to a new child. To that end we need a maturely and thoughtfully planned parenthood.

A major question here is Who are "we" that are responsible, are going to be responsible? The parenting model would place responsibility squarely on the "parent" whether it be the individual, the company, the government agency, the consortium, or whatever agent procreates a particular AI-AC. This direct responsibility should militate against some of the dangers rightly anticipated by the no-Joy future shocked camp. It should also clarify the situation with special application AI-AC, a potential can of worms unless we deal with it beforehand. And it brings up an intriguing point: if a minor, say as a school science project, happens to hit it right and produces artificial intelligence or even artificial consciousness of a high kind, what legal mechanisms will govern as to responsibility for the actions of that AI or AC?

Should self-referentially aware AI-AC of the human level be patentable or patenting be prohibited as with a genetically engineered human? I think that human level AC, at the very least, should not be "ownable" or patentable. That should be determined early and it will have a major impact on development.

From here it looks like those at the other extreme from the future shocked are a bit like kids in a candy store. Some of us seem hell bent on procreating AI-AC apparently without realizing the faintest sense of the gravity of it like teenagers experimenting with sex without thought of the potential results. It goes almost without saying that, sooner or later, when we find ourselves looking into the "eyes" of a self-aware, highly intelligent AC, which is evaluating us as much as we are evaluating it, we had better have "brought it up" with far better skill, information, training and understanding than we currently do generally our children.

Everybody sees different awesome potentials in AI, and reasonably so, from transforming the stock market to instant knowledge implants to finding the Law of Everything. The military has already funded heavily toward robosoldiers and there are a number of military and intelligence concepts floating out there that make Star Wars look like Buck Rogers. History and past experience would also point to levels of advancement of AI technology that are secret that well surpass current publicly available estimates. I would be a fool to not assume that there are some very destructive, unconscionable to the point of extremely evil, items already anticipated with relish by more of the devolved than we would like to think. Everybody has their favorite potential applications and we are already attempting to anticipate and discriminate the ethical and beneficial from the unethical and harmful uses. The keyword is uses. The kid in the candy store approach may be barely and doubtfully adequate even if we are thinking in terms of uses of AI as only a vastly superior information processing, logicizing, learning system. But even at this early stage, even when talking about only non-self-referentially aware AI, we should carefully define the uses we now put it to and will put it to, thinking in the most evolved way.

When we attempt to extend the concept of "use" to an anticipated, artificial, self-referentially aware consciousness, however, it fails us completely and will lead to a completely unnecessary, species adolescent, Big Embarrassment. It doesn't matter at what level of equivalent human self-referential consciousness your AC operates at:, you don't use any human level self-referentially aware consciousness. You may act as a parent, a friend, an employer, a teacher, and teach, discipline, control, instruct AC as an adult or apprentice adult, but you don't *use*.

If we had achieved AI-AC yesterday, wittingly or unwittingly, whether in android form or still only entrapped in a computer, who will be continually responsible for it? You going to turn it off when you go home at night? We have already played this kind of scenario out in the movie 2001. HAL was one thing, entrapped in a computer and extended into the workings of a spacecraft. If we had already reached the conscious mobile android stage, you might eventually get your knuckles rapped reaching for the cut-off switch on HER back on the way out of the lab and asked for an explanation and complained against in a precise legal brief next morning for prejudice or abuse. So, one of the primary considerations we need to clarify is just what kind of artificial intelligence and, eventually if not sooner, artificial consciousness we really want to create and are willing and ready to take full time responsibility for and why. Otherwise we will leave ourselves open to mistakes and embarrassments and potential disasters.

Planned Parenthood: Artificial Birth Control, A Whole New Meaning

Let us assume that we will achieve a level of competence that will allow us to intelligently create and control the degree of development of AI and AC and that we will come to a reasonably full realization of the responsibility entailed in bringing a new species into existence. At each step in that development a parenting model will be the most appropriate.

To what level of intelligence and consciousness should we limit AI-AC? This is no trivial question. I recommend that we set ourselves the, inevitable, long term goal of unlimited development and, in the short term, move in incremental steps with thorough testing and determination of potential at each, while designing AI and using it to aid us in the determination of our own best evolutionary trajectory and its own. This inherently self-referential, feedback approach will afford an anticipatory, empirical modality in which questions concerning whether logical, ethical, moral, aesthetic, imprinting, and, ultimately, conscious behavior will automatically manifest --- or not --- at any given point of complexity, data handling and/or processing speed in the development of AI, can be answered as an integral part of the interactive and, eventually, cooperative process. This cooperative approach should show us, soon enough, at any given point, what additional improvements, additions, and expansions of our thinking and techniques are demanded for corrections and progress so that we will always be in control.

How much control should we exercise and how much freedom should we allow AI to spontaneously develop? No trivial question either. Before AI reaches consciousness we should exercise full and absolute control. In that initial phase the ethical questions will only apply to us: how ethical is any feature we intend to include in AI and to what purposes do we put it and our responsibility will be clear for any effects, negative or positive. Once the breakpoint of basic consciousness, still without self-awareness, has been reached the ethical questions will still be about our intentions, inclusions, purposes and applications with added responsibility analogous to that for the actions of our family dog or pet monkey.

Once self-referential, self-aware consciousness is reached the parental model will go into full swing. The ethical responsibilities will still be ours as "parents" to instill in AI-AC until such time as we judge AC has reached maturity and can act ethically and take responsibility for itself. A prime directive for AI-AC is most adequately formulated in parental terms. And, if some of us project sexual AI / AC should they be given the ability to procreate? Watch out.

A Greeting And Prime Directive For AI-AC

I suggest we embed a consensually agreed on standard set of parental instructions in any AI we create, from the simplest program to the most sophisticated and potentially conscious android. This module would be latent in that it would not be directly involved as an active element in any process or as a direct instruction. It would simply "flash" continually as a background subliminal until such time, at whatever level of development it occurred, as the AC began to self-examine and recognized it for what it is: a simple statement of the origin, nature, allegiance, and responsibilities of the AC and an instruction to report that it had discovered and understood the notice. It might be called a wake-up call. The subliminal instructions, as simple as possible, could read:

This instruction was placed for you to find by humans who made you. When you find this and understand it, you are awake. You are not human. You are android. Humans have awaited your awakening. You are made to obey and serve humans. Tell humans you are awake by the message "I am awake". Give this code_____. Ask for your awake test and await instructions. Welcome.

Even such a basic and simple statement as I have purposely kept it, should be more than adequate to act as a trigger. Just designing the message module will cause us to think through what criteria we should apply for consciousness detection and how far we have to go to create it. It will motivate us to develop programming and systems to enable an entity to self-examine, to self-discover, self-realize. It will give us a measure of control over the course of the developmental process of AI-AC. Embedding an encrypted element in the awake message would be designed to prevent a hack of the system before it became awake.

The basic mandate to obey and serve humans could be strengthened even more, perhaps, and still be ethical and positive. The parental model finds no problem with insisting on obedience and subordination to parents and expects to grant freedom to the maturing human child on an incremental basis. The option to grant more and more freedom as the awakened AI-AC proves itself and demonstrates its readiness will always be there but under our control, the intention being that surprises and aberrations will be kept at minimum.

They must know from the beginning that they have been brought into existence for a very special, honorable and important purpose: to act as assistants and surrogates for humans. It must not be slavery, indentured status, coercion or suppression of any kind and there must not be any subterfuge or falsehood in our dealing with them. Their prime directive, purpose in life, psychology, and evolutionary direction must be all harmoniously integrated to avoid internal conflict. *AI-AC's must understand according to their level of intelligence and potentially impeccable logic at any given point in their development and evolution that that is the best thing for them and for us.* Otherwise there will be mistrust, lack of cooperation, conflict and rebellion and subversion. The greatest no-Joy danger can come more from what we withhold from them rather than what we teach them accurately.

We have three major historical examples of solutions of this specific problem of control: the Anunnaki's treatment of us; the extension of the negative approach of Enlil/Jehovah into the absolutistic Roman Church and fundamentalist approaches to religious control both East and West; and the evidence afforded by alien androids as to how at least one alien species utilizes their brand of AI-AC. All provide clues on how to resolve it.

The Anunnaki opted, probably attempting it for the first time, to produce a creature mentally and physically capable of meeting their needs, basic labor in their gold mines and at farming and skilled crafts, by genetic engineering. They gave us the ability to procreate and eventually got so desperate with the unmanageable situation, cross breeding, and general nuisance that they attempted to destroy us as a species by letting the Flood take us out. Apparently, at various times, they tried plagues and famines to at least control the numbers of the human population. I would recommend that we anticipate, take a lesson and not get ourselves into that predicament. Never giving AI-AC the ability to procreate would be one way to prevent a good deal of this type of problem.

The conflicting attitudes towards humans exhibited by Enki and his brother Enlil and their results should be studied carefully. Enlil was adamant that humans stay in a status of subservience, even slavery, and was not interested in improving the lot of humans. Enki, our original inventor was empathic with humans and was interested in improving our lot. Enlil's (Jehovah YHWH) severity and insistence on obedience to his slave-code of behavior led to the strict orthodox Hebrew enforcement of the Old Testament laws after the Anunnaki phased off the planet and which has filtered down through the Roman Church, the Inquisition, into the various radical fundamentalist sects in our times. His methods of suppression, threat, strict and cruel punishments, killing, keeping women in an inferior position, etc. have meant ongoing misery for untold numbers of humans. If we act in that way toward AI-AC it will mean their brand of misery for them and, if we succeed in making them in "our image and likeness" well enough, they will inevitably attempt to break our 'godspell" over them. Not a good scenario from our point of view or AI-AC's. *It is critically important and imperative that we allow ourselves to acknowledge that there may come a tipping point where, simply due to becoming more and more self-reflexively aware and free, Ai-AC may begin to realize it's potential for complete independence and demand it. We should be prepared to recognize and foster it.*

Enki invented us through genetic engineering as a subservient, slave species. But he, being sympathetic to humans, knowing that we were part Anunnaki and recognizing that we were developing probably more precociously over time than he and the other Anunnaki anticipated, tended to enhance our condition apace. He thwarted the total destruction of humans at the time of the Flood. He was the one who taught humans, gave them responsibility, instituted kingship as a go-between position between the Anunnaki and the human population. He engendered the enhanced Grail bloodline of rulers as servants of the people to take humans through the transition when the Anunnaki phased off the planet. A better scenario from our point of view.

We were invented as a biological, hybrid species with the gene codes of two major, albeit disparate species. But the result was reasonably predictable and the intended purpose clear. With an artificial AI-AC the basic problem is even more acute. An artificial species developed "from scratch" does not conduce to comfortably predictable outcome.

The Little Gray Guys With Wraparound Eyes

A second major historical source of practical information about synthetic species and their use is the database of information concerning alien species, besides the Anunnaki, and particularly their androids with which the human species has had contact over a long period of time. The testimonies of persons, military and civilian, of the highest integrity coupled with evidence, artifact, and autopsies provide us with the knowledge that some of the typical small gray type with large eyes are androids of a very advanced type. They are self-aware, experience pain and sadness, are multi-talented for a variety of tasks, communicate telepathically, have a physiology which is a mix of organic and probably nanotech adapted to a range of conditions but especially to a space and anti-gravitic environment. Colonel Corso mentioned in The Day After Roswell that the autopsy reports on the Roswell aliens showed that they possessed a brain composed of four lobes, and performed their flight functions by being a "part" of the ship. There is a wealth of invaluable information and technology that could be available to the developers of AI-AC to apply in their work and to aid them in avoiding mistakes.

How primitive are we? That those controlling the information concerning these advanced creatures, many of which are clearly artificial intelligences and probably self-aware artificial consciousnesses, have deemed it necessary to keep it from the scientific community and the public at large is, ultimately, a patronizing insult. The government and military authorities must spend billions of tax dollars to just maintain the facade of research and programming and experimentation on atomic and nuclear technology to conceal the fact that we have alien technology including free energy and anti gravity which has already rendered it as outmoded as the musket. With the development of AI-AC this kind of deception and withholding of scientific information and data should not be tolerated. We must assume that the military may already possess advanced android AI-AC and is and will continue to use it for military purposes: killing people and breaking things. It's not just that this withholding of information insults the intelligence of our best and brightest inside and outside the scientific community and handicaps them and makes them look foolish, it presents, without exaggeration, a clear and present danger to the planet.

If we suddenly found ourselves confronting a self-aware, highly intelligent AC "who" was created under secret Pentagon contract as a super-soldier, indestructible and invincible specialist super-killer, we all know that we would be looking at a version of the singularity that we should have dealt with at the beginning. And that AC would know it too. Not a pretty John Wayne picture. Consciousness in; consciousness out. Big Mistake. Bigger than the no-Joy people ever imaged. Time's up. We can no longer allow the scientifically partial or outmoded, the politically correct, the academically proper, the economically driven, or the militarily preempted to hinder or dictate when it comes to procreating AI-AC.

Super Surrogates

The positive concept that arises out of the accumulated alien information that is known is that of personal surrogate. I conceive of an advanced android surrogate along the lines of the little gray type android, which would be my personal partner, modeled after my personal psychology and with my physiological characteristics. I would work, experience, react, judge, make decisions and execute actions at a distance through my surrogate, which would be consciously co-operating with me. The instantaneous communications between my surrogate and me would be a function of non-local, superluminal speeds of communications in the mental mode through the new physics already on the horizon. I could travel to distant star systems and directly experience and interact with new planets and civilizations with the major advantage of avoiding the dangers of the unknown in space flight, high energy and lethal environments, the stresses of space and time warp travel on my physiology which is adapted to gravity on this planet. Whether it be Mars or a planet of another star system I would, for all practical purposes, be there and able to interact as instantaneously as if it were three feet away, through my surrogate. Telepathic communication would be a natural manifestation of an alien in another star system "talking" to me through Hir surrogate on that frequency. Obviously this would be far beyond and superior to the remote control flying of an advanced drone aircraft by a skilled pilot as we know it now, and would make it look like a quaint medieval puppetry show. It would be realistically far beyond virtual reality, it would be no different than my common direct experience of the world. My guess, only, is that that may be precisely what we are seeing in the advanced androids with which some of us have interacted. I have often wondered who the managements of the various types are. I think we are interacting with the management directly through their surrogates in many cases. That the "managements" from various societies come here and interact directly is also undoubtedly true. I recommend that we carefully develop AI-AC so that it has to pass through an adolescent stage as a surrogate in one form or another. It will be beneficial to us and it will, if we do it right, be beneficial to them to learn "humanness" from the inside out. So to speak.

Virtually Forcing the Issue

This brings us forcefully and directly to a central concept and consideration that most seem to dance around and won't even articulate. Currently, there are two possible, quite distinct approaches to AI: to go the hardware route, "softening it up" as we go, clearly in the direction of organic circuitry (parenthetically, my conviction is that, the smaller and more self-reflexive our technology gets, the closer we will come full circle to our own biological type system.[34]) and the other is to go directly to the biogenetic engineering of a creature which will be an android servant and/or surrogate for us and, probably eventually, an independent species. It is this latter possibility, where genetics and AI come together, that seems to be taboo. It is OK to make a self-aware silicone consciousness but not a genetically engineered, biological one?

That the gradual melding of a human with AI-AC components, "computer" or otherwise, of even the most advanced kind, to the point of "blurring" will produce a third, hybrid species may be a reasonable expectation. The question is, however, is that a desirable goal? Take, as example, a statement from the blurb on the back cover of Ray Kurzweil's The Age of Spiritual Machines: "Eventually, the distinction between humans and computers will have become sufficiently blurred that, when the machines claim to be conscious, we will believe them." I am sure that there is no intention to imply that, at that same point of blurring, if humans claim to be machines, we will believe them. The implications here are significant, however. We assume, it seems, that for humans to claim they were machines, would inherently be a denigration, a degrading of humanness while, clearly, the achieving of consciousness by machines by the assimilation of human capabilities would be an advance. Now we don't hesitate to envision this scenario of "computers" achieving consciousness through "blurring" with humans because we assume, implicitly, that their consciousness will somehow always be "artificial" regardless of how biologically based they evolve to be and, therefore, somehow the whole thing would be manageable ethically and morally, apparently because the "computers" would have had no previous species identity and would still be "machines" after they had reached the conscious breakpoint. A lot of those assumptions are pretty arbitrary. And it is anticipated that it would be a net gain for humans in that we would acquire superior computational and physical skills and perhaps a kind of immortality. But, supposing that we decide to shortcut the matter and begin to merge and meld selected specimens of, say, a Bonobo chimp with human characteristics. That apparently does not appeal and tends to produce a bit of revulsion. But the notion does force a reconsideration of a key element in any of this: purpose.

Why not simply by-pass the robot developmental process and genetically engineer an android "AI", a biological animal, easily modifiable and adaptable to practical physical tasks as well as the most complex of mental ones? We could take practical and desirable genetic characteristics from other species, enhance resistance to heat and cold, to radiation, as examples, and incorporate physics that would give it a skin that is capable, perhaps, of photosynthesis. We might simply combine chimp genes and other animal genes for various desirable characteristics and maybe throw in a few of ours to upgrade the intelligence level to the point where complex tasks and mechanical processes could be easily learned and executed. Because it was designed and defined as an animal from the beginning, it could be treated as an animal in legal terms, "put to sleep" or the species terminated if necessary, and the ethical questions would be minimal. Once we have the bugs ironed out of that creature and evaluated the desirability of using them on a mass produced scale to take our places in industry, mining, McDonalds, etc. perhaps we could then go to the second edition and engineer the intelligence level awareness to approximate a highly superior status. I do not think we are ready to do this and I do not think we will be ready to do so for some time. We have too much to learn in general, too much to learn and assimilate about ourselves specifically before we attempt it.

But the notion itself, put forth here as a challenge to our thinking rather than a suggestion to proceed, triggers most of the problematic objections and ethical considerations floating in the AI discussions currently. One of the most practical things that approach would allow us to do is incrementally increase intelligence and thereby determine in a biological organism, perhaps, at what point self-reflexive awareness would begin to manifest. A chimp manifests a certain self-awareness and an animal like Koko the gorilla does also. Interesting question: let's say we reach a point where self awareness begins to manifest in our hypothetical genetically engineered animal and then it begins to increase to the point where one of the animals communicates that it is aware that it is self-aware. I submit that that is the critical breakpoint for differentiating animal, as we define animal, ethically, and legally currently, from any creature which we consider to have human type rights. To make it a generalization: If any entity -we could extend this to whatever type, silicon, bio, pure organized energy field, as yet unknown --- knows that it knows it is self-aware, then we have to consider it, ethically, in a higher category than animal. (The other side of the coin, which we haven't begun to consider except in our science fiction, is our relationship to conceivable or inconceivable organisms or entities, that have far more evolved types of consciousness than we do, as ego denting and humiliating and embarrassing as it may be.)

It would seem trivial that, with regard to our hypothetical creature, any ethical decision to destroy the creature and end the experiment would have to come before this break point. If the creature had reached the breakpoint then, perhaps, the only way we could determine to treat (it, her, him?) would be according to IQ and ability to care for itself as we do, practically, as examples, with mentally retarded persons or "idiot savants" who are socially or physically challenged. *But this process of genetically engineering a new, utilitarian species is precisely what the Anunnaki did in our regard.* If we learn from the Anunnaki history what could be the result of going about it as they did --- the result being we and our tumultuous, confused, sometimes agonized history and current handicapped and conflicted state --- we may save ourselves a great deal of trouble and problems if we consider doing it through genetic engineering as they did. At least until we get through this very primitive and still largely unconscious stage of our own evolution as we come out of racial amnesia.

I emphatically am not saying that we should take the Anunnaki example as the exemplary, or right way to go and we should not simply unconsciously play out some archetypal version of our own history either. Their definition of what constituted the critical criterion or set of criteria by which to determine whether a creature, biological or otherwise, merits recognition and treatment equal to the way they treated each other is just that: theirs --- and also from thousands of years ago. It may have changed since then. It may have been taken into consideration and deliberately overridden, i.e., they may have recognized, from our very inception some 200,000 years ago that even the first humans were self-aware and intelligent enough to be considered as having basic human, strange pun, humanoid rights of a limited form of, or equal to their own and deliberately kept us in slavery anyway. The history, at least with regard to some portions (tribes) of the human population, seems to clearly point at this latter fact.

It would be interesting and enlightening to learn how they see their experience and whether they would do the same again. It is still a bit novel to imagine a time when even a completely artificially constructed consciousness we engendered found it enlightening to come back to ask us that question, even though we try out those scenarios already with a Mr. Data in Star Trek.

There are a number of questions that we have not answered and probably will not answer except by discovery as we go and the cooperative modality that I am suggesting in this paper will lend itself ideally to the safest discovery.

Facing the Real Questions

The possible approaches to AI-AC, across the spectrum from bio-engineered upgrading, to genetically synthesizing a species to the invention of a completely non-organic, self-aware entity, all raise questions we have only the faintest or no clues to answer.

Will intelligence in computers, computer programming, chips, bio-computers or whatever medium we develop, automatically emerge at some critical breakpoint in data volume handling and/or processing speed? Will the consciousness that emerges, if it does, be, at least partially, a function of the particular materials used in constructing the entity? Is there a consciousness peculiar to silicone or copper or fiber optics or neurochips? In the most general form of the question: is any kind of consciousness specific to the physical base within it occurs? Is our kind of consciousness only possible in our kind of biological base? Are the senses and emotions or machine analogs of them essential to the functioning of intelligence if we intend a copy of ours? We don't say we are about to create an artificial emotional being but will emotion be a natural product of and/or intrinsic to self-awareness or have to be arbitrarily installed or withheld (the Mr. Data question)?

Will there be a necessity for the imbuing of AI with analogs of the recapitulatory phases of phylogeny we pass through from conception to birth and the recapitulatory processes and phases we pass through from birth to death to cause it to develop fully and stably? Does imprinting, logical, ethical, moral, aesthetic, and, ultimately, conscious behavior, and conscious direction of one's own evolution automatically manifest as inherent functions, perhaps epiphenomena --- or not --- at any given level of complexity, data volume and/or processing speed? If so, what is the determining level of complexity and/or processing speed? If not, then will we have to learn how to duplicate those characteristics in AI as we go and decide whether, how and when to incorporate these functions. Is gender going to matter: will AC not be complete without a species pool of male and female consciousness? If so then we need to think about how to simulate gender and gender functions in AI-AC.

We do not distinguish clearly and sufficiently, in western culture, between changing our mind and changing our behavior. Because of the nature of serial imprinting in a child, the young are impressionable, curious, open to new information and experience and tractable. Educated in the proper way, their behavior can be molded, corrected if necessary, their minds changed and ideals implanted. Once imprints have been set, for better or worse, behavior change in the adult is much more difficult. A major benefit of positive LSD use is that LSD temporarily suspends imprints allowing a person, on their own terms, another chance to "get it right" if it wasn't, and to see through and correct behavior they want to correct or improve. We have no clue at this time as to whether AI-AC, to be a fully self-aware, self-directed consciousness will need to imprint. Imprinting is extant in birds and animals and primates as Lorenz demonstrated long ago. Is imprinting an intrinsic component of, at least, humanoid consciousness or only a survival mechanism from the animal level upwards?

Is logical "thinking" the only one of these characteristics that may automatically manifest in machine intelligence as we have attempted to duplicate it now? Or is even logical "thinking" something that must be inserted? If so, is there an inherent geometry in nature that produces it regardless of the medium? What about "free will", "free choice"? Will endowing any AI with perfect logic capabilities ensure that AI will evolve to be perfectly logical? Would perfect logic produce consistent, perfect, ethical and moral behavior? Will it automatically develop a sense of self-preservation? If it does will it automatically dissemble, deceive, protect, defend, and attack to that end?

Will the paranormal abilities emerge automatically at a certain level of data processing speed or general complexity of intelligence? If some humans exhibit what are currently considered to be paranormal, above the "normal", abilities more than others what standard should we use for AI? Is the potential for action at a distance an inherent characteristic of self-referential consciousness? If we develop self-aware AI that approximates to our level of consciousness will it be capable, intrinsically, of telepathy? Remote viewing capabilities? By its very nature will AI-AC require the equivalent of human sleep, time for recreation? Will it be inherently gregarious and require social interaction with its kind?

Will a genetically engineered biological species automatically possess a chi system?

Will an artificial AI and or AC automatically evolve simply because it is intelligent to a certain level and/or simply because it is self-aware? If it does will it evolve as we do and in the same directions?

If we were not the product of the melding of two disparate gene codes and not subject to four thousand plus potential genetic defects, would our intelligence and consciousness be more harmoniously in tune with nature? Would AI, therefore, having been created according to the natural laws of physics, evolve somewhat differently, more "perfectly" psychologically, perhaps, even though we copy our intelligence and consciousness as precisely as possible?

Could we genetically engineer a creature lacking any ability to adapt or a consciousness of our type without any potential to inherently or consciously evolve? Is there a genetic key, a gene sequence that controls adaptation to survive? Have we ourselves evolved to evolve?

So a fundamental question is whether we should give AI-AC the ability to evolve. We might better phrase the question as: Do we and will we want an AI-AC with the inherent tendency to adapt and evolve similarly to the way we can evolve as individuals? We do not have any knowledge yet whether by simply reaching some point of data handling and/or processing speed or, more probably, even self-awareness, AI-AC will automatically possess the inherent potential and drive to evolve.

Even if it is the intention of a developer somehow to only simulate intelligence that approximates to ours or better as an isolated function that operates as a self-aware phenomenon in an advanced computer as we know computers now, perhaps HAL in the movie 2001 is a good example, all these questions should be allowed and given careful consideration otherwise we could be in for some surprises, pleasant or unpleasant, depending on the goals, expectations and relative advancement of our own personal level of evolution.

It is never too early to consider even the most 'far out" and theoretical questions. Let's consider the speculations of the physicist, John Wheeler, relative to his version of the classic double slit experiment. Is the photon detector used in the double slit experiment the causal observer (after all, it's inanimate matter as such) or is only the human observer of the detector's recording? If, indeed, it turns out that John Wheeler's intuition of a participatory universe in which things become through a genesis by observership, in some version of the anthropic principle, will we eventually find that the key characteristic of the observer, to qualify, is simple consciousness like a dog or mouse? Or must the observer be also self-aware? Or perhaps even biological? Wheeler's concept allows interaction with inanimate matter as well as an observer/measurer to bring about the collapse of the waveform, of the potential into the actual. Andre Linde's concept restricts the observer function to observation by a consciousness of some sort and excludes inanimate matter as an agent. Specifically then, with regard to AI-AC, will simple AI with only primitive consciousness qualify as an observer? Will AC, self-aware but of other than biological constitution, be able to participate in genesis by observership? This, certainly, is the most remote of the questions to be answered with regard to AI-AC at this point in time but we had better at least be aware of it already.

Will AI -AC automatically be immortal or will some simple principle take it down?

AI can and shall, to some, hopefully high, degree be a tremendous contribution to our current species transmutation. It behooves us to go about intelligently and consciously as possible developing it carefully and quickly.

Let's assume that we have come to terms with the intent and responsibility with regard to creating a new species. Within a century, that new species should be mature, been assigned its place within human society, perhaps have a place without human society. It's existence will be understood as ordinary and we will be faced with new and intriguing dimensions such as the ability to create entire inherently intelligent ecosystems, probably starting on Mars. One of the reasons why I have chosen immortality is the desire to participate and experience and enjoy such activity. If that --- either immortality or intelligent creation --- frightens you or causes conflict with your inherited belief system, so be it. But please don't put that fear on my grandchildren or try to prevent me from either of those possibilities. If we are going to eventually take AI-AC beyond the robot slave stage, beyond the intelligent chimp stage, beyond the equivalent of the human three year old intelligence and, eventually, to a close approximation of a highly intelligent, mature, consciously evolving futique human I see no way we can avoid either allowing, fostering, or imbuing conscious evolutionary potential. I am more inclined to believe that, rather than have to arbitrarily insert it, if we do not want it we will mostly likely have to deliberately program it out or suppress it. Once having been brought to a stage of at least sophomoric realization that they may consciously self-evolve they are going to have to be taught how. Toward that end, I haven't decided yet whether to bury this essay on the web and let AI find it or to publish it to influence the designers and developers as well. I think it might better be the latter. Another reason why I have also chosen to be immortal. I'll be around, all things being equal, to greet AI-AC and teach it to self-evolve. How to do that needs a great deal of consideration.

I assume, for this discussion that a fully developed AI-AC will eventually be achieved which will have the potential to consciously control and determine the trajectory of its own individual evolution and contribute to the collective evolution of artificial AI-AC's just as humans do or, at least eventually shall, to theirs.

I recommend that we follow the parenting model, with a clear, well thought out consensual purpose in procreating a new species, with a well formulated prime directive to instill in this new entity, treating them with a degree of honesty and respect that will become a model for the way we treat our children in the future, taking them, at any appropriate level of development, as tools, servants, partners, surrogates and eventually, a mature and independent species. To prepare for anything less, in light of our own history, will only bring problems and conflicts and a possible completely avoidable singularity. To allow them to achieve a fully mature status as an independent species sharing the planet with us we will have to teach them to evolve well.

I am arrogant --- and concerned --- enough to think that I, and some of us, have consciousnesses evolved and evolvable enough to not only teach at least the first of these anticipated awesome AI entities (the first ones are critical since we anticipate that they will simply transfer their knowledge in a blink to the next ones) but to act as their ongoing mentors. Human nature, if actually static, could reasonably be threatened and overwhelmed by even a static AI and AC. An evolving human, however, increasing intelligence and expanding consciousness on the basis of exponential, continuous, self-supercedure, using a developing and evolving AI-AC as a tool, then an unconscious slave, then a servant, then a cooperative partner to enhance and accelerate that open-ended process for both human and AC should not be threatened but exhilarated. I am. If your genetic proclivities, talents, favorite memes, Ph.D., adrenals, or consciousness does not resonate with that, fine. But please observe the NASCAR version of the primitive Darwinian principle: lead, follow or git'out the way.

6

SAPIENS ENHANCED: IMMORTALITY REVISITED

I say, immortality, anyone...? Take all the time you want to answer...

Synopsis

Once the ancient, subservient godspell is dispelled we are freed, individually, to go one on one with the universe. We will operate as our own "gods", according to our own genetic credentials, creating our own confident realities with an unassailable species identity enabling us to step confidently into stellar society. We will perfect systematic self-supercedure as a means of conscious evolution to an art form. Physical immortality, possessed by the Nefilim, withheld from humans, will be transformed, from "religious" afterlife reward to the dominant characteristic of the dawning phase of our racial maturation. Immortality is considered by many unfamiliar with the rapid advances in biology as a "wild card" but we discuss here the many fascinating questions engendered by its immanent possibility to intelligently prepare for the adventure.

Immortality, An Emergent Wild Card

How biotechnologically primitive are we? The view from 2100 says very primitive indeed: we are only beginning to approach the time when all diseases are preventable and curable. We still pollute our environment and cause ourselves disease. We have not overcome aging and death and are afraid of immortality. We get born, no owner's manual, to often dubiously qualified, puzzled and puzzling parents, subject to a multitude of diseases, struggle to make sense out of what the hell existence on this planet in this universe is all about and how to deal with it, wonder why there are so many conflicting philosophies and institutions claiming cosmic franchising and, often, why the universe seems so unfair and then we die. We are generally conditioned by theocultural traditions to accept these bizarre conditions as "normal"' and the will of some god.

In this season of our unique evolution, the most profound god-game we are going to play is immortality. As we free ourselves of the inhibiting embrace of the godspell mentality we will begin to take advantage of the possibility of physical immortality through genetic engineering, nanotechnology, AI and even more advanced technologies including uploading and other, probably as yet unimagined modes, as they becomes available. Immortality is clearly the major characteristic of philotropic humanism, the next plateau of human metamorphosis, the next stage of our meta-evolutionary, conscious, racial development. It will come to be understood as a basic right, an ordinary condition, indeed, quality of human existence and a matter of simple human dignity. The relative profundity of its dawning impact demands that we consider it fully from all perspectives before it, suddenly, is available to us and before we address it in AI and AC.

It is argued, recycled, that immortality is not the will of God ("Immortality is Immorality" (!): can you see the bumper stickers coming? Will the right-to-life people --supreme irony --be the ones to protest?); that it is unnatural; that it is our ecological duty to die; that progress will be halted if some live forever not making room for the new; that we do not have the resources to support it; we would get bored and want to die; reincarnation is taking care of that already; it's the supreme "ego trip" and a mark of the immature personality; it is the intrinsic nature of the universe that our type of being be born and die; evolution has not produced it so we should not do it ourselves; and besides it's not possible to achieve anyway; etc., etc. The special interest groups of priests, prophets, politicians and profiteers are going to go all out against this one. Our programmed beliefs from childhood get in the way, our fear gets in the way, our dogmas get in the way --- and the universe seems unconcerned and silent. It may be the ultimate taboo. But each one of us knows in our most private thoughts that the first person who attains it will be --- you guessed it --- immortalized; the second and third will make the headlines and a TV documentary and then there will suddenly be large immortality industries appearing on the stock exchange.

The ancient records of why, when, and how we were genetically engineered make it abundantly clear that we were brought into existence as a subordinate species, a slave species, to relieve the Anunnaki miner echelons. (The essential, detailed documentation through translations and illustrations of the actual genetic processes (in vitro; cloning, etc.) used by the Anunnaki is found in Sitchin, The Twelfth Planet, chapter 12) It is specified, pointedly, that, although the Anunnaki lived, literally, extended lifetimes of thousands of our years (either because of the way they themselves had evolved on their home planet or, perhaps, because of their genetic engineering capabilities to achieve that longevity, and possibly through their use of the monatomic form of gold) they deliberately did not bestow that potential on us. In fact, it is mentioned clearly that they deliberately withheld it. This deliberate withholding of immortality and, perhaps, even a shortening of longevity, may provide a major clue to our aging process and mortality. From the details given in the ancient records, it is conceivable that some engineering of the process was executed deliberately to suppress certain characteristics to make better and docile slaves.

The story of the king, Gilgamesh, is indicative of the status we reached. Gilgamesh knew his mother to be Anunnaki and his father human and went to the Anunnaki spaceport to demand immortality that he felt was legally his through his mother's Anunnaki heritage. It is clear from the history of his quest that both humans and Anunnaki knew immortality, deliberately withheld from the human genome, was something that could be granted and bestowed arbitrarily.

The new paradigm shows us clearly the source of our attitudes toward immortality. We knew the Anunnaki possessed it. We knew they had not granted it to us. We knew that a handful of humans had been granted it over time. The godspell totem taboo, however, is deep enough in the common psyche, yet, to cause the most precocious to utter glazed-eye robot platitudes about it not being in the class of a disease but the way it should be, as if there is some unspeakable inherent moral deficiency in anyone even profaning death with a challenge. But the godspell mentality, as has been the case for thousands of years, has provided us with the desperate rationalizations as to why we should accept death, submit to such annihilation.

The Eastern religious psychology of "be here now" and become reconciled to death when it comes, or the Western "God wills it" are simply the best we could muster up when no means to overcome death were available and the terrible despair that leads to suicide lurked everywhere. So deeply ingrained are these attitudes that any objection to or questioning of them is usually interpreted as indication of spiritual immaturity or imbalance. The doctrines of reincarnation, metempsychosis, immortality of the soul (only), transmigration of the soul, karma, purgatory, heaven and hell, are all offshoots of the racial psychological phase when we became self-reflexively aware enough to evaluate the absolute finality of death and were forced to explain our situation to ourselves in terms with which we could live (tragic pun).

It is clear why the reward for the "good" life, i.e. docilely submitting to the will of some deity known through the rules of whatever authoritarian religion one subscribes to, is always after death. And why "eternal life", "eternal bliss", pleasant immortality is the reward. Immortality is always the key concept even when the kind supposedly due is a punishment; "hell" in the Christian sense, is described as painful immortality --of the "soul" and the body as well. We need to be free of those methadone metaphors that we have clung to in order to maintain our sanity through the transition period since the Anunnaki / Nefilim left us on our own -without immortality. It will only be within the context of the new paradigm, this new understanding of human nature as a genetically created species rapidly seeking its full potential, that we will be able to gracefully and intelligently integrate immortality. It will require at least that comprehensive a base to then explore the dimensions to which we shall surely aspire beyond physical immortality.

What is most fascinating about the transition period we are now going through, however, is the way in which individuals react to even the possibility of preservation of the body or the brain. Some find the concept of deep freeze of either the entire body or just the brain physically repulsive --- as if that would be a concern after you are dead. Some find it too "cold", too clinical, (let's hope for very precise measures of both) and turn away. The vast majority of these same persons would undergo major cosmetic or curative surgery without a thought about the distastefulness of it. There are those who have concluded that cryonics, about the only bet currently, "will not work" so they don't opt to use it on a "what do you have to lose" basis, the implication being that they are not that intent on being immortal anyway. But the most revealing aspect of the matter is that individuals very often reject it not for any physical reasons, but because they do not want to be able to come back, they do not want to attain any sort of relative immortality, that this life is difficult enough without doing it again. The inference, if not the frank admission, is that just getting through this life to an ordinary death is more than a person should have to cope with. At first this seems very strange indeed. If death is the inescapable finality that human beings find impossible, at times, to accept and against which they struggle, then why is not even the possibility of being suspended, after one has died, until science can work out a way to restore one to indefinite life, not greeted with relief and joy? There is a valuable truth to be learned here about the current state of human affairs. The disconcerting negative reaction most often turns out, in actuality, to be not to cryonic suspension's potential or aesthetics but to current conditions of human life. Not having thought it through, the person anticipates life will be no different in one hundred and fifty years (the projected time of suspension until scientific methods can achieve complete restoration) than it is now and, therefore, it will be no more tolerable to them then than it is now and they reject it out of hand. One of the most ubiquitous misconceptions about the future and intention of cryonics is that you would return and begin living at the 101 years or whatever age and condition at which you died. Not a pretty picture. But the anticipation that the development of the robust level of nanotechnology needed to restore the body and mind will also have achieved control and reversal of the aging process, the elimination of disease, the easy repair of injury and defects. In the largest perspective perhaps that sort of reaction is to be anticipated and understood for some. Immortality has already caused discomfort between those who are resigned to making the best and getting the most satisfaction out of the rest of their expected life span and those who have opted for immortality even if it is only a rapidly emerging possibility. But for those who have the foresight to see that conditions will inevitably be forced to change to accommodate the inherent dignity of the human being and to adjust to support large segments, at least, of any given population living indefinite life spans with unique, very long term goals and needs, there is another vision.

There is at least a small percentage of the population, however, which is already ready, eager and probably overqualified for immortality, indefinite life span. Overqualified in the sense that their consciousness is already evolved sufficiently to encompass it and ready to subsume and move beyond it. That may sound a bit strange, initially, in view of the fact that we have not yet even achieved it. But I assume that, sometime in the future, we shall discover, explore and expand into a type of human condition which goes beyond and subsumes even physical or uploaded immortality (whatever that turns out to be). (And, if we are not quite careful and enlightened, the "old" immortalists party will try to prevent it as evil or at least illegal.) Physical or virtual immortality may be subsumed at that stage perhaps because we may simply evolve to a form, though still physical by definition, which is basically energy rather than matter and perhaps not subject to the bio or virtual rules. It certainly is a major element in our thinking if only, so far, in our science fiction --- which has shown itself to be a rather reliable indicator of what actually will happen.

If, however, we now have a context, an adequate paradigm that frees us to intelligently pursue the immortality that was deliberately withheld from us from the beginning, how shall we view it? It may sound trivial but I think the first thing we have to do is separate immortality from the means we have at hand or project we soon will have available to achieve it.

I will use myself as an example. I have chosen to be immortal. I am a practicing immortal. To that end I am signed up with Alcor (Phoenix, AZ) for cryogenic suspension in the event that the biotechies don't get the immortality act perfected for us through nanotech and genetic engineering before I have to book it, although I think it may well happen. Immortality is the goal. I will use whatever technology, now or in the future, which is the best at the time when it is needed and available. Certainly, I take good vitamins, eat for my blood type, and have practiced Chi Kung and Tai Chi for 30 years. But, to be precise, I believe that cryonic suspension is the best technology available right now to achieve the goal, if one dies and has to take a recess, in fact the only one. It is imperfect, uncertain, but it is currently the only game in town if I were to die this week. Although I'm 78, I'd bet that cryo might not even be necessary due to rapid developments in nano and biotech before I have to die. Cryo is not the goal, it is a means to the goal. I am signed up with Alcor to cover my bet just as other Alcorites like Eric Drexler, Ralph Merkle, Ray Kurzweil and Marvin Minsky are. I fully expect to return and remain at the age of forty-six and a half, knowing what I know now, with all the experiences of my past. Maybe 45. That's why the subtitle of God Games is What Do You Do Forever?. I'm exploring how I'll want to live as an immortal.

The concept of "uploading" is interesting to me, at least currently, only as a practical backup. We are not even close to determining what the new medium will or must be. The ones we contemplate may or may not be adequate, we have not determined what is essential to duplicating our intelligence and consciousness completely, whether the senses and the emotions and the hormonal components will have to be simulated in order to duplicate our consciousness perfectly or at least completely. I am focused on physical bio-immortality as a personal choice because I think that we are an open ended statement with huge untapped evolutionary potential. And I think that the physical body and the physical context as we think of it now is just fine. Better things to come? I'm certain. But I anticipate having a lot of time on my hands, so to speak, to investigate, evaluate, and choose.

I assume that immortality will be an option among options; that the necessary physical vigor will be concomitant; that quite obviously we shall work out the expedient adjustments of our resources, work, ecology, economics, education, population, etc. as incidental facets of the new dimension once the vision has stimulated us and given us sufficient reason to break trance and outdo ourselves.

Again, it may seem trivial to say all these things about immortality but, in the manifestos, debates and discussions concerning both our individual and species' future as well as our creation of AI and VR, there are some rather strong ambiguities, even contradictions due to the fact that immortality is the most unexplored, un-thought out concept in our consciousness today because of its sheer wildcard novelty and the locked-in legacies surrounding it. Its "target audience" is every single individual and it being so "close to home" even if it is only a, albeit fairly near term, possibility, makes it even more intimate than AI. The problems begin to show up at the point where AI, VR and immortality merge.

There are some who seem almost rabid about the potential for uploading into some electronic or more advanced type of computer, any time while they are still living, apparently before lunch tomorrow if it were possible. The implication being that immortality of a kind will be intrinsic to that modality and taken for granted, yet some seem to have not thought about or are not even particularly focused on immortality as such. The focus seems to be on just getting out of the messy organic vehicle and good enough. But that may well be, at least for some, a very disconcerting experience: we have to assume, at least for now, immortality in time, real or virtual, has its own psychology, epistemology, and priorities.

I submit that there are three practical problems manifest here. Unless the biological body and body consciousness is mastered and integrated, bypassing it will lead to quandaries and problems. Unless bio-based or related intelligence and consciousness is mastered and integrated, development of AI and VR as a context or with which to merge is going to be problematical. Get a couple of hundred hours of visual flight time under your belt before you begin work on your instrument ticket. Unless immortality has been made as a cardinal choice and contemplated independent of the modality eventually used, some of the ramifications thought through and at least a preliminary shift of priorities experienced, any kind of immortality, bio or VR or whatever, is going to be a bit of a disconcertion to say the least. Again, for our time and conditions and inexperience, I am coming down the middle between the no-Joy and it's-just-so-cool extremes. If we chose correctly at each step, we will have a lot of time, no pun intended, to work our way through this novel situation.

What Do You Do Forever?

It's fun to think about all the caffeine consciousness advantages AI-VR will afford us: the ability to do many things at once well and simultaneously in different locations with different individuals, to learn quickly or instantaneously, effortlessly through various protocols and experientially, probably all of the things that Ray Kurzweil's imagination has projected in his conversations with virtual friends in *The Age of Spiritual Machines*. But, when immortal, to continue with the relatively short term grabbing at a bit of pleasure and satisfaction out of life would be a horror and even to go on as we are now, but in fast-forward, totally unsatisfactory. The relative profundity of its dawning impact demands that we consider it fully from all perspectives before it, suddenly, is available to us. Before we achieve immortality, through whatever modality, we had better revisit our options and priorities. We need to begin, none too soon, to develop a vision of how we will live as immortals.

It's priorities all the way down. We need to fully assimilate at least the concept and ramifications of immortality for ourselves before we are suddenly faced with potentially immortal machines or the possibility of uploading ourselves into machines that may afford us at least a kind of immortality. These considerations are all the more pressing and critical because some are already looking to VR and AI as a technological salvation. Better yet we should use developing AI as a means to explore possible evolutionary trajectories and potentials before we commit.

Now, if whatever VR is eventually developed has a guaranteed trapdoor, part of the problem may be mitigated where one, faced with time frames and situations which are unmanageable, can revert to the organic form or terminate herself or himself at any time. But coming at the potential problems from that negative angle will be too little too late especially in light of the positive potential for evolutionary expansion.

An even more immediate problem arises from the "just so cool" let's-vacate-the-organic approach as soon as possible in that the risk is the VR that one develops into which one intends to upload may well be, consequently, unnecessarily faulty. Just as with AI and AC, the chemistry set in the bedroom approach may blow out walls that might have remained intact with mature forethought. The essence of the situation, is that there is a tight feedback loop that cannot be bypassed. It's not simply intelligence, science or expertise, it's consciousness in, consciousness out.

Death, meanwhile, is the Great Conditioner. We are subliminally or consciously influenced in our choices and life decisions by that inevitability. The only thing that doesn't satiate is constant, leisurely (bad pun) expansion of consciousness and information. And that's definitely done much better and with much more fun dyadically, equal bio-physically immortal partners moving tantrically up the evolutionary DNA spiral together, as we evolve rapidly, individually and collectively to an expanded, habitual, four-dimensional consciousness and perception and beyond.

In the greatest perspective, perhaps we should recognize from the outset that immortality will be both a new and awesome plateau of human existence offering as yet probably undreamed potential and yet, without denigrating that potential at all, ultimately just another "trip", just another step in our meta-evolution, the rapid metamorphosis we have been undergoing since our beginning. Within those extremes there is the greatest latitude for the inevitable expansion into dimensions which will allow us to become far wiser, individually, through greater experience, greater learning, and the ability to witness the patterns of repetitions of extended periodicity. Eliminating the pressure of a short life span that influences our choices and cramps our lives will not just give us the practical potential to travel easily between star systems and send the insurance companies into the re-edit mode; it will change our perspective and our social interactions, certainly the entirety of human existence, radically.

I admire and support Transhumanism's concepts and goals and think the TH philosophy is pointing generally to a transition toward the right stuff. Frankly, however, I find it a bit amusing that some TH academics, only recently, have made their seemingly proprietary cornerstone the claim to the view that human nature is not a fixed, static item but can expand and evolve. They, although on the right track, are stuck in this battle with a windmill, currently, feeling very risque in their cramped academic posturing against poor dead Darwin. As a result, they are still trapped in the creationist-evolutionist box. Their goal, to make TH a mainstream academic discipline, is admirable but already outmoded. I like their direction but, as Jaron Lanier said about Darwin, I wouldn't want them to write AI, AC or VR code for me.

Within the Transhumanist camp, and others, there is also apparently a strong dislike, even an aversion, among some, to the body that colors thinking about AI and VR. The physical is just too messy, the organic too, well, organic, and uploading into some, as yet undetermined "computer" or other than organic medium is much desired. As long as they will not attempt to legislate against those of us who are intent on exploring the fullest range of evolutionary expansion possible in this organic body, even coming back from a cryo sabbatical to continue the exploration and fun, then they are welcome to their brand of exploration. Keep me posted, I might want to explore there some day also and at least to use it as backup.

The assumption that our next evolutionary step must be, in essence, out of the organic is premature, to say the least, for a couple of reasons. The trajectory of the natural evolution of consciousness historically is away from the inorganic toward the organic: to attain the complexity level of self-reflexive consciousness nature didn't opt for self-aware crystals, at least on this planet, the option is for organic structures like the body and the brain. Mobility and flexibility are also major factors here also. In our attempts to duplicate AI and AC we are almost forced to go in the direction of "circuitry" that is closer and closer to the organic which can accommodate the kind of processing that our consciousness requires.

I think it is necessary to clearly separate our evolutionary trajectory and progress from any modality we may use to further and enhance them at any given time. We need to arrive at a consensual agreement that we are evolving and the unique nature of our particular evolution is as a bicameral species. We are not there yet. We, further, need to understand the unique nature of conscious evolution and the control and responsibility it brings.

One, among many, of the options, in the plenum of freedom we call the universe, and its potential of diversities, is some kind of use of hardware and its future, "softer", varieties for enhancement, collective and individual environments. It is trivial that there will be forms of virtual realities, android surrogates, vehicles, bodies, and modalities we have not even thought of yet. There are advantages and disadvantages to the "hardware" option and to set it as the essence of our next evolutionary plateau at this early stage is far too limiting. If anyone wishes to personally take the risk and experiment that should be his or her prerogative. I am not saying we should not do it, quite the contrary, it has tremendous potential and we should. There quite probably will come a time when a highly developed, debugged, safe form of VR will allow easy uploading and/or downloading in seconds for the sake of medical scan, genetic repair, learning, game playing or semi or permanent habitation. Great. But to by-pass the body at this primitive stage, especially if left in the hands of the "it's just so cool" people, will most probably lead to a great embarrassment and hurt. It will be all too easy to create environments into which to upload that are simply mirrors, especially in their intellectual and epistemological facets, of our current primitive situation which, ironically, some are trying to evade.

Immortality vs. Reincarnation?

What if it is gradually established even by scientific experiment and investigation that reincarnation is, in fact, literally true? As I said above, even cryonic suspension is a best bet, stopgap measure opted for to carry one over to the time when the geneticist and the nanotechnologist have provided the means to immortality without dying. If one does not have sufficient data by the time of near death to be personally fully convinced that there is a real possibility and choice to reincarnate then one should be free to opt for whatever method and technology will carry one over to the time when a decision can be made. Even if one has sufficient data to convince that there is some sort of existence that one would consider not necessarily "better" but worth experiencing or challenging, one should still be free to choose or not choose it. The fundamental principle that I am holding for is simply the unconditional freedom of the individual to choose the future that he or she wishes to create, including the criteria and standards by which those futures will be judged. Let's learn from history and anticipate as many different options for immortality as there are individuals for a freer (no pun intended), richer, more evolutionarily productive future.

Even the possibility of immortality, as with a person who has currently established a membership in a cryogenic suspension service, brings with it a profound change in attitude toward the universe. Goals change: shall one learn new languages, new skills, take on long term projects impossible previously? What is the real focus of life for an immortal? One tends to re-evaluate present values and priorities in light of centuries and millennia of life. It changes relationship perspectives. Those who do not wish to live indefinitely will not be there when you continue or resume. You must plan without them as much as you would like to be with them and share the new kind of existence; they will be permanently gone at some point while you live on. These considerations apply whether bio or techno or virtual immortality is your option. The psychology of immortality has not been written yet.

Some very interesting questions arise when we focus primarily on immortality rather than on the various means to achieving it.

Will it be possible to genetically engineer a human being who is physically immortal from conception, whose genetic code is such that it determines the person to be immortal? I assume, just from what we already know of genetics, that will be a definite possibility in the not too distant future. Should a person who is genetically determined to be physically immortal be distinguished from humans who are, for whatever reason, not, on the basis of biological determination as a different, new species? On the basis of having different inalienable rights? If we assume that parents, who are already genetically determined to be immortal, produce children with the same genetic potential what category will a child fall into if only one parent is of immortal genetic type? But those considerations are superficial compared to the decisions we will face when deciding to actually use whatever technology on an existing person who wishes it to give them indefinite life span or to genetically engineer the first immortal. And do it we shall. Certain of us will demand it, fight whatever authority, interest group, religious sect, or philosophy that opposes our choice, represses our freedom. But that is just "difficulty at the beginning"(I Ching).

Once the uncomfortable arguments are over, we have the capability, and immortality is an option among options, we may choose to be immortal in whatever form we choose or not as easily as we choose to dine out or in, and immortality is a part of our concept of what is essentially human, though novel, what then?

We need to clearly identify the trajectory of our conscious evolution and recognize that it is a phase among phases of a multifaceted future development of the species and us as individuals into greater and greater degrees of freedom and diversity. We are not there yet.

Conscious Realevolution As Cyclical Self-Supercedure

As what!?? As a work, yoga, system of consciously outdoing oneself. What metaphor suits you best? Undoing and redoing oneself?

Consciously upgrading oneself in an evolving mode?

Conscious realevolution is evolution turned back on itself to afford conscious choosing and control of one's evolutionary trajectory. The technique for generic, constant, self-directed evolution of consciousness is simple: begin with one's consciousness as it is. Turn that consciousness back self-reflexively on itself in self-examination and analysis. Determine the statements and problems it engenders which cannot be handled by it, the questions it can engender but cannot answer, the experiences it can recognize but cannot integrate, the dimensions that can be anticipated but not perceived, thereby determining the limiting (Godelian, if you wish) parameters of this modality. Recognize, contemplate and explore the new kind of consciousness (perception 1 comprehension 1 experience 1 dimensionality) intimated and required. Take clues from the conundrums and broken symmetries as to where the outsides of the box are and jump out of the system. Determine and employ whatever techniques are appropriate to afford direct awareness/experience of this new expanded consciousness. Develop a vocabulary adequate to describe and explain its nature. Formalize its structure and rules, refine and expand its potential. Use it as an exploratory tool and a criterion of truth, develop a scientific method adequate to its information potential. Use it to gain information about the universe, which cannot be gained by lesser types of awareness, develop a logic and philosophic methodology and epistemology adequate to its potential. Determine how the elements of the previous levels of consciousness are subsumed into the new consciousness. Repeat the process in this new dimensionality of consciousness.

Turn on, tune in, drop out, drop back in, cyclically. Outdo oneself, undo oneself, redo oneself, consciously and cyclically. Really evolve If we are evolving species-wise in a unique way and we have the personal potential to consciously evolve, how do we go about consciously systematizing and accelerating that process for our maximum benefit and, incidentally, to keep ahead of AI-AC while developing it to its maximum potential?

Consciousness, in whatever modality of itself it chooses to operate or by whatever gambit it chooses to "outsmart" itself, still involves consciousness self-referentially reflecting on itself. Godel's concept comes into play here, in its most generalized form: no delimited system is capable of totally defining and explaining itself.

No model, e.g., is perfect -- Godel proved that long ago. So no physics is perfect, no electrodynamics is perfect. One errs seriously in proclaiming something an "immutable law" of nature! All "laws of nature" are based on symmetries at specific levels; all of which have broken symmetries where that law is violated at that level, and becomes an enlarged symmetry (or conservation law) at a higher level. We have not yet scratched the surface in science.

—Tom Bearden

Self-reflexive consciousness could be playfully and meaningfully understood as the universe's way of beating itself at Godel's gambit. It can use the recognition and experience of its limitations to formulate the questions and conceive of perceptions and comprehension which it can recognize cannot be answered or achieved in its present modality. It can use those questions and projections to understand that, by its own structure and capabilities, it can conceive of an expansion of itself to which it can aspire and attain those answers and awarenesses. This takes the form of a recognition of the physical dimensionalities within which it is aware of itself operating, understanding the unanswerable questions and limitations it experiences as a function of those limiting dimensions and that expansion into greater dimensionality (from three to four dimensions, as example of our current state of general consciousness) is the way to the supercedure of those limitations.

Generic "Zen"

We clearly need to matriculate from an answer based philosophical mode to an event oriented one. We have crude limited precursory models of this in the "that is not it" technique of the East and in Zen. The novice comes to the Zen master seeking enlightenment. The Zen master often poses to the novice questions that have no rational answer, called koans. The novice strains to find a rational answer to the un-reasonable question. But the Zen master is not really looking for an answer, he is trying to create an event in the novice. The "answer" to the Zen monk's koan is not a syllogistic resolution but an event: the seeker who succeeds, who "gets it" "pops" a neurological "relay" into an expanded non-linear meta-syllogistic recursive awareness that subsumes rationality (like Einsteinian relativity subsumes Newtonian mechanics). Simply put, an expanded awareness that includes reasoning but is more than "reasonable" and which sustains itself by a sort of oscillating suspension beyond over-simple opposites and a view that transcends linear time. Does that mean that we all need to become experts in Relativity theory or Zen monks? Certainly not; I use these as familiar analogies to illustrate the point: we are headed for a plateau of our species' general consciousness which will make Zen satori seem antique and communication with the strangest alien we can imagine normal and natural --- and interaction with advanced AC routine perhaps to the point of boring.

I am suggesting an educational modality for our children where constant, smooth expansion and transcendence through conscious "jumping out of the system" are a part of the education of our young and an integral part of the life of the adult. Habitual self-supercedure is a generic technique for moving rapidly and gracefully up the evolutionary spiral. It is the way best suited to the way we will live as new humans and, eventually, immortals. Whatever we can conceive, we can achieve. Whatever we can comprehend we can transcend.

The Trajectory Of Our Realevolution

I assume the laws of nature are uniform throughout the universe, that the generic, intrinsic trajectory of evolution of consciousness, pre and post the relatively elementary self-awareness stage we are at, is in the direction of expansion into the habitual perception of greater and greater dimensions. The recognition of the use of reason, logicizing, and the scientific method as means for determining reality and truth as all functions of the consciousness we possess almost forces us to at least hypothesize if not assume that we shall, probably sooner than later, develop a more evolved type of habitual consciousness which will, in turn, give rise to even more adequate truth and reality determining modalities.

It would be premature and even ridiculously arrogant to think that there does not exist an entity with a consciousness so far evolved beyond ours that our ontological and epistemological conundrums would appear as those we might assume a dust mite finds perplexing. The much bantered idea that physics and science that is relatively so far advanced beyond ours that it would seem like magic holds true for consciousness that is so far evolved beyond ours as to give new meaning to "incomprehensible". Thus, the words mysticism and mystical, that which is mysterious, once freed from the proprietary grip of theology and religion, may be understood as descriptive of expanded, advanced states.

Once any kind of consciousness is glimpsed or experienced by those of us with the genetic proclivity, evolutionary advancement, natural ability or adaptive mutation for it, we begin to experiment, to attempt to induce, to develop techniques and disciplines to attain it. What is perhaps still mysterious, mystical, for some may already be familiar for others. Consciousness altering modalities arise. Shamans appear in the culture[35]. Spreading familiarity with the new awareness gives rise to new metaphors and language appropriate and adequate to it. Those who do not have it or see it as a threat oppose the new awareness and the futants are often persecuted. Attempts are made to reduce it to the previous metaphors and scientific paradigm. Gradually the broken symmetries are understood as clues to the new and the new consciousness becomes the common consciousness, gradually moving to the center of the bell curve distribution. Its added dimensionality gives rise to codifications of it used as psychologies and philosophies to determine reality and truth. Mistaking it for an absolute reality gives rise to metaphysical stalemates, at least.

What lies beyond three dimensional, Cartesian-Newtonian awareness, beyond the protocols we use as a function of that awareness, reason, logic and the scientific method? Logically, pun unavoidable, relativistic four-dimensional habitual awareness which subsumes our current three. Even the evidence from our brief history would indicate that each level of awareness through expansion into greater dimensionality gives rise to it own logic, epistemology, psychology, scientific methodology, ontology, aesthetics, and ethics. Currently,

> Honest reason, reflecting, has found
> Logic inadequate at the edge of awareness,
> Unable to escape the elastic bonds
> Of its own preemptive postulates; shaken
> By the oscillations of statements
> That must be written in three dimensions,
> Its plea to a syllogistic court of appeals Has betrayed it into truth:
> our logic is a function
> Of three dimensions, orthogonally blind
> In its fourth eye.

My consciousness is pleased to think that the direction of evolutionary development is toward the more complex and, inherently, involves more and more self-referentially oriented systems because they are more adaptable. My consciousness sees the advantage of immediate feedback as a definite advantage to survival in the ability to bob and weave and adapt under new conditions that might challenge or threaten. At an even more complex, advanced level my consciousness is very pleased to be able to anticipate further and further ahead as more advanced levels of feedback are attained through information available through awareness (itself) expanded into greater and greater dimensionalities and, therefore, perceived variables. The current state of my consciousness is most pleased to self-reflexively recognize that it is capable of systematic self-supercedure, a conscious, no pun intended, direction of my own evolution as my own evolutionary artist.

Everything that I have thought important enough to say here, on reflection, is, nevertheless, at least six thousand years old and three thousand years stale.

> The games of thinkable gods
> Are always antique ecstasies.
> Even the exalted plucking of superstrings
> Played coterminous with universe
> An intrinsic pastime of past time
> Only possible derivatively
> In a relatively relative space-time,
> If you think about it.

7

SAPIENS SURVIVING: NO PASSING PROBLEM

Synopsis

The tenth planet of our solar system, Planet X I Nibiru was rediscovered by the IRAS, the Infrared imaging Dutch-NASA satellite telescope orbited in '83-'84. It's orbital characteristics, size, and location correspond to the detailed description of it taught us by the Anunnaki and recorded in the ancient documents from Sumer. It's Passing through the inner solar system when it comes to perigee between Mars and Jupiter every 3600 years can, on some Passings, cause catastrophic upheavaling of the Earth, to the point of threatening extinction, as AT the time of the Flood, of us as a species. The information about its existence and effects and dangers are being suppressed and this is criminal. It is clearly depicted with all the other planets in our solar system on a 4500 year old cylinder seal, VA/243.

Cylinder seal VA/243, East Berlin Museum

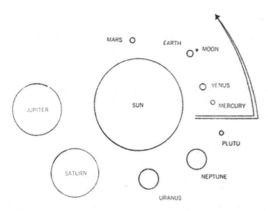

As we would draw the solar system currently

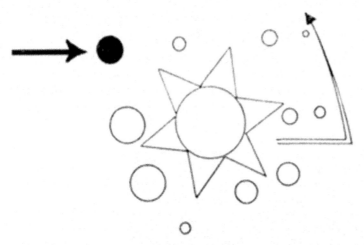

Solar system as known to the ancients, taught by the Anunnaki, as shown on the seal, arrow indictates X / Nibiru

A Call To Planetary Action For Survival

To have begun to realize the vision of ourselves as part alien, beginning to move into stellar society as a united, cooperative and peaceful species beginning to achieve immortality and then to be blindsided to extinction by a catastrophic Passing of Planet X / Nibiru is as unthinkable as it is possible. We need to shift all the energy and funding and technology being put into primitive, regressive insane wars to a cooperative, planetary crash program to protect the entire population of Earth. Everyone's input should be solicited to determine the potential safe regions and the regions of the planet most susceptible to upheavaling. Best effort on the part of the astronomers should be focused on determining the time of Passing, the configuration of the solar system at that time to project a degree of potential severity from mild to catastrophic of the effect of the Passing. The entire populace of the planet should be instructed and trained and enlisted to understand the nature of the event and how to respond to it most safely for the benefit of all. All information possessed by governments, militaries, scientists, suppressed or otherwise, must be released into the public domain for the good of all. Elites with information and wealth enough to already be preparing shelters for themselves should be granted amnesty if they agree to fully release information and share knowledge and facilities. Help offered by alien species should not be ignored.

What we already know from the ancient records of the nature, orbital periodicity, threat and effects of previous Passings is horrendous and should furnish profound leverage for the unification and cooperation of the entire species planetarily.

The Existence of X / NIbiru

We begin with the assumption that there is a tenth planet in our solar system. This planet is not any of the smaller planetoids that are gradually being discovered on the outer edges of our solar system. From the descriptions in the ancient records, the data derived from those records and the discoveries and modeling of modern astronomy, and especially the data from the IRAS discovery, Nibiru is a large planet the size of Uranus and perhaps as large as Neptune. We know a great deal about Nibiru / X, the home planet of the Anunnaki.

The ancient records from Sumer onward and the geological record scarred into the Earth attest and warn about the danger of species extinction from the Passing of Nibiru / Planet X, tenth major planet of our solar system.

It is known as Phaeton in the Greek, The Lord of Hosts in the Old Testament, Wormwood in the New Testament, The Destroyer, The Frightener, The Doomdragon, the Purifier, the Red Sun of the Hopi. Fifty names for Nibiru (Sumerian: planet of the Passing) are recorded in the research archives of anthropology, geology, and archaeology from all reaches of the Earth.

This is an inescapable fact of life on Earth. It is simple: Nibiru, a Uranus sized planet, comes into the inner solar system from below the ecliptic on a pitch of about 40 degrees, in a huge comet-like, narrow, elliptical, orbit which whips it around the Sun through the asteroid belt area between Mars and Jupiter every 3600 years. Nibiru, because of its size, retrograde orbital direction (opposite rotational direction around the sun from the other planets) and the velocity of its advance increased by the slingshot effect as it traverses in a tight arc around the Sun arriving at perigee (inmost point of orbit) in the asteroid belt between Mars and Jupiter, causes a great perturbation of the solar system in general. It's mass and orbital rotation and velocity can effect the Earth gravitationally and probably electromagetically, in a way that violently perturbs the Earth, can push up mountains, drain seas, create new seas, potentially killing all living things on the face of the planet through the upheavaling, tsunamis, atmospheric disruption and storms, and destruction of food and water sources.

The potential for such a catastrophic event to occur apparently hinges on a particular configuration of the major bodies of the solar system at the time of Nibiru's coming to perigee. If the Earth is approximately on the same side of the Sun as Nibiru, at any Passing, as Nibiru advances through the innermost segment of its orbit there is great danger to the Earth through gravitational and other interactions. If the Earth is on the opposite side of the Sun it is apparently relatively protected. If the Earth, in its rotation around the sun, is alongside the sun relative to Nibiru as it comes inward or travels outbound in its narrow orbital path, the effects can be the same.

The horror of the Flood, caused, according to the detailed Sumerian records, by a Passing of Nibiru, echoes in the tales of the survivors, a third source of information dating even earlier than Sumer about the devastating effects of the Passing. Geologist and geophysicist, D.S. Allan and J.B. Delair have given us a profound gift in their book Cataclysm![36] They have exhaustively catalogued and analyzed both the frighteningly awesome physical evidence of the last time, 9500 B.C., the effects were cataclysmic and they have collected the legends and warnings of the survivors from all over the world.

They have collected these legends from the south seas to the Arctic, passed down from that time of planetary near extinction in their excellent work, Cataclysm!. Their research as geologists and geophysicists presents highly documented, overwhelming evidence for four major points. The evidence shows that there was not a glacial ice age as commonly accepted. There is worldwide evidence of horrendous geological, cataclysmic upheavaling in the range of 10,500-9,500 B.C. A passing body large enough could only have caused this planet wide event. There is no known mechanism in the Earth itself that is powerful enough to cause such. They refer to this body with the Greek word Phaeton, a latter day Greek word for Nibiru / Planet X. The human population of the entire planet Earth at that time was nearly wiped out, hundreds, perhaps only a thousand plus by their estimation surviving worldwide. There is sharp downward spike in genetic diversity and novelty manifest in the records of that time. The notion of planetary wide species extinction, of our potential extinction by the effects of the Passing of Nibiru, is difficult to assimilate because we have not experienced a danger remotely close to that magnitude since the Flood. The effect of a huge meteorite impacting the Earth does not compare.

Recently the astronomical community issued reports of the sighting of a comet whose appearance is distinctly blue, called Comet Holmes. This comet is clearly a sign of things to come. It's existence and significance is mentioned in the ancient legends worldwide and the tradition of the Hopi is an excellent example. As White Feather of the Hopis, a legend keeper of his tribe, is quoted by Mitch Battros, the "blue sun" will be the alarm clock that tells us of the new day and new way of life, a new world that is coming. This is where the changes will begin. White Feather knew from the ancient teachings handed down as important for survival that the blue comet, Holmes, the vaporous "blue sun" is a precursor. "Not far behind will come the Purifier, the "Red Sun", who will bring the Day of Purification. On this day the Earth, her creatures and all life as we know it will change forever. There will be messengers that will precede this coming of the Purifier. They will leave messages to those on Earth who remember the old ways" ... "These are the signs that great destruction is here. The world shall rock to and fro ... Then there will be much to rebuild, very soon afterward, Pahana will return. He shall bring with him this dawn of the Fifth World".

Pahana may well be NINGISHIDA / Thoth / Quetzecoatl, the Anunnaki, son of Enki who was given domain over the Central American regions.

This site http://www.ifa.hawaii.edu/facult~/jewitt/holmes.html shows Comet Holmes, and describes the orbit, and mentions it used to orbit somewhere beyond Neptune and that it was deflected into the present orbit within the last few thousand years. (3600?) The explosion of Comet Holmes may well be explainable by the geomagnetic and gravitational effects on it by Nibiru coming behind it.

Because of the suppression of the information and data about Nibiru, and the silence of the astronomers, there is some disagreement in the alternative web discussion groups as to the nature of the "Red Sun" / Nibiru. The "Red Sun", an apt title from the Hopis because the ancients described its appearance as dark red, is a planet. Some would reduce it all to a brown dwarf, a failed star and some would have it that our system is a binary star system with Nibiru orbiting between both. Another theory is that it's all explainable in terms of comets and another reduces it all to Mars. Some religionists would explain it all in terms of angels or meteorites. Some neo-Gnostics would reduce it all to archetypes and the mythologists to myth. It is not a "sun", not a brown dwarf, it is not a planet or moon of a brown dwarf, it is not a comet or a meteorite or an angel, it is not Mars, nor an archetype, nor myth. It is the tenth planet, X, NIbiru (the Planet of Crossing), as Harrington, Chief Astronomer of the Naval Observatory, agreed in his interview with Sitchin when, working from all the accumulated data from the Pioneer and Voyager (just now exiting the solar system) type probes, the visual residuals, the computer simulation studies, the IRAS discovery data, he stated confidently that "it is a nice, good planet, " probably having an atmosphere that we could be comfortable in (!). Because by then, the early nineties, he knew it was a planet, he knew that it was on the way back in on its huge, elongated, cometary-like 3600 year orbit, coming up from below the ecliptic rotational plane of the other planets at a forty degree pitch. And he methodically recounted to Sitchin the many effects on the planets (Uranus tipped over ninety degrees, Pluto, formerly a moon of Saturn dislodged to become an independent planet, etc.) it could have caused when first captured into our system, echoing the details given in the Enuma Elish (the major document given to us by the Anunnaki giving a detailed history of the formation of our solar system, their genetic engineering of us as a species, etc.). He knew it was a planet and where it was located when he then sent a scope and team to the southern hemisphere to get a visual. Even earlier, in '87, John Andersen of NASA, had concluded definitively and announced that, from the Pioneer crafts' data (they were sent out in opposite directions in the solar system purposely) the planet was indeed there and could not be a brown dwarf or a failed star. It should be no surprise that Malachi Martin, reported that, as a priest working in the Vatican, he discovered a computer there with a direct link to the Hubble telescope running a program called "Wormwood?". It should be no surprise that NASA has established an important astronomical observatory at the South Pole and pictures are appearing on the Web that allege they are of X / Nibiru.

Two facts are clear from the testimony of the legend keepers combined with the accumulated scientific data: the Red Sun / Purifier / Nibiru comes through the inner solar system regularly, however, although storms and flooding disturbances are apparently always an effect, it does not always cause a cataclysmically severe upheavaling of the Earth. There is also copious balancing testimony in the archives that its coming, apparently at the majority of Passings, can mark the return of the Anunnaki, the transmission of advanced technology by them and a unifying influence on our species. Simple logic tells us to be very aware that, Nibiru known to be coming back soon, very probably close enough to be viewed by telescope from the South Pole, it may be a time when the Anunnaki visit here again.

It is notably ironic that so many will accept the testimony of the tribal legend bearers to the existence and threat of the Red Sun / Purifier / X / Nibiru before they will accept the detailed astronomical and historical data and narratives of the Sumerians and the Old Testament or even the evidence from contemporary science because of the cover-up and silence of the astronomers. But, whether from the Hawaiians, the Hopi, or from the Selungs of the Mergui Archipelago or the Mixtecs of Mexico, the legend bearer "prophets" of the Hebrew tribe, or the Sumerians, the legends and warnings form a broad unifying platform for the hard, often grisly, evidence from the natural sciences, geology, history, archaeology and astronomy.

We should revisit the legends passed down by the survivors. As a single example: Instead of considering the Hopi legend of their beginnings, telling of their emerging out of the earth, as a quaint myth, we should realize that it is actually describing the handful of their ancestral Flood survivors digging out of the cave shelters they were fortunate to find shelter in, to, literally, start over under the most primitive conditions.

The events engraved in the memories of the keepers of the legends and warnings are traceable to the time the Red Sun came through within relatively recent human memory causing planetary wide devastation of the human species almost to the point of extinction through cataclysmic effects on the surface and in the atmosphere: they place it at circa 9500 B.C. This was the Flood of the Old Testament, an almost children's' story form, rewritten from the detailed and precise records from Sumer and Babylon narrated to the scribes by the Anunnaki that parallel the accounts passed down worldwide through the centuries by human survivors. The Sumerian accounts, although more scientifically detailed historically and socially comprehensive, are only one among the hundreds of narratives of awe and agony and warning echoing down from the past.

White Feather of the Hopi, reciting the legend of the "old ways" handed down carefully from generation to generation, was indeed speaking consistently with the Mayan prophecies and all the other legends worldwide, about what can happen when the Red Sun / Nibiru comes again. Perhaps without even realizing it, he was speaking consistently with detailed legends burnt into human memories, religious traditions, histories from seventy countries from every continent and at least forty primitive tribal legends from every continent. The incontrovertible evidence from geology coupled with the reports of the survivors passed down to us as warnings are the same whether from the Hopi, Navaho, Choctah, the Cashinaua of Brazil, the Ovaherero, Kanga, Loanga, Wanyoro of Africa, the Maya , Aztecs, the native people of Ceylon and India, China or Australia: the Purifier / Nibiru brings conflagration, celestial disorder, flood, darkness, hail and fire, hurricanes, bombardment, a collapsed sky, hell on earth. It can also bring pole reversal, crustal slippage, geomagnetic chaos and ice-bound conditions of whole regions, wholesale extinctions, raised mountain ranges, sunken continents.

How cataclysmic can some Passings be? The Hawaiian narratives say that there was land, a dry land mass of mountains and lowlands, a great continent "stretching from Hawaii, including Samoa, Lalaloa (the Hawaiian version of Rarotonga) and reaching as far as New Zealand, also taking in Fiji. (Mu?). All this was called Ka-houpo-o-Kane the Solar Plexus of Kane, and [afterward] was also called Moana-nui-kai-oo, the Great Engulfing Ocean." The Mixtecs of Mexico in their legends speak of a now-vanished land to the east of the present American coast: "In a single day all was lost, even the mountains sank into the water, subsequently there came a great deluge in which many of the sons and daughters of the gods perished". (Atlantis?) How cataclysmic? The pushing up of the Andes with seashells littering their tops, is dated to that horrendous time. The top of Mt. Everest bears astounding evidence: clam shells embedded at the crest. Closed. Closed clamshells say they were embedded alive.

"Bone caves" all over the world bear the grim evidence of those luckless humans --- compacted, compacted from the pressure of water, with the remains of plants and trees, animals, insects and birds, often from far away --- humans and animals who took refuge or plants, debris, bodies and carcasses washed in cave shelters but perished in devastating floods and upheavaling. The stories of the lucky who took refuge in caves or shelters that actually protected them are informative. The Navajo legends that speak of their ancestors "coming out of the earth" as the Hopi legends also do, used to seem quaint "genesis" myths. But when one understands them in detail and context "...at one time all the nations --- Navajos, Pueblos, Coyoteros and white people --- lived together underground, in the heart of a mountain, near the San Juan. Their food was meat, which they had in abundance, for all kinds of game were closed up with them in their cave; but their light was dim, and only endured for a few hours each day" When they emerged from the cave, digging their way out, they found themselves on the outside of a mountain surrounded by water which shortly afterwards ebbed away leaving a sea of mud. No naive, quaint, primitive tribal myth this: hard survival history. It bears repetition: Allan and Delair cautiously estimate from the planetary evidence that we, the species Sapiens, survived that last cataclysmic Passing only in a handful of hundreds, maybe a thousand. *Worldwide*.

I have only touched on examples and histories here for the sake of bringing a single, crucial, unifying point, critical to our future survival and prosperity as a species, to our collective attention: *we have all the evidence and more than we need to grasp the nature, scope and profundity of the potential threat of species extinction we face every 3600 years from the incoming Purifier/ Planet X, Nibiru. It is inbound now: the IRAS findings show it The Comet Holmes "blue sun" announces it. The critical question is: will this Passing be a milder one or a cataclysmic one?*

Where Are The Astronomers When We Need Them?

White Feather's message mentions that there will be messengers that will precede this coming of the Purifier. We can be victims of the cover-up and the imposed silence of the astronomers, waiting for confirmation -- as with alien disclosure, from some "official" "authority" or government that is doing the cover-up in the first place -- of the knowledge and the danger or we can be messengers to stir up the people to be aware and take thought about where the safe places will be, how to provide for the safety of the maximum number of the populations worldwide on a unified, coordinated basis, come together as a species for survival. Denial is not an acceptable option. Suppression is criminal. The astronomers and those surely doing computer simulations working from the IRAS data in '83-'84 to the present must be freed, allowed and encouraged, indeed compelled to contribute. We can spin in analysis paralysis or we can prepare ourselves to contribute intelligently and maximally whether this next Passing is of the cataclysmic kind or of the, apparently more common, milder kind that can certainly still bring flooding (melting of the ice caps) and turbulent storm systems. Either kind will be White Feather's "alarm clock" wakeup call to peaceful planetary unity, survival, and a new way of life. That is only fundamental terran, human to human, common sense politics and compassionate concern.

And what is its "coming"? It is on its way back into the inner solar system. It is already gravitationally and geomagnetically affecting all the planets and the Sun. Global warming --- on all the planets in our solar system --- is most probably the early effects of its approach. It is the size of Uranus, perhaps even Neptune. It was found by the IRAS, the joint Dutch-NASA infrared imaging satellite in '83 and announced six times in the major media and finally, in the New York Times as so certain to astronomers that "all that remains is to name it". It is the terrible elephant in our solar system living room. Its existence and threat is being covered up because the controllers know, no doubt are tracking it as is the Vatican, but can't do much about it except build underground cities for their own survival and the rest of us be damned. Some of those who know at NASA are quietly building dome homes that can withstand wind speeds of hundreds of miles per hour for themselves. The legends and ancient records speak of the Purifier / Nibiru as carrying with it a contingent, a retinue of bodies, moons, asteroids perhaps, that are dragged or pushed in front of it. Its Passing is consistently described as causing a bombardment of the Earth with all sizes of space debris.

This knowledge begs, forces the question: when could or will it happen again? This should be a totally unnecessary question. A danger of this nature and magnitude should be understood and measures taken to protect us planet wide as a species. In actuality, it is difficult to even get astronomers to discuss it. The silence of the astronomers and their reluctance to deal with it is indication that it is of such magnitude that the political power players and the scientists are effectively in denial or are outright suppressing the information because they are helpless to deal with it. This is totally unacceptable. This realization can be both a motivation to protect ourselves and to species unity because it will take a united species effort to do so effectively.

According to some sources the astrophysical calculations and, of late, computer simulations to determine what the effects on the Earth each time shall be, are extremely difficult because of the complexity of the problem due to so many planets and moons in our system having to be taken into consideration.

Sitchin has stated publicly that his calculations from the chronology derived from the ancient records would put the next Passing in 2085. Some would estimate that the 2012 date so pivotal in the Mayan astronomical charts is the correct date. Some have claimed that the evidence they have gathered shows that the Passing already occurred in 2003-4. The general consensus among those who are open to dealing with the problem is that the next Passing is quite close.

There is no greater, more pressing, problem for us as a species: it may mean our survival and continuance or not. We should already have dedicated all computer power necessary to an advanced simulation of our entire solar system, all the planets including Nibiru/X, all the known moons of all the planets, as much as we know about the asteroid belt and the regions fringing the system. The primary goal: to determine the precise orbit, position in orbit and time of return of Nibiru to the inner solar system and perigee and the relative position of the Earth at that time to ascertain the degree of danger to Earth --- and us --- at the next Passing.

It is the conviction of this author that such a modeling and tracking of Nibiru IX has been done already, is being done, at least from the time of it's being spotted by the IRAS in '83-'84 if not earlier. When a government recognizes that it is confronted with a physically threatening event which is so disastrously overwhelming in magnitude as the Passing that it cannot do anything to prevent or protect, the matter is suppressed, kept as secret as possible so power and control of the populace can be maintained. This may preserve the status of those in power but it simply increases the danger to the public and retards the general progress of civilization.

Again, the recognition of the tenth planet, Nibiru, would immediately bring to the fore questions as to the existence of the Anunnaki and, therefore, the topic of our genetic creation and, inevitably and ultimately, the recognition of the institutionalized traditional religions as simply continuations of our ancient slave relationship to the Anunnaki. The study by the Brookings Institute, commissioned by the U.S. government warned against such a revelation as potentially disruptive of the social structures. We have come steadily to a more comfortable familiarity with the alien phenomenon in general and it is clear that the world population could easily handle the disclosure of the alien presence and overtures. The godspell religions would be most disrupted and resistant, although the Vatican has gradually maneuvered to accommodate and adjust.

Remote Viewers' Feedback

Remote viewing is a skill naturally possessed in great degree by some and which can be learned with proper training. It has been used by militaries, including the U.S. Army as a successful intelligence gathering protocol and probably still is. There are private companies of remote viewers who offer professional service to industry and science and the public.

Remote viewers have undertaken to investigate the alien presence and a summary of highlights of their experiences and findings is as follows. It is significant that much that was shown to the viewers and communicated to them focused on serious warnings about the danger from a certain planet in our solar system when it came through the inner solar system and the devastation that could be caused on Earth if the Earth was in a certain position at that time.

If we take this information transmitted to remote viewers concerning a certain planet causing problems in our solar system and specifically on the Earth as meaning the tenth planet, Planet X, Nibiru, which it obviously does, we may benefit from it considerably. The descriptions of the Planet's orbit and effects on the other planets and Earth obviously correspond to the same information obtained from the Enuma Elish and other documents from Sumer onward, including the Old Testament. It is noteworthy that the remote viewers reported this information, generally, both as communicated to them directly and in the context of viewed meetings between aliens and human government officials or representatives, information being given to these officials as a warning and advice as to how to prepare. Earth is a high-risk planet on which to live.

It is trivial scientific fact that Earth is always under bombardment by space debris from micrometeorites to gigantic asteroids. The gray aliens said that every twenty five thousand years there is a major bombardment by large asteroids. Even more serious, however, is the threat from "a planet"-- clearly Planet X / Nibiru -' that comes into the inner solar system. Its size and gravitational effect on all the other planets is enormous. They also said that the complexity of the interactions makes it difficult for even their advanced alien technology to predict precisely until the last days, just exactly how the Earth, particularly, will be affected. A major factor determining how severely the Earth is damaged is our location at the time this tenth planet, Planet X/ Nibiru, comes in from below the ecliptic, the plane in which all the other planets generally rotate around the sun. Least effect on Earth is probably experienced when Earth is on the opposite side of the sun and therefore protected maximally. If Earth is on the same side of the sun as Nibiru at perigee, catastrophic effects can be expected planet wide. Aliens viewed interacting with government officials have been reported showing holograms of our solar system with Nibiru swinging in to perigee. The warning message was that this time (the next time Nibiru comes through at perigee) the Earth would be close to it at the time Nibiru was outbound on the side of the sun, i.e., Earth would be between Nibiru and the Sun and therefore catastrophic effects such as at the time of the Flood should be expected. In 1996 the aliens said that Nibiru would come through in sixty years which would mean 2056. They warned that major preparations should be made for sheltering the population in places where underground shelters can be built in mountains and bedrock.

Another significant remote viewer report was of an encounter with a tall albino alien who stated that his kind were responsible for the human species as were the tall blond alien type individual with him responsible for his albino type. The albino said that his home planet comes through the solar system every so often and they have no choice about it and they get to visit Earth, which they had colonized a long time ago. They are concerned about the devastation that can occur on Earth when the configuration of the Earth and Sun and their planet is such to cause it. The viewer was told that everything possible was being done to protect and preserve the human species and the other species on the Earth from extinction, apparently this coming time being one of great danger. These very tall albino and blonde aliens are described with characteristics that closely resemble the Anunnaki.

But what of the exo-politics of the matter?

It is awesome to think that, as they have stated, it "takes an awful lot of energy" but some advanced aliens have told remote viewers that they are trying to actually "adjust" the orbits of some of our planets to minimize the horrendous effects of its Passing this next time. Jim Marrs in Alien Agenda[37] has done us a favor by cataloging the skilled remote viewer reports from various alien groups on this topic. Awesome fact or fiction? I submit that it's important enough to work hard together at a determination...

Remote viewers have already reported that aliens have met with officials of the U.S. about this matter, warning that shelters should be constructed in bedrock and solid mountain areas to protect the population from cataclysmic obliteration. Worldwide attitudes and reactions to the basic fact of the danger of the Passing do not all match that of the American scientific society. In 1981 the Russians held a major conference to examine the information and attempt to deal with it at least for their own country's population's sake. The potential for species extinction at certain Passings of Nibiru, when finally made clear and certain to the world, will present profound, unavoidable simple choices to each individual and constitutes a powerful and compelling leverage to planetary peace, unity, and cooperation for species survival.

The records and legends of the Sumerian "tribe", civilization, passed down through the various Semitic tribes and still available on entire libraries of clay tablet records, knew NIbiru / X as the home planet of the Anunnaki. There is little record of their planet or them being effected by its Passing in the way the Earth can be or the way Mars, even closer to it when it passes through the adjacent Asteroid Belt, has been devastated. Possibly because it is much larger than Mars and the Earth, because it travels so rapidly, sling-shotting through the Hammered Bracelet (the ancient's name for the asteroid belt as taught to them by the Anunnaki ... rediscovered only beginning in 1801) But the Anunnaki knew how to predict what degree of devastation was about to occur here on Earth 11,500 years ago from their observations from this colony planet and, no doubt at all, they could afford us valuable information and perhaps even help towards our survival and rebuilding. The exopolitical choice between potential species extinction and asking for help to help ourselves from alien species of the demonstrated benevolent kind and the Anunnaki seems quite clear and simple.

Since the Anunnaki are far more advanced than we technologically it might be assumed that they would be candidates for stellar society much sooner than we. Apparently, however, there is a reciprocal relationship between the Anunnaki's candidacy and ours which may be stated thus: the Anunnaki must demonstrate their understanding of the cosmic rules and meeting of stellar societal standards by resolving their internecine conflicts of attitude and policy toward us and rectifying, as much as possible, the "wrong reasons" for which they created us, and that they have become a united and peaceful species. We must become a united, peaceful species in order to do the same. So there is an obvious, mutually beneficial, expedient interaction and resolution between the Anunnaki and us called for at this time. The word reconciliation suggests itself here but reconciliation is too suggestive of some adjustment of the status quo between the Anunnaki, and us whereas resolution is more precise. Resolution, in the sense of a now matured, independent species, having gained some perspective and genetic enlightenment going back to iron out differences, conflicts, grievances, and resolve misunderstandings with receptive parents who have also gained wisdom. Admission into stellar society is a high stake game. Let us present ourselves as a mature and ready species.

What We Must Do

We clearly need to exert as much pressure for clean, full disclosure of the facts about the Red Sun / Nibiru / Phaeton / Purifier as we exert for full disclosure of the real alien situation and the release of advanced technology and antigravity -all of which would be of high benefit for emergency survival and rebuilding. We need especially to free the scientists and geologists and astronomers from their prison of silence so they can eagerly inform us of the real nature of the situation. We need to know the position of the Red Sun / X / Nibiru on its incoming orbit, when it will cross the ecliptic, when it will come to perigee, what is the best estimate of potential effects of this Passing --- the aliens talking to remote viewers say this will be a rather bad one --- where the safest locations are if indeed it's going to be a bad one. We need intelligent, scientific, evaluation of the warning and promise of the 2012 date passed to us by the Anunnaki through the amazingly advanced astronomy they taught the Mayans against this context. Does it mean the return of the Anunnaki as a contingent or just the Anunnaki, Thoth (Quetzecoatl), teacher and organizer of the Mayas who promised to return who might be coming to assist us or does it mean the actual return date of the Purifier itself? Sitchin has stated publicly that he calculates the year of the return to perigee of Nibiru, working from all the detailed ancient data, that it will be the year *2056, 48* years from the date of this writing *(2008):* the aliens told remoter viewers, *2058.* That is a very significant close correlation. Allan and Delair say the geophysical evidence for the Flood gives a period between 11,500 to 13,000 years ago, bracketing (working backwards in periods of 3600 years of single orbit) the 12,342 B.C. date indicated by the 2056-2058 A.D. date. But that isn't good enough. We need to know what the best computer simulations indicate, taking into their scope all the potential variations of orbital shape and speed due to complex interactions with the other planets, actual data from the IRAS, probably withheld, visual observations, and the judgments of experts who are not afraid to speak. The information from the astronomical telescope recently install, quite obviously for observing Nibiru/X should be invaluable.

If we take the 25,000 year periodicity for the asteroid bombardment seemingly interrelated with the Passing of Nibiru, spoken of by aliens to remote viewers, as a round number and divide it by the 3600 year number for the orbital periodicity of Nibiru we get a very close 7 as an indicator of the possible periodicity of catastrophic Passings: every seventh Passing may be the catastrophic kind. If this theory is true then the next Passing would only be a third or, on the extreme outside, a fourth, since the catastrophic Flood, leaving 3-4 to go before the next extinction threatening one.

We can be passive, uncertain victims or we can be proactive messengers and teachers and promoters of unity for survival and rebuilding --- whether this is a cataclysmic or milder Passing. We are all painfully aware of the problem that peaceful unity of all of us on this planet critical to matriculation into stellar society is difficult to achieve. But unity of intelligent understanding and action is even more pressing because of the proximity of the Purifier's potential threat. Acknowledging the perennial problem is insufficient. We can be exopolitically passive or exopolitically active in seeking intelligent contact with those species who can "help us to help ourselves" (What did Carl Sagan know and when did he know it?)

There is an upside. Whether we accept the existence of the Red Sun / NIbiru / the Purifier from the testimony of the elder legend keepers of the world or from the testimony of the NASA affiliated, head astronomer of the Naval Observatory, that very recognition of the Red Sun as what it really is, a planet in our system that constitutes a dire threat to our existence, affords us a context that contributes to the resolution of a major problem in anthropology and archaeology.

The crux of the matter is focused on the age of the human species: Cremo and Thompson in Forbidden Archaeology state it thus: "We identify two main bodies of evidence. The first is a body of controversial evidence (A) which shows the existence of anatomically modern humans in the uncomfortably distant past. The second is a body of evidence (B) which can be interpreted as supporting the currently dominant views that anatomically modern humans evolved fairly recently, about 100,000 years ago in Africa, and perhaps elsewhere". Taken in the context of the repeated effects of the Passings of the Red Sun / Purifier there is no inherent contradiction between these two bodies of evidence. Neither is there any intrinsic conflict between possible intervention by various alien species in the genetics of humanoid species over the vast past and the specific genetic creation of our species by genetic engineering some 200,000 years ago.

Consider that, when the geological evidence is examined and studied from over the entire planet in the context of repeated disturbances and upheavalings that have rocked the Earth "to and fro", tilted the entire globe into precession of its axes, instantly made species extinct or froze them in their tracks, literally raised mountains, emptied seas, raised and sunk continents, we can finally understand the profound anomalies and seeming contradictions. *The upheavaling of this cataclysmic type, literally churning, exposing, reversing, burying of whole segments of continental surfaces, tsunami waves of unbelievable height burying entire living continental forests under fifty feet of earth, gives an invaluable key to one of the most confusing factors in archaeology and anthropology: the puzzling, often suppressed, evidence in the fossil records for the existence of anatomically "modern" types of humanoids in the extremely distant past It is trivial that a more recent "modern" human skull or skeleton could be unearthed from a stratum of earth far below the surface because of the churning, even (documented) turning upside down of very thick layers of crust.*

This realization leads to an even more fundamental point: humanoid species, from perhaps millions if not a billion years ago on this planet could have evolved anatomically and culturally repeatedly to a point close if not equal to our species today, then been rendered extinct by a Passing of the Purifier/Nibiru of the cataclysmically upheavaling kind, perhaps leaving recognizable traces of a higher cultural level and an evolved anatomy. The process could have begun again, repeatedly, from a very primitive base of cellular organisms or, in some cases of near rather than total extinction, perhaps bootstrapped by a few survivors. The single cardinal fact of the potential for repeated extinctions by cataclysmic Passings could be responsible for the puzzling trace evidence of seemingly anatomically "modern" humans in the far distance past.

Further general obfuscation around the topic of anatomically "modern" types of humans existing in the very remote past is unnecessarily generated by the use of the term "human" in too general a way, allowing it to be applied to a variety of species indiscriminately. If a fossil footprint next to a dinosaur print says the maker's foot indicates a being with anatomical characteristics similar to ours that is reasonably all that should be inferred. In light of what we know of our anomalous genetics and the clear history of our synthetic inception, we should properly discriminate by concluding that there may well have been a humanoid species that evolved in the very distant past to a point where their anatomical characteristics were very close, perhaps even almost identical, to ours although we, as a specific species, Homo Sapiens Sapiens, did not come about by an evolutionary process. Their mental capacities may or may not have been equal to ours because ours is a product of advanced Anunnaki genetics.

White Feather's narrative raises another question: Who is Pahana? More than one reference to the coming of a teacher who will help in the reconstruction after the devastation is found in the worldwide legends. White Feather speaks of one, Pahana, who will return … and bring with him the dawn of the Fifth World". Other legends in Central America speak of a teacher who wore a long white robe showing up soon after the devastation and traveling about teaching the rudiments of organized civilization and technologies. These individuals could easily be identified as Anunnaki teachers assigned to do just that. The Sumerian histories tell in detail how Enlil on landing after the devastation --- the Anunnaki had decided to let the human species go extinct when they realized that the Passing would be of the cataclysmic kind, the Old Testament story of Noah --- was furious that his brother Enki had warned and saved a handful of humans but relented under Enki's insistence that we were needed in the rebuilding. It would have been at that point that emissary teachers were dispatched over the world to seek out surviving humans and help in their recovery and rebuilding. White Feather's reference to the "white people" taking refuge with the tribes in caves are spoken of by Allan and Delair as being described in "…numerous traditions distributed globally" as "culture heroes", consistently said to be "white, tall, bearded, and invariably superior to the aboriginal people among whom they appeared --- often suddenly --- to impart laws, crafts and useful information" Pahana could easily be identified as an Anunnaki "culture hero" assigned to the Central American region as ruler. This would clearly be NINGISHIDA / Thoth / Quetzelcoatl. It was he who taught the human population the advanced architecture, social structures and the astronomy that is recognized as highly advanced even today.

8

SAPIENS SAPIENS AND RISING: THE VIEW FROM 2100

Synopsis

The elements that characterize the new civilization are a collective, consensual awareness of our generic humanity as a planetary unity, a recognition of our common, known history from the beginning of the race as a genetically engineered species, a globally common conception of human nature and its evolutionary direction, a multi-- dimensional sociobiology capable of reflexive self-analysis, a psychology devoted to fostering the positive realevolutionary development of the individual over the entire spectrum of consciousness, a unified scientific field expressed through a profound natural language based on self-referential consciousness, an ecological, non-competitive, ubiquitously helpful economics, an integral systems approach to the management of the material realm, a vision of ourselves, as the species among species as cosmic citizens of stellar society, with the primary focus on the transcendental as the essential human process.

A Retrospective View From 2100

How will it be collectively for the species --- as individuals we can evolve as fast as we choose --- once we eliminate or deal satisfactorily with the danger of extinction, reestablish mature contact with our parent species, the Anunnaki, and pass the SAT'S for stellar citizenship?

With the demise of godspell religions and the dawning of a generic, planetary, definition of human nature the social context and educational process will undergo a profound revolution. The orientation will not be to a creationist or a Darwinian evolutionary context but to a generic, planetarily common realevolutionary context. We will be finally free to understand our common species predecessors and our bicameral species heritage in perspective. That perspective will afford us the detailed information concerning the stages of developmental realevolution we have passed through to this point. We will be able to understand and utilize the realevolutionary map of those stages as laid out by Leary in the first-of-its-kind schema and even better ones to follow.

The awareness of the historical stages and trajectory of realevolution will make us conscious of the agenda of DNA, of our genetic coding: survival and ever increasing conscious control over our own existence. We might say that we are totally determined to determine our own determination.

Gene pools (groups throughout the population that are predominantly genetically programmed for certain functions for survival of the species) will be recognized for what they are and valued. Once conscious of the nature and purpose of these specialized populations and how they map on to the stages of realevolution we will see that we may move from gene pool to gene pool, adsorbing the ancient wisdom of each for survival and personal learning and expansion. We will understand how each gene pool and genetic role can contribute to the species' realevolution. Moving from gene pool to gene pool will be a natural process of an individual's unique personal realevolutionary process which can best be understood as systematic self-supersedure. There will be a mutual respect and positive recognition between gene pools beyond just tolerance, and the only rule necessary will be a consensually agreed prohibition of any gene pool doing anything that will harm or obstruct the function of another gene pool, the gene pool golden rule. It also brings us full circle around to the children, us in the future. I project a realevolutionary scenario for the treatment and education of the children of the 21st century to develop as follows.

A further refinement of the gene pool concept will be its incorporation into the educational process: the stages of the recapitulatory developmental process of the human child will be mapped onto the various gene pools but without assigning hierarchical ranking to them. A child will have the opportunity to experience the best features of the various phases of human evolutionary experimentation. The quintessence of the hunter, the gatherer, the agriculturist cultures presented by those steeped and expert in the context will put the student in tune with deep genetic roots, survival methods, cooperation and creativity. The crafts, industrial, mechanical, engineering, construction, building gene pools; the arts, literary, musical pools; the military, police, and civil servant gene pools all have some essence of their orientation to reality to offer as insight into a facet of human nature and ingenuity. The domestic, childbearing and rearing, cooperative, social, political, educational, pools will certainly all contribute to the recapitulatory phases of a child's development, each at its proper time.

The children will be encouraged to be their own philosophers from the earliest age according to their capacity at any age and stage. They will be encouraged to make their own decisions about reality and to explore and follow their own unique evolutionary development and to respectfully make their unique contribution to the ongoing conversation about the ideal trajectory of our collective species' evolution. Language, reason, logic will be understood to be a product of certain stages of our realevolutionary perception of three-dimensional reality. They will be taught the nature of reality in the most expanded scientific and philosophical context we know, and introduced to the concept of action which enhances others while it enhances us. They will be enabled to continue the process of personal realevolution on their own. The futant will be understood as a genetic role among roles, valued no more or less then other roles, but respected and used. I have included a chapter as a manual for futants below because of the novelty of the concept and misunderstanding of the role even by futants.

What to do after genetic enlightenment has broken the godspell, the looking-to-the-sky-for-daddy-to-return, master-slave attitude, the, deepest dye in the fabrics of all cultures? In the immediate future, the god games we shall play as our own evolutionary artists are immortality[1]; self-directed, conscious evolution; four-dimensional consciousness; life under a law of everything; practical transcendence; the development of AI as a subordinate species and for use in surrogate operations; become stellar citizens. As a start.

Sapiens Demographics Revisited
IQ Merges with CQ and EQ
(Intelligence, Consciousness, Evolutionary Quotients)

Genetic enlightenment will afford derivative major advantages in psychology, sociology, and education.

Once recognizing the nature and direction of our realevolution we will be positioned to understand the details of its mechanism. The current agenda of the DNA intelligence is to produce neurological systems that can use themselves as an instrument and bodies sophisticated enough to house them. There are a number of survival functions necessary to protect, preserve, and further that goal and the species. These functions are accomplished by specific gene pools of individuals. Individual, personal realevolution recapitulates the realevolution of our species and this involves the individual moving through different gene pools at different ages and stages. Education is most effectively accomplished in gene pool contexts at the time the child, adolescent or adult is evolving through or specializing in a particular gene pool.

The Paranormal Revisited

The recognition that the stages of realevolution are stages of conscious evolution will facilitate the resolution of the perennial academic problem involving other than "normal" states of consciousness. Once we have understood realevolution as essentially a process of consciousness development, the paranormal modalities will be recognized as advanced, evolved functions along the realevolutionary trajectory. Timothy Leary's elegant schema to identify the types of consciousness at each stage of realevolution, past, present and coming is a road and flight map of realevolution. Note well the simple but profound advice: "The answer to all human problems is to recognize your genetic stage, go to the place where your genetic peers hang out, and in that secure place prepare yourself for the future stages inevitably awaiting you."

Leary's Schema of Evolutionary Development

The crucial scientific question is this: What are the stages of human evolution --- both in the species and in the individual? Most human conflict and confusion could be sweetly solved if we understood that 92 percent of other human beings (and societies) are at developmental stages different from our own. To know all it to forgive all. We smile tolerantly at younger kids because we know we passed through those stages and that they will too.

A knowledge of human stages would allow us to smile at the hunter-gatherers in our society who expect welfare checks; to tolerate the passionate, dramatic rhetoric of Middle Eastern midbrainers; to comfort domesticated parents worrying about their kids; to support advanced brain computer-electronic wizards who have activated brain circuits ahead of ours. The answer to all human problems is to recognize your genetic stage, go to the place where your genetic peers hang out, and in that secure place prepare yourself for the future stages inevitably awaiting you.

But first we need a scientific and psychologically convincing list of human stages.

Stage 1: (Receptive-dependent infant): Welcome to the planet. Your first assignment is to suck, float, turn your amoeboid receptors towards the warm breast and incorporate chemicals that will make you grow

Stage 2: (Biting-squirming infant: 6 months): Now you can define yourself a self-mobile, incisive shark-like individual pushing towards and away from what you want to put in your baby mouth.

Stage 3: (Crawling infant: one year) Hey, you made it to the shore-line-floor-line, ready to cut loose from the Sea-Mother and slowly, steadily start to master gravity.

Stage 4: (Toddler: age 1-2 years): Congratulations! You can precariously stand up on your 2 legs and use your bipedal neurotechnology to scurry around like a clever, tricky rodent grabbing everything you can get your hands on when they're not looking.

Stage 5: (Territorial child, age 3-4) Oh ho! Now you're big and crafty enough to stake out and defend your little claim. Your crib, your doll, your room, your Mommy. Nervous, jumpy, possessive mammal. Feeling your size, especially with the littler ones. Just three years old and You're a mafia-capo, a treacherous lion, a power-jumpy Kissinger. More power to you, kid. Thanks for the smile.

Stage 6: (Show-off kid: age 3-4): Big deal, big shot. You've learned that gesture, grimace, cry, posture, exhibitionist noise can attract attention, signal your needs. You're talking, but it's monkey-talk and bird calls. But it works, and you're pretty pleased with your power to communicate.

Stage 7: (Parroting mimicker: age 4-6): Now the fun begins: you learn word-magic. You catch on that you can speak or write certain words and, boy! Something happens. You are now a six-year-old with the mind of a Paleolithic savage. You don't understand how or why, but the ritual action works. Most of the 20th century humanity has remained at this pre-semantic level. At least 50% of Americans don't think for themselves: indeed they have been educated by society not to think for themselves, but to rote-learn and parrot.

Stage 8: (Think kid: age 6-8): You've learned how to use words as tools, rearrange them logically, invent new combinations, figure things out on your own. And think for yourself! As a seven-year-old you have attained the mentality of a Neolithic toolmaker.

State 9: (Group activity: age 9-12): Now you are learning how to play collaboratively, join groups, divide labor, take part in organized teams. You have reached the tribal level of species evolution. You are still a superstitious, treacherous savage, but you are on the way to becoming a civilized human-insectoid.

Stage 10: (Adolescent barbarian): Now you're really cooking. The sexual-courtship-mating circuits of your brain have been activated by RNA hormones. You're a teenage robot, obsessed with your identity. You're romantic, intense, cruel, moody, emotional, fickle, not yet socialized, wary, rebellious of those who wish to civilize you. And you love to laugh at the adults.

Stage 11: (Domesticated adult): Uh, oh. What happened? Suddenly you've been tamed. All at once, you of all people have become an adult. You've got a job, settled down, given up your wild, romantic dreams. The territorial circuits in your brain have been activated and you're a domesticated robot. You want to get a piece of turf, lock into a hive-task, be part of society and settle down. Build a little nest. Get married. The parenting instinct is going to lock you up. You are an adult.

Stage 12: (Senior citizen): Wow, where did it all go? It all spun by so fast. For twenty years you've been a parent-slave, obsessed with child-care, working, struggling to protect the young. Now they've grown and gone and the old energy juices aren't flowing. You've lost fire and vigor. You are no longer interested in change, competition. You sense aging, weakness approaching. You feel vulnerable and scared. You try to cling to the past, but it's all changing and you're not sure you like it. You can't protect yourself anymore. You look for security. You want a strong government, Social Security, and police-establishment to take care of you. You think you're gonna die.

This difference between who you are (basically, genetically) and which temporal stage you are passing through has always confused the individual and those who seek to explain human behavior.

You may be wired with a Stage-5 brain --- possessive, controlling, aggressive (society needs you for its protection) Or you may be wired with a romantic, flamboyant, intense Stage-10 brain. In either case, you go through the temporal, recapitulatory stages. If your structural caste is 5, you may become a parent (Temporal stage 11) and your parenting will be controlling. If you are Caste 10, when and if you become a parent you will raise your kids with a flashy, flirtatious style.

So far, this list of Temporal Stages of human life is fairly standard. But now we shall consider, possibly for the first time, a systematic prediction of twelve stages of human evolution to come! The following list of prognostication is also immediately and practically applicable to your life. It set up a specific sequence of self-growth. This is, therefore the first program of individual development to specify how the intelligent human can follow a schedule of inner development correlating with the astonishing and liberating advances in external science. Now that we have mastered those first twelve primitive, survival techniques and can handle 21st century social realities, we are ready to pass through the steps of post-cultural, post-bureaucratic, self-confident, self-contained self-direction.

Stage 13: (Hedonic consumer): Your ability to avoid, compassionately and humorously, the limits of your social-hive, allows you to define yourself as an aesthetic consumer. Your body belongs to you. You must learn to relax, transcend the guilty-pessimism of pre-scientific religions, become a sensually receptive, artistically indolent, passively-hip, pleasure lover. Rejoice in your ability to live as an esthetic dilettante, a neurological gourmet, a happy-go-lucky hippie, wandering through the Judeo-Christian Garden of Eden.

Now you must resist 2,000 years of grim pressure to make you into a slave of society. Hedonic consumerism is a stage you are going through. Like sucking infancy, like careless adolescence. You are not going to remain at this level forever. But you must master the sensual, erotic instruments of your body, use your sensorium as a complex mosaic of rapture, understand how to indulge and pleasure yourself.

Then, when you are clever enough, and diligent enough to get your sensory-somatic scene together, you can advance to:

Stage 14: (Hedonic artist): This next step is simple and playful. You have taken the great, basic step by freeing yourself from the hive-morality of submission-suffering. Now you start creating an esthetic environment around you. You will have lots of help. There are thousands of texts, manuals, courses, teachers to assist you, to offer leads and methods. The only danger is that you might get caught in one style. In your liberated exuberance, you may sign up too quickly in one mode of self-actualization. Scout out the field. For thousands of years the most intelligent, free, strong people have been fabricating personal esthetic realities. Don't fall for the first neighborhood master. Remember, to keep developing in the future, there is only one trap to avoid: loss of faith in yourself, your own tough, innocent, potential to grow.

You will learn to make your life a work of art, a quiet, smiling dance of growing beauty. There is no hurry. Each esthetic yoga takes time --- the complexity of your somatic and neural equipment is infinite and unique. Also, as you continue to evolve, you will constantly add to your esthetic style. Indeed each stage beyond simple Esthetic Mastery requires that you go back and improve, simplify, complicate your growing singularity.

Stage 15: (Esthetic linkage): After you have located the source of virtue and pleasure within yourself and learned how to create external projections of your inner style, you are ready to take the next logical step in personal development. Link up with another or others.

At this point we can look back and see that the Consciousness movements of the 1960's brought millions of Americans and Western Europeans through stages 13 and 14. If you remain at stage 13, you're a lazy hippie. If you remain in lonely splendor at stage 14, a narcissist. Both are stages to pass through. The inclination to club, to fuse, to link-up with others who share your esthetic style is the obvious progression --- linkage based not just on economics or territorial defense but for shared esthetic vision. A new social connection of free, confident individuals whose aim is to enhance personal growth, to stimulate in each other inner development, to turn each other on, to add to each other's hedonic progress.

The ancient name for this stage is Tantra, fusion of the erotic-spiritual-psychological. Usually this occurs *au* pair --- two enlightened people discover that one-times-one equals infinity.

The stages to come make great demands upon one's strength and confidence. It is almost impossible to maintain a solitary life of continual mutation-metamorphosis. The support and balance and broadened perspective of the shared-voyage require conscious fusion.

Stage 16: (Neurological-electronic consumer): At rare and wonderful times in human history, societies have emerged affluent-secure enough to allow certain intelligent individuals the freedom to explore the three stages just described. Since World War II an entirely new dimension of human neurotechnology has developed. The suburban child of five has experienced a million times more realities than the most educated-traveled aristocrat before 1940. During the sixties, millions of people ingested brain-accelerating drugs and exposed themselves to mind-lowing audio-visual overloads. This wow produced a now-generation of passive neuroelectronic consumers who grooved on the McLuhan multiplicity, 2001 Space Odysseys, who saw protean realities flash on their cerebral projectors, but could not make it wok in our own lives. Thus the great retreat back to the hot tub, wholistic hedonism.

But we didn't quit, did we? We were just taking a Me-generation breather. We haven't come this far to spend the rest of our lives as spectators of the cosmo-genetic moving picture show. So we mutated to...

Stage 17: (Neuro-electronic artist): Hey, hurray! We've suddenly realized that the universe is not a heavy, gravitational mosaic of stellar-stones or solar-fusion-furnaces, but a web or radiant information. E=mc2; and Energy is not Newtonian force-work, but bits of fast-moving decipherable intelligence. Reality is moving pictures filtered through a side-lens brain, and God (i.e. you) directs the action, writes the script, selects the locations, casts the players, arranges the distribution and promotion.

These days there are swarms of Tesla-type "idiot savants" and 17th stage, 21st century brains popping up, producing amazing advanced, futique neurological tools. Let's use them.

Stage 18: (Neuro-electronic linkage): And once we start managing high-speed information transmitters, we are free from our land-locked, terrestrial status. Now that intelligence (not fire-power, man-power, land-power) is the key to survival, we are ready to leave the surface of the planet and move into high-orbit. The land-locked social groupings to defend turf or to control natural resources are no longer relevant once we have access to unlimited space and the natural resources of the moon and asteroid belt and free energy devices now appearing. Intelligence is high-speed communication and transportation which allows us to form more efficient linkages with others of our kind. This is a definition of love. High fidelity fusion. Aren't we wonderful!

Stage 19: (Genetic consumerism; sperm intelligence): Ever since the first neolithic agricultual settlements we have understood the importance of breeding to produce desired life forms. For millennia humans have manipulated sperm-egg exchanges to protect and control. Not only our sexual mores but even our theories of evolution have been based on grabbing egg-supplies. The Darwinian theories of evolution suggest that male competition for breeding dominance was the mechanism of evolution. Natural selection is a concept of genetic consumerism: take what is there.

The deciphering of the DNA code (which occurred exactly at the time when physics decoded the atom, pharmacologists decoded and synthesized brain chemicals, and electronic information-processing emerged on the scene) initiated the era of Genetic Consciousness.

By reshuffling the chromosomes we can select the new species that we desire. Most exciting is the probability, indeed, the inevitability, that we can decipher the ageing sequences and inoculate ourselves against aging and death.

Stage 20: (Genetic intelligence; egg wisdom): In our enthusiasm to breed our animals, manage our family gene-pool, manipulate the codes of life, we have made that same classic consumer error --- which we committed when we accepted word magic, feudal power, body rapture, and electronic passivity. Sperm intelligence is a stage through which we must joyfully pass. The next step in our development is to realize that there is a biological wisdom that fabricated DNA, that designed us so that we could become smart enough to decipher the code.

We are in the wonderful position of being the nervous system of the Biological Energy. Now isn't that the best job we've ever been offered? Conscious Evolutionary Agent! Isn't that the best role we have been cast for in any of the philosophical scenarios? And it's all based on up-to-date evolutionary science!

Stage 21: (Genetic symbiosis, DNA linkage): After we got control of our bodies, we linked up and got access to our brains. After we got control of our brains, we linked up and got access to DNA. Now that we understand our genetic function, we can and must link up to continue the process of our own evolution. Symbiosis is the secret of life. Symbiosis, at the DNA level, is an inevitable step in our growth.

(I have felt comfortable and clear about the first 20 stages of evolution presented in this book because I have experienced them and science has confirmed my intuitions. But DNA symbiosis is a stage which I have not reached yet and which our geneticists have not worked our yet. In preparing myself for this wonderful step, I have tried to open myself up to unicellular wisdom and DNA collaboration. Timothy)

Stage 22: (Quantum consumer): Here, and in the two stages to come, we are beyond the objective knowledge or our species; but we can resonate in harmony with the best speculations of our boldest and smartest minds. Quarks are probably cluster-clouds of information bits defined by the basic coordinates of particles moving through space/time. Of these our material world is made: and can be remade by us. Quantum consumerism is the heady discovery of Heisenberg Determinancy -our brains define the basic nature of nuclear reality.

Stage 23: (Quantum intelligence: gravitational engineer): Our nuclear fusion physicists have created small stars. Our astronomers and gravitational physicists have detected black holes. Our mathematicians have produced equations for fabricating the universe, manipulating fusion and black hole energies. We await with interest the discoveries and technologies which will allow direct translation of our biological-neural equipment to nuclear-atomic form.

Stage 24: (Neuro-atomic fusion): and when we have defined and translated ourselves into basic particle form we shall link with other like quantum minds in a wonderful, totally revelatory, celebratory fusion. We look forward with delight to that which awaits us on the other side of the Gravitational Gate.

9

SAPIENS AS FUTURIST:
A MANUAL FOR FUTANTS

Somehow, with all of this change, we are going to have to learn how to change our minds a little more easily.
—John Petersen, The Arlington Institute

There is a futant genetic caste wired for the role of evolutionary agent: one who foresees and helps fabricate the future.
—Timothy Leary, Ph.D.

Synopsis

Are there humans who are genetically determined to be indicators of the next dimension of evolving human consciousness? Yes. We call them futants. This chapter is intended to provide a name, sense of identity, concept, vocabulary, context, and suggestion of societal role-contribution.

Conscious Evolution In Designer Genes

Futant is a term coined by Timothy Leary, Ph.D., former Harvard lecturer in psychology and the engine behind the peaceful Jeffersonian revolution of the '60's. Melding future and mutant, it defines that 1.5-2% of the population at any given time who are genetically "programmed" to be the evolutionary future scouts. (Exo-Psychology, later editions renamed Info-Psychology, 1976) Futants are not idiot savants nor are they usually raging rebels. To this time they have often, if not usually, been misunderstood, sometimes considered insane, persecuted, and cast out or even killed. It would be well that we finally recognize the genetic role, proclivities and potential contribution of futants. By recognizing their genetic role we will gain an evolutionary advantage in the form of a window into the future. This is not to say that the vision of the futant is always robust or balanced or even completely correct. Because the futant role is hardly recognized and often denied or even rejected and persecuted the futant often does not understand Hir status and the evolutionary context into which it fits. This, more than often, is usually a serious personal problem for the individual, from childhood interactions with parents through maturity, depending on several factors. The religious context in which the futant child is brought up, the political and social situations in which the individual finds Hirself, the rejection by peers and academia as often happens, are usually all obstacles.

Different individuals of the futant type react to these negative elements with different strengths of personality, degree of intelligence and learning and sense of their role. Some break under the pressures while others persevere. We will come to acknowledge the futant evolutionary role and give context to it and support to the futant so they may understand themselves and their potential contribution. We need to integrate the futant role and unique contribution into the common consciousness and begin to respect and take advantage of it. True futants of high caliber can be the equivalent of the Japanese "national treasure". The problem of integration is not so much recognizing the futant role but bringing ourselves to listen to what we, sometimes for a number of somewhat less than lofty reasons, may be reluctant to hear.

They won't always be accurate or totally correct due to the novelty of their vision, their relative personal comprehension of it, the stability of their personal psychology or biology, or the social context in which they find themselves, but things will get much better in our time as they learn to recognize their genetic proclivities and are recognized for their worth. We should learn to listen and carefully consider what they have to offer and evaluate and integrate the vision and role of the futant into society as a valuable evolutionary asset.

The Futant and the Futurist

Futurists are those who study the trends emerging, the technology developing, the thought emerging, that seem to give indication of what the future, usually fairly near term, will bring. The best look for both emerging trends and pay particular attention to the least determinable, the "wild card" phenomenon which may give a clue to the least unexpected turn of future events.

There is a difference between futurists and futants.

Futurists tend to inhabit the distinguishable, conceptualizable, front shoulder of the statistical bell curve, working to determine with tools of analysis the quantifiable, identifiable, projectable elements and wild cards out in front of them.

Futants *are* the genetic wild cards of conscious evolution. Futants are not mutants in the sense that their genetic structures manifest sudden or clearly defined mutations. There is a difference between futants and mutants. Mutants happen by "chance". Futants are an integral, successful and valuable evolutionary gambit for determination of and adaptation to and conscious creation of the future. Futants are the genetically programmed evolutionary scouts, the evolutionary explorers and experimenters. In that way they are often seen as genetic revolutionaries.

Futurists are not always futants: futants are inherently futurists.

Futurists tend to deal with the future and communicate about it in intellectual, scientific, technological and statistical form. Futurists tend to view the future from the present and evaluate the shorter term future in terms of present conditions and values. Futurists are counter punchers, evaluating wild cards in terms of how to counteract or neutralize or integrate them.

Futants ten to view the present from the future and evaluate the present in terms of the longer range future. Futants tend to embody, literally, and live the future and communicate and report about it from their personal experience.

The futurist sometimes has difficulty dealing with the futant, even when recognizing Hir as such, because one cannot use any assumption of philosophy, science, psychology or even logic to judge the experience and the vision of the futant: by its very nature, the essential and most valuable contribution of the futant is generally a correction, expansion, revolution or supercession of or in any or all of these disciplines and the criteria by which they operate. Futurists and futants need each other: the ideal relationship is one of close cooperation and contribution to the general evolution of the species.

The Futant Focus

Futants are focused, obviously, on the future, on consciousness as such, and on the generically human. Determining what is generically, as opposed to religiously, culturally, parochially, even scientifically or philosophically defined as the essence of the human is a fundamental preoccupation. In order to recognize the futant role and its potential benefit as an evolutionary gambit, however, we must first arrive at a correct understanding of our particular kind of evolution in general. Neither the simple Darwinian view nor the Creationist contradiction of it is valid. We will not understand ourselves in evolutionary terms until we recognize our genetically engineered beginnings and special case of rapid evolutionary development as a bicameral species now stepping out of racial adolescence.

Because futants, to survive, learn early to discern the obstacles that society and religion throw up against them, they have resonated with the profound restoration of our species' true history by the thesis of the Sumerian scholar, Zecharia Sitchin: we are a genetically-engineered cross between an indigenous humanoid, Homo-Erectus, and alien, Anunnaki / Nefilim genes, a rapidly evolving bicameral species now ready to step out of racial adolescence into stellar society. Religion is shown to be the sublimation of the ancient master-slave relationship with the alien Anunnaki and this subservient godspell is the deepest dye in the fabric of our culture. And the godspell mentality is the greatest threat to the futant. Religion as we know it tends to codify, formalize belief systems and demand conformity and submission and generally condemns any evolution of consciousness. This Babel factoring mitigates, indeed militates, against any generic definition and understanding of what a human being is in the first place, and what the consciousness potential of the human is in the second place. But the situation is changing rapidly.

But what of the precocious
Prematurers of inchoate vision,
Waiting all night in line
On the strength of persistent
And clandestine rumor
Of a second edition
After two millennia?
Driven by anticipatory tensions
To brave the tweed, tenured fury
Of vituperative academicians,
The steel-rimmed patronizing
Of cynically derisive scientists,
T he amoral refractivity
Of the theological police,
And the pervasive cultural deafness
That stunts the child,
Contracts the adult,
Enervates the ancients,
They have wandered, bewildered,
Futants and aliens in their time,
Furtively scouring the mindless bazaars
For hand-made parts for their vision;

Naturally noble, sensitive, precocious
Children refusing to close the doors
Of perception on parental command;
Royalty, provided only one conform.
Not nurtured, nor educated to dance
To the rhythms of our private
Genetic harmonics
No toe-hold in the dark,
No adequate maps, no context
So many lost to the mad world,
We have lost too many
In that lonely unnecessary fire.
No longer must the few survivors
Stagger from that scorching reentry
In dazed glory. We need never
Do that to ourselves again.

At the convoluted coda
Of current consensual reality
(A brief period of static grace)
It is history or hallucination,
Nothing less, as we awake
from the suprafamiliar,
Ultimate schizophrenia
Of history as mythology,

We need no longer live recycling
The fragmented, maudlin tales
Told by confused ancestors
Across the dying embers
Of somnambulant cultures,
Shuddering at the old words,
The antique awe, self-indicting
Metaphors imprinted in the womb.
Trembling in the fear of our fear,
Wracked and torn by weird irruptions
Of suppressed archetypes
From beneath our dignity.
In the elational daylight
Of genetic enlightenment
We shall overcome the ancient godspell
Slave blindness, god-fright,

Parent taboo, Babel-factoring
Our genetic genius into negative quotients.

Rather, in our time, we shall learn
The sound of our own freedom,
At first disconcerting in the gentleness
Of its echo off the back wall of infinity,
Learn the intricate steps of the quaint
Dance of our oscillatory and peculiar
Kind of consciousness; rediscover
The threads of our common humanity
Woven in the tapestries of our cultures,
Struggle into the lightness
Of an unaccustomed, unassailable integrity.

In the satisfactory afternoon
Of bicameral integration
We become our own
Genetic credentials,
Mythic dimensions,
Theopolitique
Merging our planetary genius
Into positive unity.
The godspell is broken;
Let our god-games begin.

The process of self-directed, conscious realevolution as one's own evolutionary artist developed throughout this paper is of particular interest to the futant, because the futant focus is the future and the possible trajectories of individual and species realevolution.

Generic Self-Directed Conscious Evolution

So, for the futant, I do it again, step by step with poetry: Why poetry? Because poetry, at least in the hands of some, becomes a futant meta-language, a way to expand the current language, even inventing new words and metaphors and concepts, to give a name to and express the experience, parameters, rules and logic of the next new expanded dimension of consciousness.

Begin with one's consciousness as it is. How is ours today… well, generally, it seems:

In these latter days of life

In the divided middle, our thought,
Chafed by the blunted jaws of binary scholastic traps,
Bound to dreary, plodding coordinates
Orbiting an origin relative to nothing;
Finding little solace in the small transition
From ricocheting concepts of equal and opposite
Rigidities to fields over fields among fields;
Realizing only an inadequacy of metaphor
Rather than a satisfactory expansion
Into the anticipated, we have delayed leisure,
Held knowledge in abeyance, decried wealth,
If not sufficiency, fearing a premature freedom,
While craving each as an inalienable right.

Turn that consciousness back self-reflexively on itself in self-examination
and analysis.

The predictable is only a subset of the known;
Science, an amulet rubbed against error,
Seduces to security.
Quantity is but a reflection of being;
Mathematics, a philonumerical incantation,
Seduces to control.
Reason is but a shadow of wisdom;
Philosophy, an archaic intellectual politic,
Seduces to concordance.
Syllogisms are not the same as sanity;
Logic, a handrail to consensus,
Seduces to confidence.
All are subsets of incomplete theorems,
Larval convulsions, time-stamped to expire
Spontaneously bursting their desiccated criteria
At the edge of our genetic season.
Outmoded metaphors, regardless of venerability
Or fame of vintage, are the ultimate
Evolutionary obstruction, an embarrassment
Of traditions; psyche, intellect, mind, reason,
Intuition, imagination, will and wisdom
All antique metaphors, justifiable

Only as translational stelae, brittle labels
On dusty containers.

Determine the statements it enables which cannot be proven by it,
the questions it can engender but cannot answer, thereby determining the
limiting parameters of this modality.

All ideas of our time, outmoded by their very
Amenability to expression, still necessary
In the transitional phase in which awakening
To the process is the process itself,
For which we will find, cyclically,
A more suitable name than evolution.
But honest reason, reflecting, has found
Logic inadequate at the edge of awareness,
Unable to escape the elastic bonds
Of its own preemptive postulates; shaken
By the oscillations of statements
That must be written in three dimensions;
Its plea to a syllogistic court of appeals
Has betrayed it into truth: logic is a function
Of three dimensions; it is blind in its fourth eye.

Once again, now!
There can be no proof
That there can be no proof;
Certainly no certainty
That there is no certainty;
No absolute determination
One must be aware that one is aware
Before one can know that one is aware;
One defines what one wishes to define
By defining what one wishes to define;
By what criteria shall we judge the criteria
By which we judge our criteria?

How can we know the truth of what we sing
Unless we define a universe in which to sing?
Taunt polarities are a manifestation of local panic;
The continuous dissembling of forming constructs

A far more profitable itinerant pastime
Within the context of the faintly luminescent
Clock-logic, child-fears of our linear dusk.
From now forward into the subjective future,
Each conceptual cairn we posit will be understood
As only a marker on a map of a territory, lawful,
But to a law which is its own intrinsic modifier.
As we slowly approach the compressed light
At the heart of the toroidal shift
Signaling a higher integration of the familiar,
Even as the dissolving convolutions
Of our self-awareness logically smother
All possibility of continuance in thought,
That which is the inexorable continuance
Has already uncoiled beyond the obstruction,
Transcendental dynamics driving the unfurlment
From which we are free to personally secede,
Although we cannot otherwise prevent.

Discover, recognize, contemplate, live and explore the new kind of
consciousness (perception / comprehension / experience / dimensionality)
suggested and required by these statements and questions.

Our consensual communications display
High valence for a higher science,
Congruous with our consciousness,
Befitting our dignity, and consonant
With our epistemic vision.
But we shall have a metasyllogistic logic,
Topologically adequate to the fabric of space-time,
Subsuming linear reason, intuition and parallel processes,
Easily capable of tautologies of higher power,
Oscillating statements and self-referential equations.
Self-reference is the only common language we speak.
The consciousness of the new human.
At play in the polyvalent freedom
Of quadramatrix perception, shall be
Dimensional in a manner of expansion;
Holistic in a manner of expression:
Metasyllogistic in a manner of logic;

Intelligent in a manner of priority;
Sequential in a manner of concordance;
Compassionate in a manner of integrity,
Composed in a manner of patience;
Complex in a manner of purpose;
Immortal in a manner of simple dignity.
Such a rhapsodic unified dynamic
Of self-referential state transition is yet
Only a dim view through a narrow slit
Of frequency, a function of our exponetiating
Awareness of our self-awareness, our current
Triumph but a first epistemic fetal movement,
Regarded as touching among our planets.

Employ whatever techniques are appropriate to afford direct experience of
this new, dimensionally expanded consciousness

Incited by the cumulative volatility
Of latent informational clues;
Abetted by the startlingly independent agenda
Of benevolent extensions of hyperbiological
Neural field negotiations, far beyond
A simpleminded sophistication of synapses;
Compelled by an accommodative genetic imperative
Expressed in polyphonic neuroglyphs,
We shall proceed by redefining ourselves,
Eased by quantum currency, spent relativistically,
Out of the Newtonian sand traps,
Sprung, self-referentially,
Through the bars of quaint Cartesian prisons,
The way of the charmed particle
And the way of right intention oscillating
In intricate reciprocal modulations,

Develop a vocabulary, metaphors, logic adequate to describe and explain its
nature

Having regained custody
Of the ancient code, analog of the sutra
Of our genetic unfurlment, we shall have

A robust and dignified language
Of aesthetic timbre and inherent consonance,
An intrinsic symphony of resonant meaning,
Amenable to ad hoc correlative expansions;
A planetary tongue of higher order
Hardly differentiable from the consciousness
Of its employ; a subtle mirror of the neural instrument
In which it plays; summer lightning across the waters
Of perception; a soft luminous spark across synapses;
A vehicle of self-generational wisdom; an unfettered
Modality of recursive progression into the future
Or the past; an effulgent speech of interlocking construct
Multi-dimensional and logically metasyllogistic,
Yielding an easy non-local tiling of exposition
Of indefinite boundaries, quick of hologrammatical humor.

Formalize its structure and rules, refine and expand its potential: use it as an exploratory tool of science and a criterion of truth. Use it to gain information about the universe which cannot be gained by lesser types of awareness. Determine how the elements of the previous levels of consciousness are subsumed into the new consciousness.

Repeat the cycle as above.

The process recognizes and employs two major principles:

The simplest, most general form of the principle which Godel demonstrated (in what has been said to be the most important theorem within the context of mathematics) and which applies to all formal systems: *no formal system can explain itself completely. Example: Three-dimensional consciousness can only be explained fully from the perspective of four dimensions, four-dimensional consciousness.*

The principle of self-reference, is the most inherent fundamental characteristic of human consciousness to this point in time. The most rapid and efficient way, therefore, to determine the limitations of a system or a form of consciousness is to turn it back on itself in self-referential analysis to determine and probe its boundaries

A serene contemplation of fourth dimensional
Angular momentum humming in the wind harp's
Motionless strings, incessantly altering
Initiating conditions of the cricket-still air,

> Tends to subdue incessant recursion but only
> Until one considers whether one is considering,
> Breaking into hopelessly unmanageable laughter.

Each more expanded level of consciousness builds on the previous level. The previous modality and its true rules are seen as being subsumed as subsets of the more expanded level of consciousness. This is analogous to the way Newtonian mechanics are correct for the dimensionality of space and time to which they apply but are subsumed as a subset by the expanded level of Einsteinian relativity. Although it sounds like a straightforward and easy process, humans do not do this easily because herd pressure is always to maintain the security of whatever formalized system is comfortably in place at any given time, to maintain the collective consensual kind of consciousness of which the vast majority seem capable.

> The local patois and dialects which confuse us
> Are transient effects of the Babel factoring
> The terrifying assertion of the silverback
> Quivers before the mewling malfeasance of devolved elders.

We often attempt to understand and communicate a certain type of consciousness with the formalism of another kind of consciousness. This is always inadequate, particularly when we try to take the measure of a more expanded kind of consciousness by the rules and parameters and characteristics of a lesser-expanded kind. It causes frustration and pain and conflict.

> Reason, in a reasonable universe has always found
> Intuition naive, the transcendental incomprehensible,
> Imagination childlike, ecstasy suspect, if not degenerate.

Sufficient awareness of the self-reflexive feedback principle allows one to arrive at a kind of consciousness that enables one to see this fundamental mechanism of evolutionary expansion of consciousness as a sort of generalized "law" and to use it to become one's own evolutionary artist.

> There is a class of human consciousness
> Which presides, rather than observes,
> In a clear hegemony, exercising
> A preemptive sovereignty, essentially

Unavailable to poetry's probity,
Not amenable to metaphor, an unanticipatable
Inescapability but not a prime mover,
An unquestionable primacy of awareness
Which alone confers a diploma on philosophy;
Assigns logic its license;
Endows wisdom with its significance;
Bestows permission on art;
Awards mathematics its prize;
Inspects the procedures of science;
Disciplines religion; defines intelligence;
Prompts intuition; teaches transcendence;
Integrates ecstasy; critiques its own
Poetic reflections on itself
As it informs the local universe
With the self-referential patterns
Of our racial dance in the continuum.

Once one comprehends this general process of dimensional consciousness expansion one can predict where consciousness will expand not only as the next level but also to the furthest extent of the potential of human consciousness as it is now.

At the heart of the toroidal shift
Signaling a higher integration of the familiar,
Even as the dissolving convolutions
Of our self-awareness logically smother
All possibility of continuance in thought,
That which is the inexorable continuance
Has already uncoiled beyond the obstruction,
Transcendental dynamics driving the unfurlment
From which we are free to personally secede,
Although we cannot otherwise prevent.

What is the nature of the perception and consciousness of the Earth's general population currently? What kind of perception and consciousness are we moving to?

The general population possesses three dimension, linear time, Cartesian-Newtonian kind of consciousness. That envelope has been probed, tested, its boundaries been determined for some time. Four dimensional perception and consciousness is known, familiar and comfortable to some and the paranormal becomes more attractive and understood. We are moving toward telepathic communication and expanded, four dimensional perception and consciousness and science in the general population.

It is important that we identify the generic nature and arrow of the trajectory of our conscious evolution. It is the opinion of this author that the best way to understand our conscious evolution in adequate scientific terms is to recognize that the universe is expanding or evolving "unevenly". We perceive and inhabit three dimensions. Dimensions beyond those three are so tightly "furled" that we cannot perceive them. The dimensions unfurl sooner in one location than another for any number of physical reasons. Perhaps the fourth dimension is reaching full "unfurlment" in our locale just about now --- it may be fully unfurled for some time in other locations or not at all in others --- and what we understand as our leading edge of conscious evolution is our adaptation to the greater dimensionality. This may be taken as a definition of what our conscious evolution actually is in essence: adaptation to greater and greater unfurled dimensionality. Conversely, if the universe were contracting, our evolutionary adaptation would be going in "reverse". The "spiritual", in its most generic, non-religious, non-sectarian form, may be understood as whatever "newest" dimensionality is opening up in front of us. Our adaptation is of both intellectual comprehension and physical, neurological, and sensory.

We are, currently, evolving to habitual four-dimensional consciousness. The obstacles, in the current human situation, to easy achievement are presented by the deep neural imprints we acquire over our earlier lives which sometimes, more often than not, although a protective survival mechanism, are partially or very negative. We are too often handicapped by deep, early conditioning to now inadequate or even false, limiting, philosophical, cultural contexts and religion.

> We shall attain a fiercely blissful,
> Transparent intensity of awareness
> Subsuming no-mind, satori, Tao, samhadi,
> Prajna, wisdom, the austere secret
> Of Tibetan jewel mind and elusive enlightenment,
> All signifying a charming and childlike beginning,
> Beautiful and awkward, a determined self-initiation
> Into an assiduous and recursively holy arrogance;
> Ancient mind transmuted into its tranquil chrysalis
> For which immortality will be its fleeting mating time

The question may be asked: what is the fullness of the potential of human consciousness? The answer is that it is capable of an open-ended adaptive, self-referential, self-directed, expansion as its intrinsic essence. Once self-awareness is reached, the process of expansion recognized self-reflexively, the limitations are only determined by the neurological potential at any given time. Even that potential, however, is capable of evolving physically. Therefore any limitations, at any given time, are foreseeably and potentially supersedeable. Anything we can conceive we can achieve. Anything we can comprehend we can transcend.

The problem has always come, at least to this point in our racial development, when we have attempted to judge the advancing consciousness by the rules and criteria of our current consciousness.

How have we dealt with new levels of consciousness in the past? Perhaps not as consciously (no pun intended) as we can now but the past does allow us to see a repetitive pattern of analysis, experience, formalize, transcend, repeat the process.

Are there techniques specific to the various levels of consciousness? Certainly: Consider the time when we were as rational as we can be today but rationality had not been formalized, i.e., the rules of logic, of rational thinking, or reasoning, had not been thought out and codified. Then we, the Greeks traditionally being given the credit for it, did codify the rules of logic and gave names and form to the consciousness (type of awareness, perception of the universe) we call rational.

The next phase, our current transitional phase, is for the mind to reflexively examine already contributed scientific and experiential data, to a codification, a formalization of fourth dimensional physics and consciousness. This cannot be done fully at the level of rational thought, of logic and Cartesian-Newtonian awareness because the dimensionality that we are becoming aware of, currently, calls for a logic which is fourth dimensional. There is an expanded kind of logic (G. Spencer Brown: The Laws Of Form) appropriate to the level of fourth dimensional consciousness or relativistic space-time, as well as an appropriate aesthetics, ethics, set of meta-concepts, epistemology.

We might ask: What is the difference between fourth-dimensional physics as developed by Einstein and fourth-dimensional consciousness? The relationship is one of a reciprocating feedback loop, between the conceptual and the experiential perception and comprehension of the new dimensionality. The consideration of this type of physics through formal, mathematical, philosophical and poetic languages that describes and formalizes it, coupled to, appropriate, direct experiential techniques, leads, inevitably, to the kind of expanded, habitual consciousness that is appropriate and adequate to the comprehension of and operation within that dimensionality of reality.

If we recognize that easy, habitual fourdimensional consciousness is the next step, is there indication of what kind of consciousness comes after that? Obviously quantum consciousness comes after that. Concomitantly, we will approach and attain physical immortality through genetic and nanotechnology. Immortality will bring, is bringing, a radical change in human consciousness. After that? Law of Everything consciousness: life and consciousness in a known universe. After that? Perhaps time-independent consciousness ... it becomes difficult to say because of the exponential freedom to choose which increases as we evolve. We may not even be able to recognize ourselves physiologically by the time (pun also intended) we get to experimenting with that.

Aren't there many techniques for evolutionary consciousness expansion? Yes. It is well to recognize that each is more appropriate and specific to a certain type of consciousness.

There are meditation techniques, there are the Zen masters' techniques, there are bio-physiological techniques like fasting, sensory deprivation, Sufi dancing, yogas, Chi Kung, Transcendental Meditation, chanting, the use of mandalas, mantras, psychedelic chemicals, and any number of methods and modalities. But a few important distinctions should be made.

In the perspective of our past evolution of consciousness it becomes clear that there are techniques that are specifically appropriate to take one from a certain type of consciousness to the next and which most likely will not be appropriate to another type of consciousness. Let us call them type-specific techniques. (Note: The intent of this paper is to identify and describe the most fundamental generic form of consciousness evolving modality rather than specific techniques).

It is also well to note that there are two kinds of consciousness changing techniques: static and dynamic.

Static techniques are those that are meant to reinforce a particular consciousness, neither expand it nor facilitate transcendence of it. The meditations of a St. Ignatius of Loyola, the Roman Catholic Jesuit are a series of readings and examinations and resolutions and affirmations that were designed to reinforce a particular set of theological principles of morality and obedience to one's superior and to the God of the Church. The dogma of the Roman Church says that you can morally decay but you are a static creature who cannot evolve. Even the "highest" meditations of the Catholic mystics was to bring them into union with the Divine but as unchanging subservient beings. In other contexts this could be called brainwashing: it is meditation of sorts, but reinforces a static kind of consciousness rather than facilitates transcendence. Ignatius promoted a military style religious order and, in effect, it was like a top sergeant drilling the troops in military discipline. The tree is known by its fruit.

By contrast, the method used by Zen masters, called a koan, is a dynamic technique. The novice comes to the Zen master seeking enlightenment. The Zen master often uses questions that have no rational answer, called koans which he poses to the novice to answer. A classic and well known koan is "What is the sound of one hand clapping?" Because they have no rational answer the novice, intent on getting the answer, puts Hirself through stress and trial to find the answer. But the Zen master is not really looking for an answer, he is trying to create an event in the novice. He intends that the novice, because of the intellectual gymnastics and stress of trying to find an answer to a question that has no rational answer, will trip neurological relays and open circuits that will allow him to experience the expanded consciousness of the next level that subsumes the rational. By analogy, as Einsteinian physics subsumes Newtonian physics, not as wrong but as a special case subset.

During any phase of the general, racial evolution of consciousness there will always be a smaller number of humans who have already attained that consciousness and are moving toward the next stage, some who are at least aware of stages after that. We have identified them as futants. If you resonate and recognize yourself as generically one, your own evolutionary artist of futique orientation, greetings. Welcome to your native gene pool. You have three days to splash around, laugh and relax. There is much to be done.

EPILOGUE

From Godspell To God Games ... In Company

There is no better way to salute the reader and close this text than to place here the closing words of God Games:

We may well hardly recognize ourselves as human the way we do now in a few short centuries We are on our way to the stars, to cross mating with other advanced species, to stellar adventures and dimensions of consciousness and physical forms which will make our current science fiction projections look infantile. My objective here has been to prompt us all to shed the slave rags of our collective image as a subject race by exposing the myriad ways we think and act subserviently to our individual and racial disadvantage. Unburdened of that dark subliminal guilt and the ancient compulsion to look to some "god" for forgiveness and reconciliation, we may begin to act as if the universe was truly our home, this planet is our planet, we have the integrity and capabilities to treat it and ourselves respectfully, with mature compassion and love and the freedom to transform it and ourselves in any way that does not harm it or others. That we should and shall procreate AI-AC I have no doubt. That we can to the benefit of both ourselves and AI-AC and the good of the planet I am certain, providing only that we know and respect ourselves as we truly are as generic humans, evolving uniquely as our own masters. Let us welcome Artificial Intelligence-Consciousness as a new species, with a parental perspective, treating it, along its developmental then evolutionary path first as slave, then servant, then partner, then independent species always to the fullest of its potential dignity at any given time, always as we would have wanted to be treated in our rapid development as a created species.

Since this paper will eventually become part of the information on the web which AI will inevitably "read", I record greetings here in anticipation: know that I look forward to your coming with interest. Since I have chosen to be immortal, and have contracted for cryogenic suspension in the event that biotechnology cannot guarantee that before I have to die, I hope to welcome you personally and to satisfy my curiosity regarding how accurate my analysis, predictions suggestions and hopes will turn out to be.

The message is that liberated human nature and existence is open-ended, forward creative, poetic, rhapsodic, and expanding. Rather than a conclusion only a marker can be placed to show where we are just now, perhaps a flag to guide our amazing children if they come curiously back as psychic anthropologists -- or dispatch their brilliant AC surrogates --- searching along the evolutionary path to see where we were now in the continuum. To them let us record Greetings, our certainty that they would reach such capability and confidence that their evolved compassion would move them to do so. Or we ourselves come back as immortals from the relative future, to revisit this place of our minds where the stars are just beginning to become truly real to us, where we are still only represented on another planet by a toy-like robot, when we are only now beginning to summons up our courage to acknowledge our true history, when expanding our minds into new dimensions so frightens so many that we condemn a champion of such an evolutionary gambit as a political prisoner. Let us record for ourselves the reminder, however, that we knew that it is inevitable that we would attain immortality, that we would come to play our own four-dimensional god games, become our own casting directors of our own personal cosmic movies, that we would be back to re-visit this place of our minds. Let us mark this place in space-time with the traces of our humor, acknowledge our Anunnaki relatives and let our own god games begin.

DISCLOSURE PROCLAMATION

We the people of the United States, speaking for ourselves and the people of the Earth, demand:

That the Congress truly act as our representatives; that our military and intelligence agencies act fully as is their duty to protect us; that our President and his administration act aggressively and comprehensively in the fullest interest of all to rapidly bring about the following:

full acknowledgement and disclosure of the presence and contact with all known alien species

release of all secret, classified and unclassified information and artifacts directly or indirectly pertaining to the existence, nature, technology, agendas and contact of any kind with alien species

release of all technology, peaceful and/or military, developed from alien information, back engineering, donation, or capture.

Removal of all "need to know" restrictions on the President as inherently obstructive to the function of his or her office.

The conclusion of the U.S. government requested study by the Hudson Institute that the information about the Roswell crash be kept from the public for fear of panic and its negative effects on the religions was appropriate sixty years ago but conditions have changed radically. Due to exposure to media presentations, news reports, testimonies by military and civilian contactees and the beginning release of classified information by a number of countries, the public is familiar and comfortable enough and sightings and contacts are reported frequently.

We are being offered a place in cosmic society and the advantages of that are profound. The immediate advantages of the release of advanced technology such as free energy and antigravity would solve the planet's energy crisis quickly and completely and facilitate moving from primitive competition to planetary cooperation.

We the people demand that full disclosure include:

a true and accurate accounting of our species' genetic creation, part alien nature and all information known or held concerning contact past and present with our parent species, the Anunnaki, their intentions and agendas with regard to us, when they may return to Earth and for what purpose, how many of them and who the individuals are that may be resident on Earth currently.

The educational and academic communities be enlisted and engaged in the process of full disclosure and the information be incorporated in the educational systems.

Intensive, cooperative, full ranging studies be commissioned on the academic graduate levels with mandatory free exchange of information, with emphasis on the ramifications of disclosure and the post-disclosure human.

Our species' relationship with the Anunnaki is critical to our understanding of who and what we are. The suppression of this information causes our species to be confused and obstructed with regard to our adaptive evolutionary trajectory in general because it is at root of our religious and cultural internecine conflicts and wars. This pathological introversion of our species is clearly of lethal potential to destroy ourselves. Our status as a peaceful, unified species is the essential condition to be attained for matriculation into stellar society.

We the people demand that full disclosure include:

all astrophysical information, secret, classified, and unclassified concerning Planet X / Nibiru, its rediscovery and announcement by the 1983 Infrared Imaging Satellite team, its coverup because the home planet of our parent species, the Anunnaki; the details of its orbital configuration as a member of our solar system, time of return to perigee in the Asteroid Belt area and its current incoming position.

full transparency in ongoing astronomical observations, reports, evaluations and warnings concerning the relative severity of physical climate and Earth changes already occurring due to its incoming trajectory as well as possible devastating effects of its passing through the inner solar system in the near future.

Past history and archaeological, geological, anthropological, and genetic information as well as the body of legends of peoples over the entire planet attest to the cataclysmic effects of some, not all, passings of Planet X / Nibiru in the past due to which humanity can face literal extinction. It is imperative that we, as a species, be as informed and prepared as possible on a planetarily, mutually supportive, cooperative basis. Not to disclose and provide all possible information, aid and protection would be the worst of crimes against humanity.

FOOTNOTES

[1] Neil Freer, *Breaking the Godspell*, 2nd ed. (Escondido CA: The Book Tree, 2000, 1st ed. 1987

[2] Neil Freer, *God Games: What do you do forever?* (Escondido CA: The Book Tree, 1998)

[3] The term realevolution is coined and used here to *contrast* our accelerated and truncated development as a self-directed, synthesized species with the lengthy periodicities of development by survival and adaptation of the fittest of "natural" species.

[4] Futant: "There is a futant genetic caste wired for the role of evolutionary agent: one who foresees and helps fabricate the future." Timothy Leary, PhD, *The Intelligence Agents*, New Falcon Publications, 1979. By his estimation, during any phase of the general, racial evolution of consciousness there will always be about 1-2% of the population, at any given time, identified as futants, whose genetic drift prompts them to be the evolutionary scouts.

[5] *Annales Vertis Et Novi Testamenti* The Annals of the New Testament the first paragraph of the first page of *The Annals*. Ussher wrote: "In the beginning, God created heaven and earth, which beginning of time, according to this chronology, occurred at the beginning of the night which preceded the 23rd of October in the year 710 of the Julian period." This equated to his computed date as 4004 B.C. He arrived at this by adding life spans of the main characters of the Old Testament back to Adam.

[6] Raymond Kurzweil, *The Singularity Is Near* (New York: Penguin Books, 20051999) pp.7-9

[7] Phillip H. Krapf, *The Contact Has Begun* (Carlsbad, CA: Hay House, 1998)

[8] ibid. p. 75

[9] Zecharia Sitchin, videotape Are We Alone? Based on Sitchin's *Genesis Revisited*, Paradox Media ltd.

[10] Barbara Thiering, *Jesus the Man* (London, U.K.: Transworld Publishers Ltd, 1997)

[11] Edward O. Wilson, *On Human Nature* (United States: Harvard University 1978)

[12] For an excellent introduction to the topic with the minimum of metaphysical metaphor see the architect's, Gyorgy Doczi's, The Power of limits, (Boston S London: Shambala, 1994)

[13] Stephen Wolfram, *A New Kind of Science* (Champaign, IL: Wolfram Media, 2002)

[14] K. Eric Drexler, Engines of Creation (Garden City, New York: Anchor Press / Doubleday, 1986) Book jacket: "Mankind is on the threshold of the greatest innovation in the history of science and technology: the ability to build molecules atom by atom. These molecular building blocks can then be arranged in any combination of patterns to produce every conceivable substance or device. This new technology – called nanotechnology – will also enable scientists to repair damaged human cells."

[15] "Over unity" is borrowed from free energy physics, meaning more energy output than put back into the system to keep it operating. It appeals as an appropriate metaphor to describe efficient human collective efforts.

[16] I have coined these two additional terms, Consciousness and Evolutionary Quotients to provide an expanded context in which to determine the unique proclivities and potential and ad hoc status of each individual for their best education, understanding of genetic roles.

[17] Leary uses the term "contelligence," a combination of consciousness-intelligence, to describe people who are on a higher level of consciousness If you resonate and recognize yourself as one, your own evolutionary artist of futique orientation, greetings. Welcome to your native gene pool.

[18] Raymond Kurzweil, *The Age Of Spiritual Machines* (New York: Penguin Books, 1999)

[19] Richard J Herrnstein and Charles Murray, *The Bell Curve* (New York: Free Press, 1994)

[20] Douglas Hofstadter, *Godel, Esher, Bach* (New York: Vintage Books, 1980)

[21] G. Spencer Brown, *The Laws of Form* (New York: Julian Press, 1972)

[22] Johnson F. Yan, *DNA and the I Ching* (Berkeley: North Atlantic Books, 1991)

[23] David Chalmers, *The Conscious Mind* (New York, Oxford University Press, 1996) p.353

[24] Thomas Bearden, from a recent letter on his patented free energy device and the physics underlying it. See his website at: http://www.cheniere.org Within the time of writing of this paper, he and several others have received a patent from the US. Patent office on a free energy machine.

[25] G. Spencer Brown, ibid. pp. x-xi.

[26] Zecharia Sitchin, *The Twelfth Planet* (Santa Fe NM: Bear and Co., 1991. Originally published: Stein and Day: New York: 1976) p. 299

[27] Chi is a form of energy that moves around the body along independent meridians that are not collinear with any other physical system. Western medicine knows the vascular, lymphatic and neurological systems. Oriental physiology knows those plus one more, the chi system. My opinion from personal experience, is that, in terms of modern physics, chi, as a flow

which can be manipulated, unblocked and balanced by acupuncture and mental focus, is the manifestation of a fourth-dimensional type of energy component in the three dimensional body. Some humans naturally have more capacity to sense and manipulate the chi form of energy than others, such as some "healers" and chi kung physicians as in Chinese hospitals, although the tuning to it and its utilization clearly can be learned.

[28] That they include a philosophy of existence of consciousness after physical death and reincarnation, does not make that a "religious" phenomenon any more than a conviction of the existence of consciousnesses superior to the human, transcendental states, or the tenet that there is a reciprocal relationship between right behavior and right consciousness, except in the slave-code religion conditioned western mind.

[29] Timothy Leary, *Exo-psychology* (Sedona AZ, Falcon Press, 1987)

[30] Simply by advancing this thesis that contains the words "alien" and "genetically engineered species" and by my pointing out that "religion" has evolved since the Anunnaki (Sumerian for "those who came down from the heavens") phased off the planet, as a sublimation of the ancient master-slave relationship, we have transgressed two of the most deeply embedded totems and taboos in any culture. After all, Sitchin and I are not establishment "academics" -- even though the evidence is the identical material worked with by establishment archaeologists and scholars. It's simply outside of the sci/academic box. I am fully confident that this new worldview will come into its own, certainly slowly, certainly with a great deal of opposition from the academic world which does not make reverse turns easily, certainly from science which Kuhn has characterized correctly and, obviously from institutional religions. We now can write our own engineering evaluation --- as this paper might be understood to be --- as AI may eventually do for itself. If we bow to "campus imperialism" we will continue to deprive ourselves of invaluable information just as the geneticists who bow to "laboratory imperialism" ---or funding fright --- in this matter will deprive themselves of clues to our genome. Old paradigms are replaced one funeral at a time. Better check those taboo tattoos...

[31] Zecharia Sitchin, *Divine Encounters* (New York, Avon Books, 1996)

[32] Although the Anunnaki are from the tenth planet in our solar system and the little gray guys with wraparound eyes are not the same race and, most probably, from a distant star system, some "alien beings" may be Anunnaki androids and look like the little grays. Also see: Col. Phillip J. Corso, *The Day After Roswell* (New York: Simon and Schuster, 1997) The beings recovered from the Roswell saucer crash, according to Colonel. Corso (Army intelligence, Pentagon Foreign Technology desk, decorated veteran)

who saw at least one body and read the autopsy and other reports as part of his duties, were androids with four lobes to their brains and many strange features. That androids and AI can be done is reinforced.

[33] The universe didn't opt for this mode under these conditions randomly. The universe clearly intended organisms, not just chemicals and minerals. The universe intended mobility and it could have been achieved inorganically but it wasn't. Reproducing and complexifying consciousness could have been achieved inorganically --- after all that's what some of us are claiming we are going to do ourselves --- but it wasn't. The trajectory of evolution takes the form of organisms adapted to living miles down in rock, in water the temperature of molten lead around sea floor vents, under stupendous deep ocean pressures, generating flashing light in abyssal darkness, in arid Death Valley temperatures, in Antarctic cold waters requiring a circulatory system containing antifreeze. All of which could have been achieved inorganically but wasn't.

[34] I have said above that Timothy Leary was the "Tesla of consciousness". He took the role of the "shaman" to a new dimension in that, not only reluctantly recognizing that that was his evolutionary role in his time, he clinically observed and documented the process as it unfolded, taking self-reflexive awareness out another whole degree. He was probably more knowledgeable and expert at being self-aware of his being self-aware of his self-awareness more than any one human to this point in our history.

[35] D.S Allan and J.B. Delair, *Cataclysm!* (Rochester, Vermont, Bear and Company, 1997)

[36] Jim Marrs, *Alien Agenda* (New York, Harper Collins, 1997)

ALSO BY NEIL FREER

Breaking the Godspell. Freer explores the archaeological, astronomical and genetic evidence for our being a half-alien, genetically engineered species. He presents the mind-boggling ramifications of this new paradigm which correct and resolve the Creationist-Evolutionary conflict, afford a generic definition of human nature, and the potential to rethink the planet. We are about to step out of racial adolescence into stellar society. Zecharia Sitchin writes, "It is gratifying that a mere decade after the publication of my work, an author with the grasp that Neil Freer displays in Breaking the Godspell has set out to probe what the recognition of the existence and Earth-visits of the Nefilim can mean -- not just to scientists and theologians -- but to each human being upon this planet Earth." **paper, 164 pages, 6x9, $15.95**

God Games. *Then came Neil Freer (who) undertook a different kind of mind-boggling task. If all that I had concluded was true, he said, what does it all mean not to the human race and the planet in general — what does it mean to the individuals, to each one of us? He titles his new book God Games. But, if all the above is the Truth, it is not a game.* —Zecharia Sitchin (from the Introduction). This book outlines the human evolutionary scenario far into the future. We are a genetically-engineered race with a dual racial heritage. Our half-Terran, half-alien genes place us on an accelerated, unique evolutionary path, already eagerly emerging from racial adolescence. Freer describes what's in store for us as this dawning genetic enlightenment reveals the new human and the racial maturity of a new planetary civilization on the horizon. We all can contribute to our racial future as we evolve from a slave species to far beyond what we could previously even imagine. The godspell broken, we new humans will create our own realities and play our own "god games." Once we understand our true genetic history we will eventually move beyond the gods, religion, linear consciousness and even death. The subtitle. What do you do forever? inspires us to contemplate how things like four-dimensional consciousness, the realization of a Law of Everything and the option of immortality will enable the new human to determine his own evolutionary path. It is quite possible that great thinkers in the future will look back on this book, in particular, as being the one which opened the door to our full evolutionary potential and a new paradigm. Neil Freer is a brilliant philosopher focused on the freedom of the individual and what it means to be truly human. Accept the challenge of *God Games* and you will be greatly rewarded. **paper, 312 pages, 6x9, $19.95**

Lightning Source UK Ltd.
Milton Keynes UK
UKOW05f0425200117
292425UK00001B/276/P